Joan Wilkes

Spring
Wildflowers
of New Mexico

William C. Martin
and Charles R. Hutchins

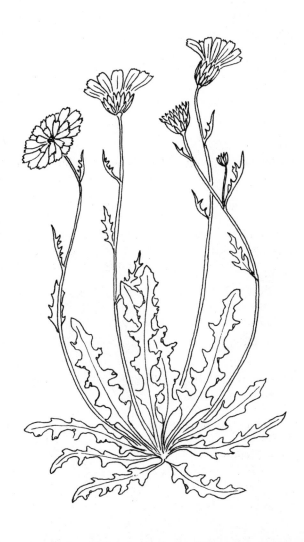

**The New Mexico
Natural History
Series**

Barry S. Kues,
General Editor

University
of New Mexico Press
Albuquerque

Library of Congress Cataloging in Publication Data

Martin, William C., 1923–
  Spring wildflowers of New Mexico.

  (The New Mexico natural history series)
  Includes index.
    1. Wild flowers—New Mexico—Identification. I. Hutchins, Charles R.,
1928– . II. Title. III. Series.
QK176.M37   1984   582.13'09789   83-25954
ISBN 0-8263-0742-6
ISBN 0-8263-0743-4 (pbk.)

Color illustrations printed in Japan.

International Standard Book Number (clothbound) 0-8263-0742-6.
International Standard Book Number (paperbound) 0-8263-0743-4.
Library of Congress Catalog Card Number 83-25954.
First Edition

Contents

Introduction

Most people, even those with little or no formal training in botany, find flowering plants attractive and interesting and have developed a certain curiosity about the identity and characteristics of the plants they encounter throughout our state.

New Mexico wildflowers are abundant in many habitats and in several life zones, ranging from desert areas in the southern part of the state to the alpine summits of the Sangre de Cristo range in the north-central part.

Of the more than four thousand species of plants growing wild in New Mexico, probably over a third of these can be designated as wildflowers depending, of course, on one's definition of the term *wildflower.* By the usual definition, these plants are those whose flowers, by virtue of size, shape, or color, tend to attract attention. The dictionary definition would include in this category all plants growing without cultivation.

In this book, we have attempted to characterize and illustrate the major spring-blooming wildflowers of New Mexico. These plants are arranged according to family; for example, those belonging to the Lily family are grouped together because of associated characteristics. The same applies to those species belonging to other families.

Originally, we considered combining all plants having similar flower colors into groups, but we were reluctant to do so because a number of species may exhibit two or more color variants. We did not want to associate plants not necessarily closely related.

We have attempted to make the initial identification somewhat easier and more efficient by providing keys to identification to families and genera, using the common names for both family and generic categories. Final separation of species can be easily determined from the descriptions in the text.

Each wildflower in this book is described briefly, and pertinent data relating to general habitat, geographical distribution, and elevational range are presented. Each plant is designated by a number and by both common and scientific names. The number designating each species is the reference number shown in both the index and the keys to identification and is not necessarily related to

1

page numbers. In the text, descriptive material is presented on facing pages. The right page contains the description of four species; the left page presents drawings representative of these four plants.

Note also, in the following section, a discussion pertaining to the use of the keys in the identification of families and genera. Of course, if one already has some idea about the identity of a particular plant, one can go to the index and find the reference number, then compare the unknown plant with the descriptions and drawings.

This book is the first of a series of three books on the wildflowers of our state. The second volume will concentrate on the summer wildflowers, and the third volume on the wildflowers that bloom in autumn. All books will be profusely illustrated.

Use of Keys to Identification

Most keys to identification are based on a series of alternative statements or couplets about the characteristics in question. Thus, identification, by use of a key, involves a simple process of elimination.

Note that major characteristics are designated in the keys by number and letter symbols, with pairs of alternatives following in succession. At the end of certain alternatives, instructions in parentheses direct the reader to another set of alternatives. This procedure continues, couplet by couplet, until one or more final categories are reached, beneath which a listing of one or more pertinent families and genera is provided. In some cases, the final category may direct the reader to additional keys to large groups, such as the Lily or Aster families.

For example, the first alternative, category 1a, is shown at the beginning of the key indicating "flower parts in 3s or 6s; leaf veins parallel." The alternative to this is the second part of the couplet or 1b which indicates "flower parts mostly in 4s or 5s, sometimes of 7 or more parts; leaf veins mostly branched." The next set of alternatives shown under 1a is that of ovary position, above or below the point of attachment of the petals and sepals. The choices lead directly to a listing of family and genus categories with an abbreviated list of characteristics, including flower color, noted for each one. Under alternative 1b, the next step is combination 3a and 3b, then successively 4a and 4b, 5a and 5b, 6a and 6b, and so on, until one or more families and genera are reached.

Let us consider an example to illustrate the use of this key. An analysis of flower parts of an unknown plant indicates that there are 5 petals present. The first alternative, category 1a, indicates parts in 3s or 6s, thus we select the characteristics for 1b; these describe the flower parts as being in 4s or 5s, or 7 or more. The instructions following 1b send us to alternatives 3a or 3b. Category 3a points out that flowers are arranged in either headlike clusters, like those of daisies or dandelions, or in some other arrangement. We decide that the flowers are not in headlike clusters, thus category 3b is selected. Because there are 5 petals, we then proceed to alternative 4b. Further examination of the flower shows that the petals are not all the same size or shape, thus the

3

instructions at the end of 4b send us to 5a. Examination of the leaves shows the leaf arrangement is scattered or alternate; we proceed to 6a. Finally, because the flowers have a backward-pointing spur or spurs at the base, we choose alternative 9a. This final category leaves us with a comparatively simple choice between the Buttercup family, the Fumitory family, and the Violet family, based on some easily determined characters of flower and leaf morphology and flower color. If the stamens are numerous and leaves are palmately divided, our selection is the Buttercup family, more specifically the larkspurs. The numbers in parentheses following "Larkspur" refer to the numbers in the text of the three larkspurs in this category. A single choice can then easily be made, based on description and key characters. All unknowns can be keyed out in much the same way down to a few easily separated choices.

In order to assist the reader in better understanding the meaning of the relatively few technical terms used in this book, an illustrated glossary immediately follows on page 5. The terms are briefly described, this description often followed by a sketch illustrating the term. We have eliminated technical terms whenever possible but are aware that in some instances the meaning of a particular term cannot be efficiently duplicated in everyday language.

Glossary

Typical Flower

stigma
style ⎫ pistil
ovary ⎭
anther ⎫ stamen
filament ⎭
petal—corolla ⎫ perianth
sepal—calyx ⎭
receptacle
pedicel

Achene. A dry one-seeded fruit that does not split open, common in the sunflower and buttercup families.

Acuminate. Tapering to a long point, as in the tip of a leaf.

Acute. Leaf tips or bases with margins that meet at an acute angle.

Alternate. Referring to parts of a plant (such as leaves or branches) that occur singly at a node.

Annual. A plant that germinates, develops, flowers, and fruits in a single growing season.

Anther. The saclike part of the stamen that contains the pollen.

Apex. The tip.

Apical. Occurring at the apex.

Armed. Bearing sharp-pointed projections.

Ascending. Angling upward, between growing straight up and spreading horizontally.

Axillary. Occurring in the axil between two connecting parts, such as where a leaf stalk joins the stem.

Banner. The upper petal of certain flowers such as pealike legume flowers.

Acuminate

Acute

Alternate

Ascending

banner ---

Pealike

5

Beak. A narrow projection on fruits or flower parts.

Berry. A fleshy fruit, not splitting open.

Bipinnate. Twice pinnate; as in one section of a pinnate leaf being again pinnate.

Blade. The expanded portion, especially of a leaf.

Bract. A modified leaf, usually subtending a flower or a group of flowers.

Bulb. An underground stem composed of fleshy scales and a very short axis.

Caespitose. Tufted or matted; occurring in tufts; many stems from the top of a single root.

Calyx. The outer whorl of perianth (flower) parts, referring to all the sepals.

Capitate. Headlike, often referring to a dense cluster.

Capsule. A dry, variously shaped fruit that splits open and has two or more compartments and usually several seeds.

Cordate. Heart-shaped.

Corm. A fleshy underground stem bearing inconspicuous, scalelike leaves.

Corolla. The inner whorl of perianth (flower) parts, referring to all the petals.

Corymb. A flat-topped or convex flower cluster with the lower pedicels longer than the upper ones, and the outer flowers maturing first.

Cyme. A flower cluster similar to a corymb with the central flowers maturing first.

Deciduous. Falling off.

Decumbent. Referring to stems with the base prostrate but with the terminal parts erect or ascending.

Deflexed. Bent or turned downward.

Dentate. Toothed, the teeth having approximately equal sides.

Digitate. With separate parts or lobes diverging from a common point of origin.

Entire. With an unbroken smooth margin.

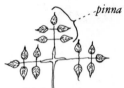

*Bipinnate or
Twice-compound*

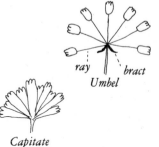

ray   bract
Umbel

Capitate

Corymb

Decumbent

Dentate

Palmate or Digitate

Entire

Epidermis. The outer layer of cells of the various plant parts.

Exserted. Projecting beyond, usually applying to flower parts such as stamens.

Fascicle. A cluster or bundle, as in a fascicle of leaves.

Filament. The stalk of an anther.

Free. With parts not united.

Fruit. A mature ovary; the seed-bearing structure of a plant.

Glabrous. Without hairs.

Globose. Spherical or rounded.

Hastate. Having divergent lobes at the base, as in leaves.

Head. A dense cluster of flowers subtended by bracts, the flowers sessile on a common receptacle.

Herb. A nonwoody plant.

Included. Not projecting beyond, as in stamens not protruding from a flower.

Involucre. A series of bracts subtending a cluster of flowers.

Irregular. Referring to a flower showing differences in size or shape of similar parts.

Lanceolate. Lance-shaped, broadest below the middle.

Lateral. Borne on the sides.

Leaflet. A division of a compound leaf.

Linear. Slender; having parallel sides, usually 8–10 times longer than wide.

Lobed. Having lobes (parts resulting from partial division).

Lyrate. Pinnatifid with small lower lobes and a large, rounded terminal lobe.

Oblanceolate. Lanceolate but attached at the narrow end and broadest above the middle.

Oblique. Slanted, with sides unequal.

Hastate

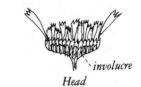

involucre

Head

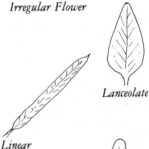

Irregular Flower

Lanceolate

Linear

Lobed

Lyrate

Oblanceolate

Oblique

7

Oblong. Elongate, with sides roughly parallel, usually less than eight times longer than wide.

Obovate. Ovate but attached at the narrow end and broadest above the middle.

Obtuse. Blunt, often referring to a leaf tip with the sides forming an obtuse angle.

Opposite. Referring to parts of a plant (such as leaves or branches) occurring in pairs on opposite sides of a node.

Ovate. Egg-shaped, broadest below the middle.

Palmate. With separate parts or lobes diverging from a common point of origin.

Panicle. Usually referring to any compound flower cluster.

Pealike. A corolla composed of a banner, wings, and keel, as in certain legume flowers.

Pedicel. The stalk of a single flower.

Perennial. A plant that lives for more than two years.

Petal. A single segment or unit of a corolla.

Petiole. The stalk of a leaf.

Pinna. A primary division of a pinnate or a pinnately compound leaf.

Pinnae. Plural of pinna.

Pinnate. Having leaflets arranged in two rows along a common axis.

Pinnatifid. Cleft, divided, or incised in a pinnate manner.

Pod. A dry fruit that splits open.

Prickle. A sharp projection from the epidermis of a plant.

Procumbent. Lying on the ground.

Prostrate. Lying flat on the ground.

Raceme. A cluster of flowers having an elongated axis with flowers borne on simple pedicels along the axis.

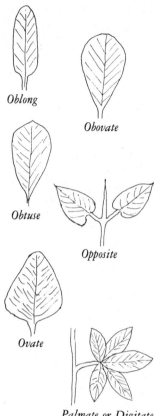

Oblong

Obovate

Obtuse

Opposite

Ovate

Palmate or Digitate

Panicle

Pealike

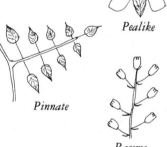

Pinnate

Raceme

Recurved. Curved downward or backward.

Reflexed. Bent sharply downward or backward.

Rhizome. A generally horizontal underground stem.

Sagittate. Shaped like an arrowhead, and with a V-shaped notch at the base.

Sagittate

Scarious. Thin, dry, and papery.

Sepal. A segment or unit of the calyx.

Sessile. Without a stalk, usually in reference to flowers or leaves.

Shrub. A woody plant, usually with several main stems and less than 15 ft. (4.5 m) tall.

Spatulate. Club-shaped, narrowed at the base, broader and rounded at the tip.

Spatulate

Spike. An elongated flower cluster bearing sessile flowers.

Spine. A leaf or part of a leaf modified into a sharp projection.

Spike

Spreading. Strongly diverging from the main axis, nearly horizontal, as applied to hairs, branches, fruiting pedicels, etc.

Spur. A hollow projection from a calyx or corolla.

Stipule. An appendage of a leaf, often attached where the petiole joins the stem.

Stolon. A modified, horizontal, above-ground stem, usually developing roots at the nodes.

stipule

Stipule

Tendril. A leaf modified into a slender, twining, holdfast structure.

Terminal. Of the end or apex.

Thorn. A modified branch, typically sharp-pointed at the tip.

Toothed. Having teeth, as in variously irregular leaf margins.

Trifoliolate. Having three leaflets.

Truncate. Having the end flattened or squared off.

Tuber. A thickened, fleshy, modified underground stem, usually a food-storage organ.

Trifoliolate

Truncate

Umbel. A flower cluster having flowers on pedicels or having rays of about equal length, these from the same point of origin at the apex of the flower stalk.

Unarmed. Not having prickles, spines, or thorns.

Undulate. Wavy on the margins.

Undulate

9

Vining. Referring to stems that trail or creep along the ground or along other supports.

Viscid. Sticky.

Whorled. Parts occurring in groups of three or more at one node, all at the same level, applied to branches or leaves.

Whorled

Key to Common Names of Families and Genera

1a. Flower parts in 3s or 6s; leaf veins parallel, not branched. (See 2a or 2b.)

1b. Flower parts mostly in 4s or 5s, sometimes of 7 or more parts; leaf veins mostly branched. (See 3a or 3b.)

2a. Ovary placed above the point of petal and sepal attachment.
Lily family. Sepals and petals usually similar; flowers rarely subtended by conspicuous bracts. See key to Lily family on page 25.
Spiderwort family. Sepals and petals unlike; flowers always subtended by conspicuous bracts.
  Dayflower (1). Petals unequal in size; staminal filaments without hairs. Flowers blue or white.
  Spiderwort (2). Petals equal in size; staminal filaments hairy. Flowers blue or white.

2b. Ovary placed below the point of petal and sepal attachment.
Amaryllis family. Stamens 6, pointing inward; sepals and petals similar.
  Century plant (25, 26). Leaves large and thickish, spine-tipped, in conspicuous basal rosettes. Flowers greenish yellow or yellow.
  Stargrass (28). Leaves grasslike. Flowers whitish or yellowish with greenish outer surface.
  Zephyr lily (27). Leaves grasslike. Flowers white, yellow, or pink.
Iris family. Leaves folded lengthwise and overlapping; 3 stamens; petals similar.
  Iris (29). Flowers more than 2 in. (50 mm) long. Flowers blue or white.
  Blue-eyed grass (30). Flowers not more than 3/4 in. (20 mm) long. Flowers blue or white.
Orchid family. Lower petal differing from the other petals in appearance.
  Coralroot (31). Leaves scalelike, yellowish or purplish. Lip petal white with purple dots.
  Helleborine (32). Leaves typical, green. Lip petal greenish purple.

11

3a. Flowers in headlike clusters resembling those of daisies or dandelions. *Aster family.* See key to Aster family on page 35.

3b. Flowers not arranged in the above manner. (See 4a or 4b.)

4a. Petals or petallike parts 7 or more.
    Buttercup family. Ovaries and stamens spirally arranged. Flowers white.
        Baneberry (49). Leaves divided into 2 or 3 sets of 3 leaflets.
        Marsh-marigold (50). Leaves heart-shaped.
        Pasqueflower (56). Leaves palmately divided; styles feathery.
        Windflower (57, 58). Leaves palmately divided; styles not feathery.
    Purslane family. Low-growing herbs with fleshy leaves.
        Bitterroot (40). Nearly naked flowering stems. Flowers pink or red.
    Water-lily family. Aquatics with broad heart-shaped leaves.
        Pond-lily (46). Flowers yellow.

4b. Petals or petallike parts 4 or 5. (See 5a or 5b.)

5a. Petals unequal in size and/or shape. (See 6a or 6b.)

5b. Petals equal or nearly so in size and/or shape. (See 11a or 11b.)

6a. Leaves opposite or whorled. (See 7a or 7b.)

6b. Leaves alternate or basal. (See 9a or 9b.)

7a. Shrubs or trees.
    Catalpa family. Flowers mostly 1¼–2 in. (30–50 mm) long; 2 or 4 stamens.
        Desert willow (301). Leaves simple. Flowers white or pink.
        Yellow trumpet (302). Leaves pinnately compound. Flowers yellow.
    Honeysuckle family. Flowers usually 2 or more per cluster, mostly less than 1 in. (25 mm) long.
        Elderberry (313, 314). Flowers regular; leaves pinnately compound. Flowers white to pale yellow.
        Honeysuckle (317, 318). Flowers irregular; leaves simple. Flowers white, yellow, or orange.
        Snowberry (315, 316). Flowers regular; leaves simple.
    Vervain family.
        Lippia (272). Leaves and bracts with resinous dots; foliage aromatic.

7b. Herbs, the stems not woody. (See 8a or 8b.)

8a. Stems 4-angled.
    Mint family. Flowers strongly 2-lipped; plants aromatic.
        Fertile stamens 2.
            False pennyroyal (274). Calyx 2-lipped; upper lip of corolla flat. Flowers pink or purple.
            Horsemint (273). Calyx with 5 equal teeth. Flowers yellowish with purple spots.
            Sage (275, 276). Calyx 2-lipped; upper lip of corolla curved. Flowers red or purple.

Fertile stamens 4.

Dead nettle (278). Calyx 5-toothed; upper corolla lobe as long as the lower. Flowers reddish purple.

Germander (277). Calyx 5-toothed; upper corolla lobe much shorter than the lower. Flowers white, blue, or pink.

Skullcap (279). Calyx 2-lobed, the lobes not toothed. Flowers blue or violet.

8b. Stems rounded.

Figwort family. Corolla usually strongly 2-lipped; 2 or 4 stamens.

Flowers yellowish.

Lousewort (297). Upper lip of corolla compressed on the sides and arching; leaves pinnately lobed, the lobes toothed.

Monkeyflower (295, 296). Lower side of the corolla tube with a pair of longitudinal ridges; leaves not lobed, often ovate to rounded.

Toadflax (287). Corolla tube with a slender spur at the base; leaves linear or oblong.

Flowers blue, white, purple, pink, or red.

Beardtongue (289, 290, 291, 292). Corolla usually strongly 2-lipped, the 5th stamen represented by a sterile, often hairy filament; leaves opposite. Flowers red, blue, or purple.

Speedwell (293, 294). Corolla slightly irregular, not obviously 2-lipped; 2 stamens. Flowers white or blue.

9a. Flowers with a backward-pointing spur at the base.

Buttercup family. Stamens numerous.

Larkspur (51, 52, 53). Leaves palmately divided. Flowers bluish.

Fumitory family. Leaves repeatedly dissected into many small segments.

Golden smoke (67). Leaves and stems hairless, smooth. Flowers golden yellow.

Violet family. Leaves heart-shaped or lance-shaped.

Violet (202, 203, 204). Flowers violet or yellow.

9b. Flowers not spurred. (See 10a or 10b.)

10a. Stamens 2, 4, or 5.

Broomrape family. Stems fleshy; leaves scalelike; plants without chlorophyll.

Broomrape (304, 305). Corolla tube curved. Flowers yellow to purplish brown.

Figwort family. Plants with chlorophyll and typical leaves; sticky hairs uncommon.

Flowers blue, purple, or white.

False snapdragon (288). Corolla throat with a conspicuous hairy cushion; leaves alternate, somewhat triangular. Flowers purplish or pinkish.

Speedwell (293, 294). Corolla slightly irregular, not 2-lipped; 2 stamens. Flowers white or blue.

Flowers yellow, orange, or reddish.

Indian paintbrush (298, 299, 300). Flowers inconspicuous, subtended

13

by brightly colored, often leaflike bracts; leaves entire to lobed, the lobes, when present, not toothed. Bracts yellowish to orange red or scarlet-tipped.

Lousewort (297). Upper lip of corolla compressed on the sides and arching. Leaves pinnately lobed, the lobes toothed. Flowers yellow.

Toadflax (287). Corolla tube with a slender curving spur at the base. Flowers yellow.

Legume family.

Ratany (136, 137). Sepals unequal; upper 3 petals constricted at the base; lower 2 petals greatly reduced and greenish. Flowers crimson.

Unicorn-plant family. Low plants; leaves long-stalked, with sticky hairs.

Unicorn-plant (303). Leaves triangular-ovate. Flowers reddish purple to white.

10b. Stamens 7–10 or more.

Legume family. Leaves compound, except redbud with simple heart-shaped leaves; 10 or more stamens. See key to Legume family on page 29.

Milkwort family. Leaves simple; 8 stamens.

Milkwort (191). Flowers white with green center.

Soapberry family. Leaves pinnately compound; 7–10 stamens.

Mexican buckeye (194). Flowers strongly irregular with petals arranged on one side; shrubs. Flowers bright pink.

11a. Stamens 8 to many. (See 12a or 12b.)

11b. Stamens 2–7. (See 21a or 21b.)

12a. Leaves simple. (See 13a or 13b.)

12b. Leaves compound or appearing so. (See 17a or 17b.)

13a. Shrubs or trees, the stems woody and having bark. (See 14a or 14b.)

13b. Herbs, the stems not woody, devoid of bark. (See 15a or 15b.)

14a. Petals united to form a somewhat tubelike flower.

Ocotillo family. flowers tubular; stems whiplike, arching.

Ocotillo (238). Flowers scarlet.

Heath family. Flowers urn-shaped; stems with many branches.

Madrone (234, 235). Flowers white or pink.

Manzanita (236). Flowers white or pink.

14b. Petals separate.

Rose family. Leaves alternate, not palmately veined.

Flowers pink or yellow.

Antelope brush (123). Low, many-branched shrubs with wedge-shaped, 3-toothed clustered leaves. Flowers yellow.

Cliffrose (124). Shrubs with glandular-dotted leaves. Flowers yellow.

Squawapple (104). Leaves sessile, clustered at the ends of the branches, the teeth minute or absent. Flowers pink.

Flowers white or sometimes whitish cream.

Apache plume (121). Leaves pinnately lobed; petals falling easily; styles conspicuously hairy. Flowers white.

Chokecherry and *wild plum* (108, 109). Bark with conspicuous horizontal markings; flowers in racemes or small umbels. Flowers white or creamy white.

Hawthorn (105). Branches with long thorns; leaves elliptic, irregularly toothed. Flowers white.

Mountain mahogany (122). Leaves unlobed, often coarsely toothed; fruits with curved feathery tails. Flowers white.

Serviceberry (106). Leaves variously toothed; flowers in small clusters at the ends of short branches, 2–5 styles, ovaries united; often small trees. Flowers white.

Saxifrage family. Leaves opposite, or if alternate, then palmately veined.

Cliffbush (97). Leaves opposite, ovate, toothed, hairy beneath; 10 stamens. Flowers white.

Fendlerbush (98). Leaves opposite, narrowly lance-shaped; 8 stamens. Flowers white or pinkish.

Gooseberry and *Currant* (100, 101, 102, 103). Leaves rounded, palmately veined, alternate, 5 stamens. Flowers whitish to yellowish, reddish, or purplish.

Mockorange (99). Leaves opposite, mostly lance-shaped; 15–50 stamens. Flowers white.

Tamarisk family. Branchlets slender, drooping; leaves tiny, scalelike, somewhat resembling juniper leaves.

Tamarisk (201). Flowers pink.

15a. Stamens 15 or more. (See 16a or 16b.)

15b. Stamens 4–12.

Evening primrose family. Leaves alternate; 4 petals and sepals; 8 stamens.

Calylophus (230). Flowers in the axils of the upper leaves; stigmas unlobed. Flowers yellow.

Evening primrose (227, 228, 229). Flowers in the axils of the upper leaves; petals mostly more than 10 mm long; stigmas with 4 conspicuous slender lobes. Flowers yellow, pink, or white.

Gaura (225, 226). Flowers in narrow elongated clusters; petals not more than 7 mm long; stigmas with 4 slender lobes. Flowers white to pinkish.

Geranium family. Leaves palmately or pinnately lobed; 5 petals and sepals; 5 or 10 stamens; fruit forming an elongate, beaklike column.

Filaree (183). Stamens 5. Flowers pink.

Geranium (181, 182). Stamens 10. Flowers white, pink, or purple.

Purslane family. Leaves fleshy; often 2 sepals.

Bitterroot (40). Sepals 2–8; petals 4–18. Flowers pinkish or reddish.

Flame flower (41). Sepals 2; petals 5; ovary completely superior. Flowers yellow.

Purslane (39). Sepals 2; petals 5; ovary partially inferior; capsule opening around the perimeter. Flowers yellow to reddish.

Rock purslane (43). Sepals 2; petals 3–7; capsule splitting lengthwise. Flowers red.

Spring beauty (42). Sepals 2; petals 5; stem leaves consisting of a single pair. Flowers white or pink.

Rose family. Leaves with usually persistent stipules.

Burnet (110). Leaves pinnately lobed; flowers greenish, in dense terminal clusters.

Saxifrage family. Leaves simple, often with a rounded heart-shape; 5, 8, or 10 stamens.

Alumroot (93, 94). Leaves rounded, palmately veined; 5 stamens. Flowers pink or greenish white.

Saxifrage (96). Leaves ovate; petals sometimes notched at the tip; 10 stamens. Flowers white.

Woodland star (95). Leaves palmate, deeply divided into 3 or more segments; petals deeply divided; 10 stamens. Flowers white.

Spurge family. Flowers unisexual; ovary conspicuously 3-lobed.

Croton (192). Stems and leaves aromatic, bearing numerous star-shaped hairs. Flowers whitish.

16a. Stems bearing spines, barbed bristles, or star-shaped hairs.

Cactus family. Stems thick and fleshy within; leaves reduced to conspicuous spines. See key to Cactus family on page 33.

Loasa family. Herbage with barbed or stinging hairs.

Stickleaf (206, 207, 208). Leaves and stems with short, barbed hairs; 20 or more stamens. Flowers yellow.

Wavyleaf cevallia (205). Leaves and stems with slender stinging hairs; flowers in whitish, feathery plumose clusters. Flowers white.

Mallow family. Herbage with star-shaped hairs; stamens united into a column.

Globemallow (198, 199). Stamens appearing at the summit of the staminal tube; carpels splitting into segments resembling orange slices. Flowers orange or orange with a reddish tinge.

Paleface rosemallow (197). Stamens appearing all along the staminal tube; calyx with several small bractlets immediately beneath it. Flowers white to pale purple.

Scurfy mallow (200). Stamens appearing at the summit of the staminal tube; calyx without small bractlets immediately beneath it. Flowers yellowish.

Poppy family. Leaves and stems with milky juice, conspicuously spiny.

Prickly poppy (65). Flowers white with yellowish center.

16b. Stems without spines, short, barbed bristles, or star-shaped hairs.

Buttercup family. Stamens and pistils in spiral arrangement.

Buttercup (59, 60, 61). Leaves alternate; fruits of achenes. Flowers yellow or white.

Marsh marigold (50). Leaves basal, somewhat heart-shaped; 6–12 petallike structures. Flowers white.

Pasqueflower (56). Leaves opposite or whorled; styles with feathery hairs. Flowers whitish to purplish.

Windflower (57, 58). Leaves opposite or whorled; styles hairy but not feathery in appearance. Flowers white to pink.

Poppy family. Low-growing, smooth, with leaves dissected into groups of 3 segments.

Golden poppy (66). Flowers golden yellow.

Purslane family. Leaves fleshy; sepals often 2.

Bitterroot (40). Leaves basal; flower stems nearly naked. Flowers pink or reddish.

Flame flower (41). Leaves alternate. Flowers yellow.

Purslane (39). Leaves opposite; capsule opening transversely around its periphery. Flowers yellowish or reddish.

Rock purslane (43). Leaves alternate. Flowers rose red.

Spring beauty (42). Stem leaves a single pair, opposite; 5 petals and stamens. Flowers white or pink.

Rose family. Leaves compound or strongly pinnatifid.

Avens (117, 118). Base of style merging with the fruit, the style jointed, forming 2 segments. Flowers yellowish to pinkish.

Cinquefoil (115, 116). Base of style jointed to the fruit, the style not forming 2 segments. Flowers yellow.

Thimbleberry (114). Leaves broadly heart-shaped, unevenly toothed. Flowers white.

Water-lily family. Aquatic with large, somewhat heart-shaped, untoothed leaves.

Pond-lily (46). Flowers yellow.

17a. Leaves having 3 leaflets or 5 or more palmately arranged leaflets.

Caper family. Stamens 6 or 12–24. Leaflets 3.

Bee-plant (91). Stamens 6. Flowers yellow.

Clammyweed (92). Stamens 12–24. Flowers pinkish.

Rose family. Stamens and pistils usually numerous.

Avens (117, 118). Styles jointed, forming 2 segments. Flowers pink or yellow.

Cinquefoil (115, 116). Styles not jointed to form 2 segments. Flowers yellow.

Strawberry (111). Leaflets 3, having doubly toothed margins. Flowers white.

Rue family. Stamens 4–8; leaves glandular-dotted.

Mexican orange (190). Leaflets 5–10, digitately arranged. Flowers white.

Woodsorrel family. Leaflets 3, wedge-shaped, notched at the tip.

Woodsorrel (184). Stamens 10. Flowers yellow.

17b. Leaves pinnately compound with 5 or more leaflets. (See 18a or 18b.)

18a. Stamens 15 or more. (See 19a or 19b.)

18b. Stamens 8–12. (See 20a or 20b.)

19a. Plants with whitish or yellowish sap; petals appearing fragile and crumpled.
Poppy family.
Mexican poppy (66). Stems and leaves smooth. Flowers golden yellow.
Prickly poppy (65). Stems and leaves prickly. Flowers white with yellow center.

19b. Plants without whitish or yellowish sap.
Buttercup family. Leaves divided twice or thrice into 3 segments.
Baneberry (49). Many flowers, in racemes. Flowers white.
Clematis (54, 55). Vines with opposite leaves. Flowers white or purplish.
Columbine (47, 48). Petals with conspicuous spurs. Flowers bluish or yellowish, rarely white.
Legume family. Leaves twice pinnately compound.
Acacia (126, 127, 128). Plants spiny; flower heads congested. Flowers yellow or creamy white.
Fairy duster (125). Plants not spiny; flower heads loose. Flowers reddish purple.
Rose family. Leaves once pinnately compound; stamens numerous.
Herbs.
Avens (117, 118). Styles jointed, forming 2 segments. Flowers pink or yellow.
Cinquefoil (115, 116). Styles not jointed or segmented. Flowers yellow.
Shrubs.
Apache plume (121). Leaves to $1/2$ in. (15 mm) long, the lobes narrowly oblong; petals fall easily. Flowers white.
Raspberry (112, 113). Leaves at least 2 in. (50 mm) long; ovaries exposed on a conical receptacle. Flowers white.
Rose (119, 120). Leaves at least 2 in. (50 mm) long; ovaries enclosed in and hidden by the fleshy calyx tube. Flowers pink.

20a. Leaves opposite.
Caltrop family. Stamens in 2 whorls; 2–5 carpels, united.
Creosote bush (187). Aromatic shrubs; leaves with 2 leaflets. Flowers yellow.
Goathead (188). Prostrate annual; leaves with 6–14 leaflets. Flowers yellow.
Desert poppy (189). Low-spreading annual; leaves with 8–16 leaflets. Flowers orange.

20b. Leaves alternate.
Legume family. Leaves twice pinnate, bearing permanent stipules. See key to the Legume family on page 29.
Mahogany family.
Chinaberry (196). Small tree with spreading crown; leaves twice pinnately compound. Flowers white to pale lavender.
Rose family. Leaves once pinnately compound.
Cinquefoil (115, 116). Leaves and stems with silky hairs. Flowers yellow.

21a. Shrubs or trees, the stems with bark. (See 22a or 22b.)

21b. Herbs. (See 24a or 24b.)

22a. Leaves opposite or whorled.

Honeysuckle family. Leaves opposite; 4 or 5 stamens.

Elderberry (313, 314). Leaves pinnately compound; flowers in large terminal clusters. Flowers white.

Honeysuckle (317, 318). Leaves simple; flowers often in axillary pairs. Flowers whitish to yellowish or orange.

Snowberry (315, 316). Leaves simple; flowers in small axillary clusters, funnel-shaped. Flowers pink.

Olive family. Leaves opposite; usually 2 stamens.

Ash (240). Small tree; flowers fragrant, with slender, elongate petals. Flowers greenish white.

Madder family. Leaves simple, entire; 3–5 stamens, pointing inward.

Bouvardia (309). Leaves in whorls of 3 or 4. Flowers red.

22b. Leaves alternate or basal. (See 23a or 23b.)

23a. Leaves compound.

Barberry family. Petals 6 or 9, in 2 or 3 rows; 6–18 stamens.

Barberry (62, 63). Inner bark yellow; leaves hollylike; petals 6. Flowers yellow.

Sumac family. Petals usually 5, in a single row; 5 stamens.

Sumac (193). Leaflets 3, aromatic; styles 3. Flowers pale yellow.

Rue family. Leaves gland-dotted; 4 or 5 petals; ovary surrounded by a fleshy, ringlike disk.

Mexican orange (190). Leaflets 5–10, palmately arranged. Flowers white.

23b. Leaves simple.

Barberry family. Petals 6 or 9, in 2 or 3 rows; 6–18 stamens.

Barberry (64). Leaves clustered, mostly elliptic; stems with 3-parted spines at the nodes; 6 stamens. Flowers yellow.

Buckthorn family. Petals 4 or 5; ovary surrounded by a fleshy, ringlike disk; 4 or 5 stamens.

Desert buckthorn (195). Leaves conspicuously 3-veined from the base of the blade; branches rigid, somewhat spinescent. Flowers white.

Heath family. Petals strongly united, the corolla somewhat urn-shaped; twice as many stamens as corolla lobes.

Madrone (234, 235). Small trees with pinkish bark; ovary hairy. Flowers white or pink.

Manzanita (236). Shrubs with reddish brown bark; ovary glabrous. Flowers white or pink.

Saxifrage family. Stamens and petals attached to the rim of a floral cup; usually 5, 8, or 10 stamens, sometimes numerous.

Cliffbush (97). Leaves ovate, toothed, hairy beneath; 10 stamens. Flowers white.

Fendlerbush (98). Leaves narrowly lance-shaped; 8 stamens. Flowers white or pinkish.

Gooseberry or *Currant* (100, 101, 102, 103). Leaves rounded, palmately veined; 5 stamens. Flowers whitish to yellowish, reddish, or purplish.

Tamarisk family. Leaves reduced to green, crowded scales, somewhat resembling juniper leaves; 4, 5, 8, or 10 stamens.

Tamarisk (201). Flowers pinkish or whitish.

24a. Leaves opposite or whorled. (See 25a or 25b.)

24b. Leaves alternate or basal. (See 29a or 29b.)

25a. Leaves fleshy.

Purslane family. Often 2 sepals; typically more petals than sepals.

Bitterroot (40). Sepals 2–8; petals 4–18. Flowers pinkish or reddish.

Flame flower (41). Sepals 2; petals 5; ovary completely superior. Flowers yellow.

Purslane (39). Sepals 2; petals 5; ovary partially inferior; capsule opening around the perimeter. Flowers yellowish to reddish.

Rock purslane (43). Sepals 2; petals 3–7; capsule splitting lengthwise. Flowers red.

Spring beauty (42). Sepals 2; petals 5; stem leaves consisting of a single pair. Flowers white or pink.

25b. Leaves not fleshy. (See 26a or 26b.)

26a. Leaves of a pair unequal in size.

Four-o'clock family. Flowers tubular, usually in small clusters subtended by greenish bracts; stamens usually projecting.

Desert four-o'clock (35, 36). Stems erect, glabrous; leaves petioled. Flowers red, pink, or white.

Sand verbena (37). Stems erect to spreading, with sticky hairs. Flowers white or tinged with pink.

Spiderling (38). Stems erect, smooth; flowers very small, less than 1/8 in. (2 mm) long. Flowers white to pinkish or purplish.

26b. Leaves of a pair or whorl equal in size. (See 27a or 27b.)

27a. Petals appearing separate.

Dogwood family. Flowers in open or dense clusters subtended by conspicuous corollalike bracts; 4 petals and stamens.

Cornel (233). Low herb; upper leaves in a crowded whorl.

Pink family. Leaves sessile, entire, usually narrow; petals often lobed or divided; 2–5 styles.

Chickweed (45). Petals 2-lobed; 5 styles; 10 stamens. Flowers white.

Starwort (44). Petals 2-cleft; 3 styles; 3–10 stamens. Flowers white.

Milkweed family. Stems and leaves with milky juice; 5 petals, reflexed, the summit of the flower bearing 5 hoodlike structures.

Milkweed (243). Leaves linear to lance-shaped; flower stalks minutely woolly. Flowers purplish.

27b. Petals united to form a tube. (See 28a or 28b.)

28a. Ovary free from the calyx tube.

Gentian family. Glabrous herbs; leaves sessile, smooth-margined; as many stamens as corolla lobes and alternate with them.

Centaury (241). Corolla tube slender, the lobes oblong, spreading.

Phlox family. Variously hairy herbs; leaves with smooth or lobed margins; stamens usually at different levels on the corolla tube.

Phlox (256, 257). Leaves linear to lance-shaped, smooth-margined. Flowers white to lilac or pink.

Prickly phlox (252). Leaves divided into 3 or more slender, spiny-pointed segments. Flowers white to pale yellow or pink.

Trumpetflower (254, 255). Leaves linear or cleft into 2 or 3 narrow segments. Flowers yellow or white, often marked with purple or red.

Vervain family. Leaves variously toothed and lobed; 5 corolla lobes, slightly unequal; 4 stamens, in 2 groups.

Vervain (269, 270, 271). Flowers in dense, spikelike or headlike clusters; individual flowers usually subtended by conspicuous bracts. Flowers pink or bluish.

28b. Ovary surrounded by and united to the calyx tube.

Madder family. Petals and stamens 4 or 5; anthers pointing inward.

Bluets (310, 311, 312). Corolla lobes and stamens 4. Flowers white to pink or purple.

Valerian family. Stamens 1–4, fewer than and inserted on the corolla lobes.

Valerian (319). Basal leaves unlobed; stem leaves of 2 or 3 pairs, pinnately divided. Flowers white to pink.

29a. Leaf bases with large stipules sheathing the stem.

Buckwheat family.

Dock (33). Flower parts 6; stamens 6; stigmas 3; fruits often 3-angled or 3-winged.

29b. Leaves without conspicuous sheathing stipules. (See 30a or 30b.)

30a. Leaves divided into usually numerous divisions; flowers in umbels; stems grooved, hollow.

Carrot family.

Chimaya (231). Branches of the umbel glabrous. Flowers yellow.

Mountain parsley (232). Branches of the umbel hairy. Flowers yellow to purple.

30b. Leaves, flowers, and stems not fitting all of the above characters. (See 31a or 31b.)

31a. Petals separate. (See 32a or 32b.)

31b. Petals united. (See 33a or 33b.)

32a. Petals 4.

Mustard family. Stamens 6, usually 4 of them longer than the other 2. See key to the Mustard family on page 31.

Caper family. Stamens 6 or 8–24. Leaves compound, usually with 3 leaflets.
  Bee-plant (91). Stamens 6. Flowers yellow.
  Clammyweed (92). Stamens 8–24. Flowers pinkish.

32b. Petals 5 or more.
  Flax family. Leaves sessile; 5 stamens and styles.
    Flax (185, 186). Leaves linear to narrowly lance-shaped; petals falling easily. Flowers white to blue or yellow.
  Geranium family. Stamens 5 or 10; styles 5, united into a slender column; leaves often palmately veined.
    Filaree (183). Stamens 5. Flowers pink.
    Geranium (181, 182). Stamens 10. Flowers white, pink, or purple.
  Purslane family. Leaves fleshy; often 2 sepals.
    Bitterroot (40). Sepals 2–8; petals 4–18. Flowers pinkish or reddish.
    Flame flower (41). Sepals 2; petals 5; ovary completely superior. Flowers yellow.
    Purslane (39). Sepals 2; petals 5; ovary partially inferior; capsule opening around the perimeter. Flowers yellowish to reddish.
    Rock purslane (43). Sepals 2; petals 3–7; capsule splitting lengthwise. Flowers red.
    Spring beauty (42). Sepals 2; petals 5; stem leaves consisting of a single pair. Flowers white or pink.
  Milkweed family. Stems and leaves usually with milky juice; petals 5, reflexed, the summit of the flower bearing 5 hoodlike structures.
    Milkweed (242). Leaves lance-shaped; flowers in umbellike clusters. Flowers yellow to orange.

33a. Stems vining or creeping, usually elongate.
  Figwort family. Flowers usually irregular, funnelform.
    False snapdragon (288). Leaves triangular, broadly notched at the base. Flowers bluish.
  Melon family. Coarse, rough, herbaceous vines with tendrils; leaves palmately veined.
    Buffalo-gourd (320). Leaves roughly triangular with shallow, angled lobes. Flowers conspicuous, yellow.
    Bigroot cucumber (321). Leaves palmately divided into triangular lobes. Flowers greenish white.
  Morning-glory family. Prostrate or climbing vines without tendrils; flowers funnel-shaped.
    Bindweed (244). Leaves somewhat oblong, notched at the base, often with a pair of basal lobes. Flowers pink.

33b. Stems not vining or creeping, mostly spreading to upright. (See 34a or 34b.)

34a. Flower clusters one-sided, often curled like a scorpion's tail.
  Borage family. Plants usually with stiff, spreading or appressed hairs; ovary 2-celled, deeply 4-lobed.

Bluebell (266). Leaves lance-shaped; corolla funnel-shaped. Flowers bluish.
False gromwell (268). Leaves and stems bristly; leaves conspicuously veined, large. Flowers greenish yellow.
Heliotrope (263, 264). Corolla funnel-shaped, the lobes represented by 5 angles. Flowers white, sometimes tinged with blue.
Hound's tongue (265). Stems coarse, to 24 in. (60 cm) tall; leaves large, lance-shaped, to 12 in. (30 cm) long. Flowers usually purplish.
Puccoon (267). Leaves linear, without teeth; corolla with irregularly toothed lobes. Flowers yellow.
Waterleaf family. Ovary one-celled, not lobed.
Nama (259). Low-growing, stiffly hairy annual; leaves linear, smooth on the margins; corolla funnel-shaped. Flowers reddish purple.

34b. Flowers variously arranged but the clusters not as above. (See 35a or 35b.)

35a. Stamens 2–4; flowers irregular.
Figwort family.
Indian paintbrush (298, 299, 300). Upper leaves sometimes with 1 or 2 narrow lobes; flowers inconspicuous, subtended by usually colorful, often lobed, leaflike bracts. Bracts greenish to purplish or red.
Speedwell (294). Leaves sometimes toothed; corolla less than 1/8 in. (2 mm) wide. Flowers white.
Toadflax (287). Leaves entire; corolla with a curved spur at the base. Flowers blue.

35b. Stamens 5; flowers regular. (See 36a or 36b.)

36a. Stamens attached opposite the corolla lobes.
Primrose family. Leaves all basal; style unbranched.
Primrose (237). Calyx with a whitish mealy deposit. Flowers pinkish purple with a yellowish throat.

36b. Stamens alternate with the corolla lobes.
Bluebell family. Calyx tube united with the ovary; style single but 2- to 5-lobed.
Venus's looking glass (322, 323). Slender annuals; corolla wheel-shaped. Flowers bluish.
Nightshade family. Flowers usually folded lengthwise; style single; stigma unlobed or 2-lobed.
Desert tobacco (280). Stems erect, with sticky hairs; stem leaves with earlike basal lobes. Flowers greenish white.
Groundcherry (284). Calyx greatly inflated, papery, and ribbed at maturity; corolla somewhat bell-shaped. Flowers yellow with dark basal spots.
Horsenettle (285). Leaves and stems with silvery, star-shaped hairs and often bearing slender spines; anthers conspicuous, yellow. Flowers purplish.
Prostrate groundcherry (286). Low perennial with sticky hairs; leaf margins lobed or wavy; corolla hairy within. Flowers yellow to purple.

Wolfberry (281, 282, 283). Shrubs with leaves broadest toward the tip and arranged in clusters; corolla narrowly funnel-shaped. Flowers white, often tinged with purple, or purple.

Phlox family. Stamens often at different levels; style one, with 3 branches; flowers tubular, funnelform, or salverform, rolled lengthwise in the bud.

Collomia (258). Leaves linear to lance-shaped, the margins smooth; flower clusters with conspicuous bracts. Flowers white or pink.

Gilia (248, 249, 250, 251). Leaves usually with slender lobes; upper leaves much reduced; calyx membranaceous. Flowers white to purple with yellow center.

Ipomopsis (245, 246, 247). Leaves often with linear lobes; upper leaves not much reduced; calyx green. Flowers white to pink or purple.

Jacob's ladder (253). Leaves pinnate, the segments oblong or oval; plants aromatic. Flowers yellow to white.

Prickly phlox (252). Plants shrubby at the base; leaves palmately parted into 3–7 needle-shaped segments; flowers solitary in the upper leaf axils. Flowers white to yellow or pinkish.

Key to the Common Names of the Genera of the Lily Family

1a. Petals united for at least one-fourth of their length. (See 2a or 2b.)

1b. Petals separate or nearly so. (See 5a or 5b.)

2a. Leaves elliptic to ovate.
Solomon's seal (11). Flowers greenish yellow.

2b. Leaves linear. (See 3a or 3b.)

3a. Leaves scattered on the stem.
Death camas (12). Petals each with a conspicuous glandular spot at the base. Flowers whitish.

3b. Leaves basal. (See 4a or 4b.)

4a. Stamen filaments united to form a tube, the summit of the tube with toothlike lobes between the stamens.
Funnellily (24). Flowers white to purplish.

4b. Stamen filaments separate.
Bluedicks (13). Flowers about 3/8 in. (10 mm) long. Flowers blue.
Star lily (14). Flowers at least 2 in. (5 cm) long. Flowers white.

5a. Sepals green; flowers with a large, often fringed, glandular zone at the base of each petal.
Mariposa lily (10). Flowers white, purplish, or yellowish.

5b. Sepals the same color as the petals, never green; flowers without a conspicuous glandular area at the base of each petal. (See 6a or 6b.)

6a. Leaves in rosettelike clusters at the base of the plant or at the base of conspicuous flowering stalks, stiffish and spine-tipped or with spine-toothed margins.
Beargrass (7). Leaves smooth or with minute teeth; flowers less than 3/8 in. (10 mm) long. Flowers white.

Sotol (8). Leaves with curved, sharp, marginal prickles; flowers less than $3/8$ in. (10 mm) long. Flowers white.

Spanish bayonet or *yucca* (3, 4, 5, 6). Leaf margins often bearing slender filaments; flowers at least $3/4$ in. (20 mm) long. Flowers white or creamy white.

6b. Leaves not arranged as in 6a. (See 7a or 7b.)

7a. Flowers arranged in umbellike clusters subtended by 1 or more bracts.

Onion (16, 17, 18). Plants with an obvious onionlike odor; stamens separate at the base. Flowers white to pink.

Texas lily (19). Plants onionlike in appearance but without the characteristic odor of onions; stamens united at the base. Flowers yellowish white, often tinged with purple.

7b. Flowers in spikes, racemes, panicles, or solitary. (See 8a or 8b.)

8a. Styles separate; flowers in slender spikelike clusters.

Green lily (15). Flowers greenish white.

8b. Styles united; flowers never in spikelike clusters. (See 9a or 9b.)

9a. Flowers at least 2 in. (5 cm) long; leaves whorled at upper nodes.

Lily (22). Flowers orange red with purplish black spots near the base.

9b. Flowers not more than $3/4$ in. (20 mm) long; leaves scattered.

False Solomon's seal (20). Leaves lanceolate or elliptic. Flowers white.

Fairybells (21). Leaves ovate. Flowers white or yellowish white.

Fritillary (23). Leaves linear to narrowly lance-shaped; flowers nodding. Petals purplish with yellowish white spots.

Key to the Common Names of the Genera of the Legume Family

1a. Leaves simple.

Ratany (136, 137). Leaves linear to oblong-lanceolate; low shrubs or mostly herbaceous. Flowers reddish.

Redbud (138). Leaves broadly heart-shaped; shrubs or small trees. Flowers pink.

1b. Leaves compound. (See 2a, 2b, or 2c.)

2a. Leaves twice-pinnate. (See 3a or 3b.)

2b. Leaves once-pinnte, having more than 3 leaflets. (See 6a or 6b.)

2c. Leaves with 3 leaflets, or if leaflets 5 or more, then palmately arranged. (See 9a or 9b.)

3a. Stamens more than 15, often very numerous.

False mesquite (125). Petals and stamens united. Flowers reddish purple.

Acacia (126, 127, 128). Petals and stamens separate. Flowers yellowish.

3b. Stamens not more than 15. (See 4a or 4b.)

4a. Flowers in racemes; petals unlike in shape and in size.

Rushpea (141, 142). Low, unarmed, often dotted herbs. Flowers yellow.

4b. Flowers in rounded, headlike or cylindrical clusters; petals alike in size and shape. (See 5a or 5b.)

5a. Plants herbaceous or sometimes woody only at the base.

Sensitive briar (130). Leaves sensitive to touch; stems often creeping, bearing recurved prickles. Flowers pink.

Bundleflower (131, 132). Leaves not sensitive to touch; stems spreading to erect, unarmed. Flowers greenish white.

5b. Plants woody shrubs.

Mesquite (129). Spines straight; flowers in dense, cylindrical spikes. Flowers yellow.

Mimosa (133, 134, 135). Spines recurved; flowers in rounded, headlike clusters. Flowers whitish or pinkish.

6a. Leaflets even in number.
Senna (139, 140). Stamens 10–15; petals only slightly unequal; leaves without tendrils. Flowers yellow.
Peavine (173). Stamens 10; petals strongly irregular; leaves tendrilled; styles hairy all along one side. Flowers white to yellowish.
Vetch (174, 175). Stamens 10; petals strongly irregular; leaves tendrilled; styles with a tuft of hairs near the apex. Flowers bluish or purplish.

6b. Leaflets odd in number. (See 7a or 7b.)

7a. Leaves glandular-dotted.
False indigo (177). Stamens 9 or 10; 1 petal; shrubby. Flowers blue or purple.
Indigobush (149–53). Stamens 9 or 10; petals 5, attached to the stamen tube. Flowers white to pink, purple, or rose.
Prairie clover (176). Stamens 5; petals 5; herbs. Flowers white.

7b. Leaves not glandular-dotted. (See 8a or 8b.)

8a. Flowers yellow, orange, red, or pink.
Deervetch (159, 160). Leaflets 3–7. Flowers yellow, tinged with orange.
Locust (178). Large shrubs or small trees; leaflets 9–19. Flowers pink.
Red bladderpod (180). Herbs; leaflets 15–25. Flowers dull red.

8b. Flowers blue, purple, violet, or white.
Sophora (171, 172). Stamens separate; pods constricted between the seeds. Flowers white or blue.
Locoweed (179). Stamens united; keel petals with a prominent upturned beak; pods usually inflated. Flowers white to blue.
Milkvetch (161–69). Stamens united; keel petals without a prominent upturned beak; fruit often inflated. Flowers white to blue.

9a. Flowers yellow or orange.
Deervetch (159, 160). Leaflets 3–7; staminal filaments flattened. Flowers yellow tinged with orange.
Golden pea (143). Stipules leaflike. Bright yellow.
Yellow sweet clover (158). Large, coarse plants with small flowers in slender racemes; veins of leaflets projecting into the teeth. Flowers yellow.

9b. Flowers blue, purple, white, pink, or red. (See 10a or 10b.)

10a. Leaflets 5–8.
Lupine (144–47). Leaves in palmate arrangement. Flowers blue or purple.

10b. Leaflets 3. (See 11a or 11b.)

11a. Shrubs with hooked prickles on stems and leaves.
Coralbean (154). Flowers scarlet.

11b. Herbs without hooked prickles. (See 12a or 12b.)

12a. Stems twining; keels of flowers coiled or incurved.
Wild bean (148). Flowers pink, purple, or red.

12b. Stems not twining; keels of flowers not coiled or incurved.
Alfalfa (156). Fruits coiled. Flowers violet.
Clover (155). Flowers in dense, headlike clusters. Flowers white to pink.
White sweet clover (157). Flowers in slender racemes. Flowers white.

Key to the Common Names of the Genera of the Mustard Family

1a. Leaves, at least the basal ones, deeply or shallowly pinnately lobed or sometimes twice divided into numerous segments. (See 2a or 2b.)

1b. Leaves entire to toothed. (See 3a or 3b.)

2a. Flowers pinkish, purplish, or white.
Greggia (69). Stems and leaves covered with star-shaped hairs. Flowers white or tinged with purple.
Thelypodium (78). Basal leaves lyrate-pinnatifid; fruits linear, 1⅝–2¾ in. (4–8 cm) long. Flowers white to pale purple.
Watercress (84). Aquatic; leaf segments wavy. Flowers white.

2b. Flowers yellow.
Desert plume (77). Upper leaves often clasping the stem. Flowers creamy yellow to yellow.
Tansy mustard (80, 81). Leaves twice pinnatifid. Flowers pale yellow or yellow.
Wintercress (83). Basal leaves lyrate-pinnatifid; fruits slender, 4-angled, slender-beaked at the tip. Flowers yellow.
Yellow cress (85). Leaves smooth above, hairy beneath, wavy-pinnatifid. Flowers yellow.

3a. Fruits wedge-shaped, globose or nearly so, or resembling a pair of spectacles, often as wide as or wider than long, typically less than ⅜ in. (10 mm) long. (See 4a or 4b.)

3b. Fruits linear or oblong, mostly much more than ⅜ in. (10 mm) long, occasionally shorter. (See 5a or 5b.)

4a. Flowers white to purple; fruits not obviously inflated.
Spectacle-pod (87). Fruits flattish, somewhat spectaclelike in appearance. Flowers white.
Wild candytuft (88). Fruits wedge-shaped or somewhat asymmetrically curved; stem leaves often clasping the stem at the base. Flowers white or purplish.

4b. Flowers yellow; fruits obviously flattened.

Bladderpod (89, 90). Basal leaves linear to narrowly lance-shaped or spatulate; fruit not notched. Flowers bright yellow.

Twinpod (86). Basal leaves spatulate to rounded; fruits deeply notched. Flowers yellow.

5a. Fruits mostly 1/4–3/4 in. (0.5–2.0 cm) long.

Greggia (69). Mature fruits somewhat 4-angled. Flowers white.

Whitlowgrass (75, 76). Mature fruits flattened, often twisted. Flowers yellow or white.

5b. Fruits mostly 3/4–4 in. (2–10 cm) long. (See 6a or 6b.)

6a. Leaves heart-shaped.

Bittercress (68). Flowers white.

6b. Leaves linear to obovate or ovate. (See 7a or 7b.)

7a. Calyx flask-shaped and nearly closed at flowering time; petals often twisted or recurved.

Twistflower (70, 71, 72). Flowers white, purple, or yellow.

7b. Calyx and petals not as in 7a. (See 8a or 8b.)

8a. Petals yellow or orange.

Wallflower (79). Fruits very slender, erect, 2–4 in. (5–10 cm) long.

8b. Petals white to pink or purple.

Rockcress (73, 74). Fruits hanging downward at maturity. Flowers pink to purplish.

Tumble mustard (82). Upper leaves linear, without teeth; fruits nearly erect, slender. Flowers rose purple.

Key to the Common Names of the Genera of the Cactus Family

1a. Spine pads (areoles) containing very short, barbed spines in addition to typical spines; stems usually jointed. (See 2a or 2b.)

1b. Spine pads (areoles) not as above; stems typically not jointed but may be branched from the base. (See 3a or 3b.)

2a. Joints conspicuously flattened in cross section.
Prickly pear (212, 213, 214). Flowers yellow or pink.

2b. Joints rounded in cross section, at least not conspicuously flattened.
Cholla (209, 210, 211). Flowers yellow or purplish.

3a. Stems longitudinally ribbed. (See 4a or 4b.)

3b. Stems not ribbed, the spine pads (areoles) located at the summit of conspicuous, more or less conical projections (tubercles). (See 5a or 5b.)

4a. Ribs 15–22.
Hedgehog cactus (218). Flowers reddish purple or yellowish.

4b. Ribs 5–14.
Hedgehog cactus (215, 216, 217). Flowers green, reddish purple, or red.

5a. Spine pads and ovaries with dense, whitish, woolly hairs.
Turk's head and *horse crippler* (219, 220). Flowers pink or purplish.

5b. Spine pads and ovaries not whitish woolly. (See 6a or 6b.)

6a. Tubercles grooved from the tip to at least the middle.
Pincushion cactus (223, 224). Flowers pink to purple.

6b. Tubercles not grooved or only slightly grooved at the tip.
Pincushion cactus (221, 222). Flowers whitish to yellowish to pale pink.

Key to the Common Names of the Genera of the Aster Family

1a. Flower heads similar to those of dandelions, with all the flowers strap-shaped; plants usually with milky juice. (See 2a or 2b.)

1b. Flower heads with flowers 2-lipped, the upper lip 2-lobed, the lower lip 3-toothed.
Desert holly (337). Leaves hollylike. Flowers rose purple.

1c. Flower heads with only the outer series of flowers strap-shaped (ray flowers), these resembling the flower heads of daisies or sunflowers; central flowers inconspicuous and with tubular, 5-toothed corollas (disk flowers); sometimes none of the flowers strap-shaped.

2a. Flowers white, pink, or purple. (See 3a or 3b.)

2b. Flowers yellow or orange. (See 4a or 4b.)

3a. Bristles at the summit of the fruits feathery, with conspicuous plumelike, lateral projections.
Wire lettuce (324, 325). Fruits not tapering at the summit into a beaklike projection. Flowers pinkish.
Desert chicory (326). Fruits tapering at the summit into a slender, beaklike projection. Flowers white or pink.

3b. Bristles at the summit of the fruits slender and threadlike, without conspicuous plumelike, lateral projections.
Desert dandelion (327). Upper stem bearing conspicuous stalked glands. Flowers white, pink, or purple.
Skeleton plant (331, 332). Plants without stalked glands, often smooth. Flowers pink or rose.

4a. Leaves entirely basal.
Dandelion (328). Fruits 4- or 5-ribbed. Flowers yellow.
Mountain dandelion (329). Fruits 10-ribbed. Flowers yellow.
Microseris (333, 334). Fruits 10-ribbed. Flowers yellow.

4b. Leaves scattered on the stem as well as clustered at the base.
Desert dandelion (335). Basal leaves smooth or with clumps of soft, woolly hairs. Flowers yellow, tinged with purple beneath.
Dwarf dandelion (336). Basal leaves smooth. Flowers yellow to orange.
Hawkweed (330). Basal leaves with numerous stiffish hairs. Flowers yellow.

5a. Flower heads without strap-shaped flowers, all disklike. (See 6a or 6b.)

6a. Flowers whitish.
Pussytoes (338). Plants woolly throughout; stems matted-spreading.
Everlasting (339). Plants woolly; stems erect.

6b. Flowers pinkish or yellowish.
Greenthread (363). Leaves divided into several slender lobes. Flowers yellowish.
Palafoxia (358). Leaves lance-shaped, not divided into lobes. Flowers pinkish.

7a. Outer series of flowers white, pink, blue, or purple. (See 8a or 8b.)

7b. Outer series of flowers yellow. (See 10a or 10b.)

8a. Leaves finely dissected into numerous short, narrow segments.
Yarrow (354). Plants aromatic when bruised. Flowers white.

8b. Leaves with toothed or smooth margins. (See 9a or 9b.).

9a. Flowers of the outer series purple, violet, or blue.
Daisy fleabane (344, 345). Ray flowers often 50 or more.
Aster (348, 349). Ray flowers usually fewer than 50.

9b. Flowers of the outer series white or pink.
Daisy fleabane (343, 345, 346, 347). Plants usually erect; leaves alternate or basal.
Blackfoot (366). Plants low and spreading; leaves opposite.

10a. Leaves opposite (See 11a or 11b.)

10b. Leaves alternate. (See 12a or 12b.)

11a. Leaves relatively broad, ovate or heart-shaped, mostly more than 5/8 in. (15 mm) wide.
Arnica (350). Leaves heart-shaped; fruit 5- to 10-angled.
Mexican sunflower (365). Leaves ovate; fruits flattish, 2-winged.

11b. Leaves relatively narrow, linear to oblong, usually not more than 1/2 in. (12 mm) wide, without marginal teeth.
Baeria (360). Leaves linear; fruits 4-angled.
Bahia (361). Leaves oblong-elliptic; fruits slender, 4-angled.
Zinnia (362). Leaves linear, 3-veined from the base; rays broad, persistent, papery in age; fruits strongly compressed, 2-angled.

12a. Bristles at the summit of the fruits slender and mostly threadlike.
Groundsel (351, 352, 353). Involucral bracts subtended at the base by several tiny bractlets.

Golden aster (341). Plants densely pubescent; fruits flattish.

Goldenweed (342). Leaves spiny-toothed.

12b. Bristles at the summit of the fruits mostly broad and scalelike. (See 13a or 13b.)

13a. Flower heads very small, usually with only 3–8 ray flowers.

Snakeweed (340). Leaves and flower clusters somewhat sticky.

13b. Flowers heads larger, usually with 10 or more ray flowers. (See 14a or 14b.)

14a. Leaves toothed; fruits strongly compressed and 2-winged.

Crownbeard (364).

14b. Leaves mostly without teeth or lobes; fruits not compressed or 2-winged.

Bitterweed (356, 357). Leaves deeply pinnately lobed, or else smooth on the margins and long-tapering to the base.

Paperflower (359). Plants much branched and woolly; rays persistent and papery at maturity.

Sneezeweed (359). Fruits with 8–10 ribs; plants tall and erect.

New Mexico Spring Wildflowers Descriptions and Illustrations

The 366 species of spring-blooming wildflowers characterized in this book are represented by both common and scientific names and the common name of the family to which each species belongs. These names are followed by a description of characteristics pertaining to the identification of each species, including size measurements where useful and flower color.

Additional remarks present a brief account of the maximum known range of distribution, the approximate distribution within New Mexico, the elevational range, and the kinds of habitats usually associated with this species.

Following the description and under the heading *Key Characters* is a listing of those features most useful in making a quick identification of the described plant. Where appropriate, additional remarks are included under the category of *Related Species*. These remarks deal with the identity of other closely related species which can be found occasionally as part of the spring flora.

Note also that each plant name is preceded by a number. This number refers only to the plant whose description follows and is used as a reference number in the keys to identification and in the index. These reference numbers are more useful than page numbers.

Each description is accompanied by a line drawing showing the major features. Many of these illustrations are further supplemented by the numerous color plates provided.

1. **Dayflower**   *Commelina erecta*   Spiderwort family

Perennial herb, the stems several, jointed, to about 16 in. (40 cm) long, erect when young, then spreading. *Leaves* alternate, sheathing the stem at the base, linear to narrowly lanceolate, to 6 in. (15 cm) long and about 1/5–3/8 in. (5–10 mm) wide, with smooth margins. *Flowers* with two blue petals and a slightly larger white petal, all petals 3/8–5/8 in. (10–15 mm) long, the flower arising from two long, tapered bracts. The delicate flowers of the dayflower (or widow's-tears) open about dawn and last until around noon.
Range and Habitat: New York to Colorado, southward to Florida, Louisiana, Texas, New Mexico, and Arizona. Usually found on dry hills and plains in fine or sandy soil, often in shady spots in north-central to southwestern New Mexico; 3,500–6,000 ft.
Key Characters: Dayflower is characterized by the long united bracts below the flower, and by the delicate petals, one whitish and the other two blue.
Related Species: Two other species of dayflower are similar but have longer bracts, and all three petals are blue.

2. **Western spiderwort**   *Tradescantia occidentalis*   Spiderwort family

Slender-stemmed herb from fascicled roots, the stems jointed, erect or nearly erect, to about 2 ft. (60 cm) high. *Leaves* alternate, sheathing the stem at the base, narrowly lanceolate, to 20 in. (50 cm) long and 3/4 in. (2 cm) wide, with smooth margins. *Flowers* in umbellike clusters, the three petals about the same size, blue, 3/8–5/8 in. (10–16 mm) long, usually only a few flowers of the cluster blooming at a time, the cluster arising from 2 or 3 leaflike bracts. The flowers of the spiderwort are showy, but last only a few hours, generally closing before noon. The tender shoots of this plant are sometimes used for food.
Range and Habitat: Wisconsin to Montana, southward to Texas, New Mexico, and Arizona. Usually found on dry hills and plains in somewhat sandy or fine soils, often in shady spots throughout New Mexico; 5,000–8,000 ft.
Key Characters: Spiderwort is characterized by the three similar blue petals and the flowers in an umbellike cluster.
Related Species: A variety of the Western spiderwort differs in being glabrous in and around the flower cluster, where the variety described has gland-bearing hairs in and around the flower cluster.

3. **Banana yucca; datil**   *Yucca baccata*   Lily family

Perennial without a noticeable trunk. *Leaves* in a dense cluster near the ground, narrow, elongate, rigid, bluish green, concave, 1 1/4–2 in. (3–5 cm) wide, bearing a few coarse, curved fibers on the margins. *Flowers* in a large open cluster, pendulous, 2–4 3/4 in. (5–12 cm) long, the petals lanceolate. *Fruit* 4–8 in. (10–20 cm) long, fleshy. The flowering panicle of the banana yucca remains close to the leaf cluster. The flowers, fruit, seed, and tender central leaves have been used for food. Fibers of the leaves have been used for weaving.
Range and Habitat: Colorado to Utah and Nevada, southward to Texas, New Mexico, Arizona, and California. Banana yucca is widespread on mesas, dry hills, and rocky slopes of New Mexico; 3,500–7,500 ft.
Key Characters: The wide, thick leaves borne near the ground and the flowering panicle partly within the leaf cluster are characteristic of the banana yucca.

Commelina erecta

Tradescantia occidentalis

Yucca baccata

4. **Soaptree yucca; palmilla**   *Yucca elata*   Lily family

Perennial, often with a definite, usually branching trunk, the plant to about 18 ft. (6 m) tall. *Leaves* narrow, 10–30 in. (25–70 cm) long, ¹/₄–¹/₂ in. (6–12 mm) wide, with many fine fibers on the margins. *Flowers* in a large, much-branched, open cluster borne above the leaves on a long leafless stalk, the petals white, elliptic to lanceolate, ¹/₄–1³/₄ in. (3.0–4.5 cm) long. *Flowers* dry at maturity, 2–3¹/₈ in. (5–8 cm) long, pale brown. The fruit, flowers, and young tender central leaves of this species are sometimes used for food, and the roots are used for making soap for washing woolens and for washing hair.
Range and Habitat: Southwestern Texas to Arizona and Mexico. Usually found on dry plains and hills in central and southern New Mexico; 3,500–5,500 ft.
Key Characters: Soaptree yucca is characterized by the frequent presence of an obvious trunk and the narrow leaves.

5. **Soapweed yucca; amole**   *Yucca glauca*   Lily family

Perennial, usually without a noticeable trunk, sometimes with a short decumbent stem. *Leaves* in a cluster, narrow, rigid, 8–40 in. (20–100 cm) long, ¹/₄–¹/₂ in. (6–12 mm) wide, bearing a few fine, grayish fibers on the margins. *Flowers* greenish white, in a narrow cluster (raceme), or occasionally on branches, the raceme borne on a leafless stalk to 3 ft. (1 m) tall, the petals 1¹/₄–2 in. (3–5 cm) long. *Fruit* dry at maturity, about 1¹/₂ in. (3 cm) long. The roots of soapweed yucca have been used for soap; the flowers, young flower stalks, and tender crowns have been eaten; and the leaves have been used in weaving and rope making.
Range and Habitat: Kansas to Colorado, southward to Texas and New Mexico. Usually found on dry hills and plains in northern, eastern, and central New Mexico; 5,000–6,500 ft.
Key Characters: Soapweed yucca is characterized by the normally unbranched raceme of flowers and the absence of a noticeable trunk.

6. **Torrey yucca; palma**   *Yucca torreyi*   Lily family

Perennial with stems unbranched or few-branched, 4–13 ft. (1.5–4.0 m) tall. *Leaves* in a dense cluster, rigid, rough, yellowish green, 24–42 in. (60–110 cm) long, 1¹/₄–2 in. (3–5 cm) wide, bearing coarse, grayish fibers on the margins. *Flowers* white, cream-colored, or tinged with purple, borne on a leafless stalk mostly above the leaves, the petals elliptic, 2–4 in. (5–10 cm) long. *Fruit* nearly dry at maturity, 2³/₄–4³/₄ in. (7–12 cm) long. Torrey yucca is a conspicuous element of arid land vegetation.
Range and Habitat: Western Texas and southern New Mexico. Normally found on dry hills and plains in southern New Mexico; 3,000–4,500 ft.
Key Characters: Torrey yucca is characterized by the tall, often branching trunk and the conspicuous cluster of flowers.

7. **Beargrass; sacahuista**   *Nolina microcarpa*   Lily family

Perennial without noticeable stems. *Leaves* many, in a dense cluster near the ground, narrow, somewhat flexible, to about 3 ft. (1 m) long and ¹/₄–¹/₂ in. (6–12 mm) wide, the margins rough to the touch. *Flowers* small, white, in a dense, many-flowered, open cluster (panicle), mostly not exceeding the leaves. *Fruit* a small 3-lobed capsule. Beargrass leaves have been used in weaving, and the young emerging flower stalks have been used for food.
Range and Habitat: Western Texas to Arizona and northern Mexico. Found mostly on dry hills and plains throughout New Mexico; 4,000–8,000 ft.
Key Characters: Beargrass may be recognized by the cluster of curving, wiry leaves, and the large, dense cluster of small flowers nestled among the leaves.

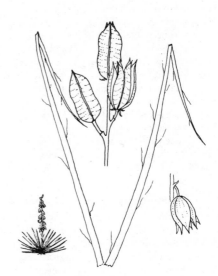

Yucca elata

Yucca glauca

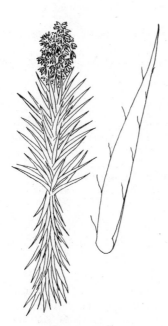

Yucca torreyi

Nolina microcarpa

8. Sotol   *Dasylirion wheeleri*   Lily family

Perennial from woody underground crowns. *Leaves* numerous, in a cluster near the base of the plant, rigid, flat, green or grayish green, to 3 ft. (90 cm) long and 5/8–1 in. (15–25 mm) wide, bearing numerous yellowish brown prickles on the margins. *Flowers* very numerous, unisexual, borne in a large narrow cluster (panicle) on a leafless stalk 10–12 ft. (3–4 m) tall, the flower segments less than 1/8 in. (2–3 mm) long. *Fruit* roundish, about 1/4 in. (6 mm) long. Sotol leaf fibers have been used for weaving, the young tender crowns used for making mescal, and the young emerging flower stalks used for food.

Range and Habitat: Western Texas to Arizona and northern Mexico. Found on dry hills in southern and west-central New Mexico; 3,500–6,500 ft.

Key Characters: Sotol may be easily recognized by the densely prickly leaf margins and the tall, narrow panicle of flowers.

Related Species: Another species of sotol is similar but differs in that the leaf prickles are curved toward the base of the leaf instead of toward the tip (*Dasylirion leiophyllum*).

9. Gunnison mariposa lily   *Calochortus gunnisonii*   Lily family

Erect perennial herb arising from corms. *Leaves* alternate on the stem, linear, grasslike. *Flowers* borne 1 to 3 in a cluster at the end of a slender leafless stalk, the petals white to purple, showy, bell-shaped, about 1 1/4–1 3/4 in. (3–4.5 cm) long, with a densely purple-bearded zone on the inside of the three inner ones, the outer segments purple-spotted. Gunnison mariposa lily is a showy plant. The plant has been used to make a thick tea to treat swellings.

Range and Habitat: South Dakota to Montana, southward to New Mexico and Arizona. Usually found in meadows and open ground in northern, central, and western New Mexico; 7,000–8,000 ft.

Key Characters: Gunnison mariposa lily is characterized by the densely purple-bearded zone on the petals, this zone wider than tall.

Related Species: A similar species, *C. ambiguus,* differs in the bearded zone, being circular or nearly so.

10. Sego lily   *Calochortus nuttallii*   Lily family

Erect perennial herb 8–16 in. (20–40 cm) high, from corms. *Leaves* alternate, linear, grasslike. *Flowers* 1 to 4 at the tip of a leafless stalk, this exceeding the leaves; the inner petals white to purple, the gland round or nearly so, usually sparsely bearded, often with a reddish brown zone above the gland, the outer segments with 1 or 2 purple spots. Sego lily has a conspicuous flower and is somewhat similar to Gunnison mariposa lily.

Range and Habitat: Nebraska to California, southward to New Mexico and Arizona. Usually found on open slopes in northern to southwestern New Mexico; 5,000–8,500 ft.

Key Characters: Sego lily may be recognized by the sparsely bearded, circular gland on the inner petal surface.

Related Species: A variety of sego lily has yellow petals, otherwise is similar to the variety described.

11. Solomon's seal   *Polygonatum cobrense*   Lily family

Perennial herb, the stems slender, glabrous, flexuous, to about 16 in. (40 cm) tall, from rhizomes. *Leaves* alternate, elliptic, glabrous, faintly nerved, 2–4 1/2 in. (5–11 cm) long, 3/8–1 1/4 in. (10–32 mm) wide, sessile or short-petioled. *Flowers* 1 to 3 in a cluster, the 6 segments greenish yellow, united to form a tube, 1/2–3/4 in. (12–20 mm) long. *Fruit* spherical, blue or black, about 1/4 in. (6–8 mm) in diameter.

Range and Habitat: New Mexico and eastern Arizona. Usually found on shaded or partially shaded slopes in southwestern New Mexico; 5,500–7,000 ft.

Key Characters: Solomon's seal can be recognized by the greenish yellow flowers on pedicels that curve downward.

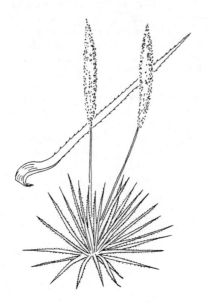

Dasylirion wheeleri

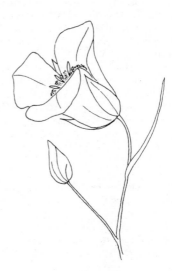

Calochortus gunnisonii

Calochortus nuttallii

Polygonatum cobrense

12. **Death camas** *Zygadenus paniculatus* Lily family

Glabrous perennial herb with relatively stout stems to about 28 in. (70 cm) tall, from bulbs. *Leaves* mostly crowded at the base of the stem, narrow, grasslike, 12–20 in. (30–50 cm) long, ³/₈–⁵/₈ in. (8–15 mm) wide, a few leaves sometimes present on the middle and upper parts of the stem. *Flowers* yellowish white, in a dense, widely branching, open cluster (panicle), the flower segments about ¹/₈ in. (3–4 mm) long, triangular, often with a short claw at the base. Death camas is highly poisonous, and care should be taken to avoid chewing on any part of the plant.
Range and Habitat: Montana to Washington, southward to New Mexico, Arizona, and California. Usually found on open plains and hills among grass or rocks in northwestern and central New Mexico; 5,000–7,000 ft.
Key Characters: Death camas resembles many other members of the Lily family but is characterized by the combination of small yellowish white flowers in a panicle, the mostly basal, grasslike leaves, and the bulb devoid of an onionlike odor.

13. **Bluedicks** *Dichelostemma pulchellum* Lily family

Glabrous perennial herb arising from corms with fibrous coatings. *Leaves* crowded at the base of the plant, linear, ³/₁₆–¹/₂ in. (5–12 mm) wide. *Flowers* blue, cylindrical or bell-shaped, borne in a loose umbel at the top of a leafless stalk 10–24 in. (25–60 cm) tall, the flower segments ¹/₄–¹/₂ in. (7–12 mm) long.
Range and Habitat: New Mexico to southeastern California and Mexico. Bluedicks usually occurs on open mesas and slopes in west-central and southwestern New Mexico; 4,000–5,500 ft.
Key Characters: Bluedicks is characterized by the blue flowers and by the conspicuous, lanceolate, leaflike bracts at the base of the umbel.

14. **Star lily; sand lily** *Leucocrinum montanum* Lily family

Stemless perennial herb from fleshy roots and short rhizomes. *Leaves* grasslike, borne near the ground, flat, 4–8 in. (10–20 cm) long, less than ¹/₄ in. (2–5 mm) wide, surrounded at the base by scarious bracts. *Flowers* white, borne in umbels attached to the tip of the rhizome, usually 4–8 flowers per umbel, on pedicels ⁵/₈–1¹/₄ in. (15–30 mm) long, the 6 flower segments forming a tube 2–2³/₄ in. (5–7 cm) long with lobes about ³/₄ in. (20 mm) long. *Fruit* about ¹/₄ in. (6–8 mm) long. This plant, though striking in appearance, can easily be overlooked because it grows and blooms so close to the ground.
Range and Habitat: South Dakota to Oregon, southward to New Mexico, Arizona, and California. Usually found on open slopes and in open meadows in northern New Mexico; 6,500–8,000 ft.
Key Characters: Star lily may be recognized by the low, stemless growth pattern and by the conspicuous white flowers.

15. **Green lily** *Schoenocaulon texanum* Lily family

Glabrous perennial herb from black, fibrous bulbs. *Leaves* from the base of the plant, linear, grasslike. *Flowers* greenish white, borne in a narrow raceme at the apex of a leafless stalk 10–20 in. (25–50 cm) tall, the 6 flower segments linear, about ¹/₈ in. (3–4 mm) long. *Fruit* about ¹/₂ in. (10–12 mm) long.
Range and Habitat: Western Texas to New Mexico and Mexico. Generally occurring on dry plains and hills in southeastern and south-central New Mexico; 3,500–4,500 ft.
Key Characters: The narrow, spikelike raceme of greenish white flowers borne on a scape from black, fibrous-coated bulbs is characteristic of this plant.

Zygadenus paniculatus

Dichelostemma pulchellum

Leucocrinum montanum

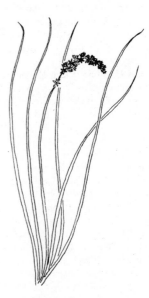

Schoenocaulon texanum

16. **Large-petal onion**   *Allium macropetalum*   Lily family

Perennial herb 4–12 in. (10–30 cm) tall, from 1 to 3 strong-scented, fibrous-coated bulbs. *Leaves* usually 2 per flowering stem, about ⅛ in. (2–4 mm) wide, nearly round. *Flowers* borne in an erect umbel, the outer pedicels drooping in fruit. The umbel subtended by 2 bracts with 3 to 5 nerves, the flower segments pink, about ¼–⅜ in. (8–10 mm) long. *Fruit* a crested capsule. This plant is a striking part of the early spring flora.
Range and Habitat: Colorado and Utah to Texas, New Mexico, and Arizona. This plant is commonly found on dry plains throughout New Mexico; 4,500–6,500 ft.
Key Characters: Large-petal onion is characterized by the reticulate, fibrous bulb coat, the 2 leaves, and the 3 bracts subtending the erect umbel.

17. **Geyer onion**   *Allium geyeri*   Lily family

Perennial herb 6–20 in. (15–50 cm) tall, from a strong-scented, fibrous-coated bulb. *Leaves* usually 3 per flowering stem, about ⅛ in. (2–3 mm) wide. *Flowers* borne in an erect umbel subtended by 2 or 3 single-nerved bracts, the flower segments white or pink, ¼–⅜ in. (6–10 mm) long. *Fruit* a capsule without obvious crests. Geyer onion has been used to flavor soups and gravy and is occasionally eaten raw.
Range and Habitat: Alberta to Washington, southward to Texas, New Mexico, and Arizona. Geyer onion is commonly found in meadows and on slopes throughout New Mexico; 6,500–12,000 ft.
Key Characters: Geyer onion is characterized by the fibrous-coated, solitary bulb, the three leaves, and the single-nerved bracts.

18. **Wild sweet onion**   *Allium perdulce*   Lily family

Perennial herb to 8 in. (20 cm) tall, from fibrous-coated bulbs. *Leaves* 3 or more, linear (1–2 mm) wide, as long or longer than the flowering stems. *Flowers* borne in an erect umbel subtended by 2 or 3 5-nerved bracts, the flower segments deep rose to purple, ¼–⅜ in. (7–10 mm) long. *Fruit* a capsule without crests. The short, wild, sweet onion is often overlooked in the grassy plains.
Range and Habitat: South Dakota to Texas and New Mexico. Usually found early in the spring on sandy plains in eastern New Mexico; 3,500–5,500 ft.
Key Characters: Wild sweet onion may be identified by the fibrous-coated bulbs, the capsules without crests, the 5-nerved bracts, and the 3 leaves.

19. **Crow-poison**   *Nothoscordum texanum*   Lily family

Perennial herb to 14 in. (35 cm) tall, from bulbs. *Leaves* basal, linear. *Flowers* few, on slender pedicels, borne in an umbel at the apex of a leafless stalk, the umbel subtended by 1–3 bracts forming a sheath, the 6 flower segments separate, yellowish white, tinged with purple on the outside, about ½ in. (10 mm) long. *Fruit* a capsule. Crow-poison resembles an onion but lacks the characteristic onion odor.
Range and Habitat: Western Texas to southern Arizona. Often found in dry grasslands in southern New Mexico; 4,000–6,000 ft.
Key Characters: Crow-poison may be recognized by the umbels of whitish flowers subtended by scarious bracts; it differs from the wild onion in not having an onionlike odor.

Allium macropetalum

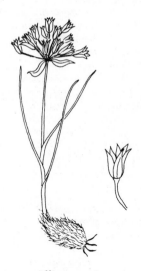

Allium geyeri

Allium perdulce

Nothoscordum texanum

20. **False Solomon's seal**   *Smilacina racemosa*   Lily family

Herb, the stems erect to spreading, usually unbranching, from rhizomes. *Leaves* alternate, ovate or elliptic, on short petioles, bearing fine hairs beneath, the nerves prominent. *Flowers* somewhat inconspicuous, borne in an open cluster (panicle), the 6 segments similar, white, about ⅛ in. (2–3 mm) long. *Fruit* a red berry bearing purplish spots, about ¼ in. (5 mm) in diameter. The bright green foliage of this forest plant is perhaps as striking and attractive as the small flowers.
Range and Habitat: Throughout much of temperate North America. Commonly found on forested slopes throughout New Mexico; 7,000–10,000 ft.
Key Characters: This plant is characterized by the relatively large, conspicuously nerved, alternate leaves, and by the terminal panicle of small white flowers.
Related Species: A variety of the false Solomon's seal has leaves that are sessile and often clasping. Star flower, *S. stellata,* is distinguished by the flowers borne in racemes, and by the berries that are nearly black at maturity.

21. **Fairybells**   *Disporum trachycarpum*   Lily family

Perennial herb, from elongate rhizomes, the stems erect, somewhat hairy, 12–20 in. (30–50 cm) tall. *Leaves* alternate, sessile, many-nerved, ovate to oblong-ovate, with rounded or subcordate bases. *Flowers* solitary or few in a cluster at the apex of the stem, drooping, the 6 segments similar, separate, narrow, white to yellowish white, ⅜–⅝ in. (10–15 mm) long. *Fruit* a 3-lobed berry about ⅜ in. (8–10 mm) in diameter.
Range and Habitat: Manitoba to British Columbia, southward to New Mexico and Arizona. Fairybells may be found in damp woods in north-central to northwestern New Mexico; 7,000–9,500 ft.
Key Characters: Fairybells may be identified by the drooping flowers in terminal clusters, not subtended by bracts, and by the rhizomes instead of bulbs.

22. **Rocky Mountain lily**   *Lilium umbellatum*   Lily family

Perennial herb, with leafy stems, 12–25 in. (30–65 cm) tall, from bulbs bearing thick fleshy scales. *Leaves* mostly alternate but the upper nodes of the stem bearing whorls of leaves, all leaves glabrous, linear to lanceolate. *Flowers* showy, solitary or sometimes 2 or 3 in a cluster, red to orange red with purplish black spots near the base, the segments separate, long-clawed, 2–2½ in. (5–6 cm) long, spreading to recurved at the tip. *Fruit* a capsule. Rocky Mountain lily is a conspicuous spring plant.
Range and Habitat: Ohio to Alberta, southward to Arkansas, New Mexico, and Arizona. Usually found in open woods from northern to south-central New Mexico; 7,000–8,000 ft.
Key Characters: Rocky Mountain lily is easily recognized by the showy orange flowers, and by the whorls of leaves at the upper nodes.

23. **Fritillary**   *Fritillaria atropurpurea*   Lily family

Perennial herb, from thick-scaled bulbs, the stems leafy, erect, unbranching, 6–18 in. (15–45 cm) tall. *Leaves* alternate or often whorled at the upper nodes, linear, about ⅛ in. (2–4 mm) wide. *Flowers* solitary or 2 to 4 in a narrow cluster (raceme), showy, nodding, purple with yellowish white spots, bell-shaped, the segments 6, similar, ⅜–¾ in. (10–20 mm) long. *Fruit* a 6-angled capsule.
Range and Habitat: North Dakota to Oregon, southward to New Mexico, Arizona, and California. Found occasionally on plains and slopes, often in wooded areas in northwestern New Mexico; 6,000–9,000 ft.
Key Characters: Fritillary may be recognized by the nodding, dark purple flowers bearing yellowish white spots.

Smilacina racemosa

Disporum trachycarpum

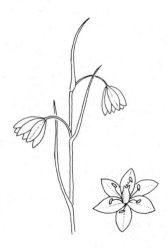

Lilium umbellatum

Fritillaria atropurpurea

24. Funnellily — *Androstephium breviflorum* — Lily family

Perennial herb from ovoid corms with membranous or fibrous coatings. *Leaves* few, basal, linear. *Flowers* 3 to 12, funnel-shaped, borne on stout, scabrous, leafless stalks 4–12 in. (10–30 cm) tall, in a terminal umbel subtended by scarious bracts, the flower stalks $^1/_2$–$^3/_4$ in. (12–18 mm) long, the 6 segments united to below the midpoint, white, purplish, or sometimes tinged with bluish purple, $^5/_8$–$^3/_4$ in. (15–20 mm) long. *Fruit* a capsule $^5/_8$–$^3/_4$ in. (15–18 mm) long.

Range and Habitat: Colorado to California, southward to New Mexico and Arizona. Found occasionally on dry, sandy mesas in northwestern New Mexico; 5,000–7,000 ft.

Key Characters: Funnellily is characterized by the funnel-shaped flowers with the segments united for nearly half their length, and by the 6 stamens with their filaments united into a tube.

25. Century plant — *Agave palmeri* — Amaryllis family

Large perennial without noticeable stems. *Leaves* in a basal rosette, from a woody rootstock, green, lanceolate, 2–4 in. (5–10 cm) wide, the margins bearing numerous spines curved toward the base of the leaf, the leaf tip ending in a spine. *Flowers* borne in an open cluster (panicle) terminating a tall, stout stalk, this to 14 ft. (4 m) tall, the flowers perfect, complete, of 6 similar greenish yellow segments, the 6 stamens exserted. *Fruit* a capsule $1^1/_2$–$2^1/_2$ in. (40–60 cm) long. Century plant in flower is sure to draw attention. In general, a century plant will bloom at an average age of about 17 years, not 100 years. After blooming, the parent plant dies.

Range and Habitat: New Mexico to Arizona and central Mexico. Commonly found on dry, rocky slopes and desert grasslands in southern New Mexico; 5,000–6,500 ft.

Key Characters: Century plant is easily recognized, especially when in bloom, by the large, toothed leaves in a basal rosette, and by the tall, flowering stalk with the flowers borne in an open panicle.

Related Species: Another century plant, New Mexico agave (*A. neomexicana*), has bluish green leaves that are usually less than 16 in. (40 cm) long. It is normally found in situations similar to those of the above century plant.

26. Lechuguilla — *Agave lechuguilla* — Amaryllis family

Perennial. *Leaves* yellowish green or grayish green, often curved, 1–$1^1/_2$ in. (2.5–3.5 cm) wide, spine-tipped, the margins bearing spines curved toward the base of the leaf. *Flowers* borne in a narrow, spikelike cluster (panicle) on a leafless stalk to 10 ft. (3 m) tall, the 6 flower segments greenish yellow to pale yellow, sometimes purple-tinged, the 6 stamens exserted. *Fruit* a capsule $^3/_4$–1 in. (20–25 mm) long. Lechuguilla is a smaller, more compact version of the century plant, usually growing at lower elevations and flowering earlier.

Range and Habitat: New Mexico to Texas and central Mexico. Common on dry hills and plains in south-central and southeastern New Mexico; 3,000–4,500 ft.

Key Characters: Lechuguilla may be identified by the tighter flowering panicle and the yellowish green, curved leaves in a rosette of mostly 12–15 leaves instead of 30 or more.

Related Species: Mescal (*A. parryi*) grows in similar situations but has more leaves, wider leaves, and an open panicle of flowers, these somewhat larger than those of lechuguilla.

Androstephium breviflorum

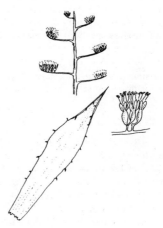

Agave palmeri

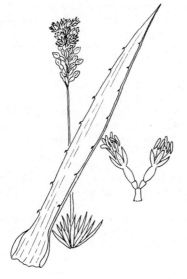

Agave lechuguilla

27. **Zephyr lily; Atamosco lily**   *Zephyranthes longifolia*   Amaryllis family

Perennial herb from ovoid bulbs 3/4–1 in. (2–2.5 cm) in diameter. *Leaves* linear, grasslike, 6–
10 in. (15–25 cm) long. *Flowers* borne singly at the top of a leafless stalk to 14 in. (35 cm)
tall, subtended by floral bracts 3/4–1 in. (2.0–2.5 cm) long, the 6 similar segments usually
1 1/4–1 1/2 in. (3–4 cm) long, bright yellow, conspicuous, the stamens included in the
perianth. Zephyr lily is usually a conspicuous part of the flora, appearing about 10 days after
a rain.
Range and Habitat: Western Texas to Arizona and Mexico. Usually found on dry hills and
mesas in central and southern New Mexico; 3,000–7,500 ft.
Key Characters: Zephyr lily is characterized by the nearly spherical, deeply 3-lobed fruit,
and by the yellow flowers with stamens included.

28. **Hairy stargrass**   *Hypoxis hirsuta*   Amaryllis family

Stemless perennial herb from corms. *Leaves* linear, grasslike, less than 1/4 in. (6 mm) wide,
strongly hairy, usually longer than the flowering stalk. *Flowers* borne singly or 2–7 in a
cluster at the top of a slender stalk, the 6 segments yellow inside, greenish on the outside.
Fruit a capsule bearing a beak.
Range and Habitat: Maine to Saskatachewan, southward to Florida, Texas, and eastern
Colorado. Not reported for New Mexico but expected to occur on plains and along foothills in
extreme northeastern New Mexico; 5,000–6,500 ft.
Key Characters: Hairy stargrass may be recognized by the narrow, hairy (villous) leaves that
exceed the flowering stalk, and by the beaked capsule.

29. **Rocky Mountain iris**   *Iris missouriensis*   Iris family

Perennial from rhizomes, to 28 in. (75 cm) tall. *Leaves* linear, glabrous, bluish green, 2-
ranked, light green, 1/4–3/8 in. (6–10 mm) wide. *Flowers* in terminal clusters, each subtended
by 2 scarious bracts, the sepals about 2 1/2 in. (6 cm) long, drooping, yellowish white at the
constricted base, the claw yellowish white, the expanded upper part mostly blue, sometimes
with purple veins. *Fruit* a capsule 1 1/4–2 in. (3–5 cm) long. Wild iris is a conspicuous plant
of moist mountain meadows.
Range and Habitat: North Dakota to British Columbia, southward to New Mexico,
Arizona, and California. Commonly found in open meadows of higher mountains throughout
New Mexico; 7,500–10,500 ft.
Key Characters: Wild iris is easily recognized by its resemblance to the cultivated iris,
though usually smaller in size.

30. **Blue-eyed grass**   *Sisyrinchium campestre*   Iris family

Erect perennial herb to 12 in. (30 cm) tall, the stems narrow, winged, without leafy bracts.
Leaves linear, grasslike, 4–8 in. (10–20 cm) long. *Flowers* in clusters at the tip of the stem,
subtended by 2 bracts, the outer much longer than the inner one, the 6 perianth segments
pale blue or white. *Fruit* about 1/8 in. (2–4 mm) long. This plant is often overlooked in
dense stands of grasses or sedges.
Range and Habitat: Wisconsin to Manitoba, southward to Louisiana, Texas, and New
Mexico. Usually found on moist mountain slopes and in moist meadows in northern to south-
central New Mexico; 7,000–8,500 ft.
Key Characters: Blue-eyed grass may be identified by the 6 similar petals, the low stature
of the plant, the grasslike leaves, and the unequal bracts subtending the flowers.

Zephyranthes longifolia

Hypoxis hirsuta

Iris missouriensis

Sisyrinchium campestre

31. **Wister's coralroot**   *Corallorhiza wisteriana*   Orchid family

Perennial from stout rhizomes, the stems purplish or yellowish, 8–20 in. (20–50 cm) tall. *Leaves* reduced to brownish, purplish, or yellowish scales. *Flowers* in narrow clusters (racemes) at the tip of the stem, the sepals and side petals 1/4–3/8 in. (6–8 mm) long, greenish yellow with purple lines, the lower petal (lip or labellum) about 1/4 in. (6 mm) long, white with purple spots, not striped or lobed, but the margins irregularly notched. Wister's coralroot, as all the coralroots, lacks chlorophyll, and often resembles an upright stick in the forest.
Range and Habitat: Pennsylvania to Idaho, southward to Florida, New Mexico, and Arizona. Common in deep, forested mountain slopes throughout New Mexico; 7,000–9,500 ft.
Key Characters: Wister's coralroot may be identified by the absence of chlorophyll and the unlobed lip bearing spots and lacking striations.

32. **Helleborine**   *Epipactis gigantea*   Orchid family

Perennial herb from creeping rhizomes, the stems leafy, to 32 in. (80 cm) tall. *Leaves* alternate, clasping the stem, ovate to lanceolate, to about 6 in. (15 cm) long, the veins conspicuous. *Flowers* few, to 1 1/2 in. (30 mm) long, borne in a slender cluster, the sepals greenish and spreading, the petals greenish purple, shorter than the sepals, the lip (labellum) about 5/8 in.
(15 mm) long, greenish with purple lines. Helleborine contains chlorophyll; thus it is neither parasitic nor saprophytic.
Range and Habitat: Montana to British Columbia, southward to western Texas, New Mexico, Arizona, and California. Found occasionally in damp woods, usually on seeping slopes, east-central to southern and western New Mexico; 7,000–8,500 ft.
Key Characters: Helleborine may be recognized by the often tall, leafy stems and the flowers to 1 1/2 in. (30 mm) long.

33. **Canaigre; Wild rhubarb**   *Rumex hymenosepalus*   Buckwheat family

Perennial herb from tuberous roots, the stems stout, glabrous, reddish or reddish green, 2–4 ft. (60–120 cm) tall. *Leaves* alternate, elliptic to oblong, 2 1/2–12 in. (6–30 cm) long, the petioles somewhat clasping the stem and subtended by membraneous stipules that more or less form a sheath around the stem. *Flowers* in compact clusters, the segments about 1/8 in. (2–3 mm) long, pinkish. *Fruit* enclosed by 3 coarsely veined wings 3/8–5/8 in. (10–15 mm) long. The tuberous roots of this plant have been used for tanning leather. With careful preparation, various parts of the plant have been used for food and medicine.
Range and Habitat: Wyoming to Utah and California, southward to western Texas, Arizona and northern Mexico. Common in sandy fields and mesas throughout New Mexico; 4,000–6,500 ft.
Key Characters: Canaigre is one of the earliest plants to appear in the spring. A reddish green, conspicuous head resembling maize arises from the dark green leaves. It differs from other members of the genus by the larger wings enclosing the fruit, and by the lack of grains on each wing.

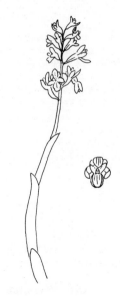

Corallorhiza wisteriana

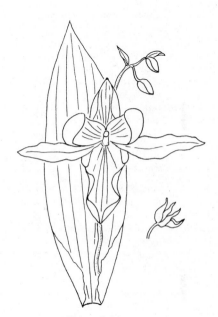

Epipactis gigantea

Rumex hymenosepalus

34. Umbrellawort   *Allionia incarnata*   Four-o'clock family

Perennial herb, the stems prostrate on the ground, bearing sticky hairs. *Leaves* ovate, often with glands and hairs, 3/8–1 1/8 in. (1–3 cm) long, the base oblique and rounded. *Flowers* in axillary clusters of 3, each subtended by 3 distinct bracts, the segments pink, 1/4–5/8 in. (6–15 mm) long. *Fruit* bearing 2 strongly incurved wings. Umbrellawort is relatively inconspicuous and has an unpleasant feel due to the sticky hairs on the stems. The flowers usually open late in the afternoon and close about mid-morning.
Range and Habitat: Colorado to California, southward to Mexico. Commonly found on dry slopes throughout New Mexico; 3,500–6,500 ft.
Key Characters: Umbrellawort may be recognized by the prostrate, sticky stems, the bright pink flowers appearing early in the morning or late afternoon, and by the fruit with 2 strongly incurved wings.

35. Desert four-o'clock   *Oxybaphus nyctagineus*   Four-o'clock family

Perennial herb, the stems nearly glabrous, 12–40 in. (30–100 cm) tall. *Leaves* opposite, triangular to ovate, rounded at the base, pointed at the apex, to 4 3/4 in. (12 cm) long, petioled. *Flowers* axillary or in loose clusters, the segments red or pink, about 3/8 in. (10 mm) long, subtended by a 5-lobed involucre, the stamens exserted. Desert four-o'clock typically opens late in the afternoon and closes about mid-morning.
Range and Habitat: Wisconsin to Montana, southward to Texas, New Mexico, and Mexico, Usually found in open, dry, mostly gravelly areas in northeastern and central New Mexico; 4,000–6,500 ft.
Key Characters: Desert four-o'clock may be identified by the almost glabrous flower clusters, the nearly erect stems, and the leaves on petioles at least 1/4 in. (6 mm) long.

36. White four-o'clock   *Oxybaphus albidus*   Four-o'clock family

Perennial herb, the stems erect, whitish, to 4 ft. (120 cm) tall. *Leaves* opposite, linear to ovate, glabrous, on short petioles or sessile. *Flowers* in clusters of 1 to 3, the segments white or pink, about 3/8 in. (10 mm) long, each cluster subtended by a 5-lobed involucre. White four-o'clock is inconspicuous unless noticed in the late afternoon or early morning when the flowers are open.
Range and Habitat: South Carolina and Alabama to Missouri, Kansas, Texas, and New Mexico. Usually found on dry slopes and in dry meadows in southern New Mexico; 3,500–6,500 ft.
Key Characters: White four-o'clock may be recognized by the typical four-o'clock flowering pattern, by the erect whitish stems, and by the petioles shorter than 1/4 in. (6 mm) long.

37. Sweet sand verbena   *Abronia fragrans*   Four-o'clock family

Perennial herb, the stems erect to spreading, usually with sticky hairs, to 40 in. (1 m) tall. *Leaves* opposite, ovate to nearly oblong, rounded to truncate at the base, pointed or rounded at the apex, 3/4–3 in. (2–8 cm) long. *Flowers* numerous, borne in verbenalike heads, the perianth long and narrow, with segments white or pink-tinged, 5/8–1 in. (15–25 mm) long, the heads subtended by thin, membranous, involucral bracts 3/8–3/4 in. (10–20 mm) long. *Fruit* 1/4–3/8 in. (5–10 mm) long, bearing 3–5 narrow wings. This plant is often mistaken for a verbena.
Range and Habitat: South Dakota to Idaho, southward to Texas, Arizona, and Mexico. Commonly found in sandy soil throughout New Mexico; 4,000–6,000 ft.
Key Characters: Sweet sand verbena may be recognized by the pale verbenalike flowers and by the strongly winged fruit.
Related Species: A similar plant, winged sand verbena, may be found in like habitats but differs in that the wings are completely surrounding the fruit and are conspicuously net-veined.

Allionia incarnata

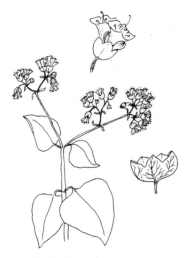

Oxybaphus nyctagineus

Oxybaphus albidus

Abronia fragrans

38. Spiderling   *Boerhaavia erecta*   Four-o'clock family

Annual herb, the stems erect, branched, glabrous except for a sticky band often found between the nodes, the plant to 4 ft. (12 dm) tall. *Leaves* opposite, glabrous, thin, ovate, each pair of opposite leaves having one larger than the other, 3/4–3 1/8 in. (2–8 cm) long. *Flowers* in loose clusters on unequal stalks, 5-lobed, pink, less than 1/8 in. (2 mm) long. *Fruit* 5-angled.

Range and Habitat: New Mexico and Arizona to tropical America. Usually found on dry hills in southwestern New Mexico; 4,000–5,000 ft.

Key Characters: Spiderling may be recognized by the small, typical four-o'clock flowers, and by the sticky band found between nodes of the stem.

Related Species: Other spiderlings—*B. gracillima, B. tenuifolia,* and *B. linearifolia*—are similar and occupy similar habitats but differ in their perennial nature, the absence of a sticky internodal band, and the dark purplish red flowers.

39. **Purslane**   *Portulaca parvula*   Purslane family

Annual herb, the stems fleshy, branched, nearly prostrate but spreading upward, to about 5 in. (13 cm) long. *Leaves* linear, almost circular in cross-section, not petioled, 1/4–5/8 in. (6–15 mm) long, bearing long white hairs in the leaf axils. *Flowers* about 1/8 in. (2–2.5 mm) long, borne singly or in clusters, with 2 sepals and 5 yellow to copper-colored or reddish petals. *Fruit* a globose, single-seeded capsule about 1/8 in. (2 mm) in diameter, the top part separating from the bottom at maturity, somewhat like a lid. This small plant is related to the common "moss-rose."

Range and Habitat: Missouri to Colorado, southward to Oklahoma, Texas, southeastern Arizona, and Mexico. Often found in sandy soil of plains and valleys in eastern and southern New Mexico; 3,500–4,500 ft.

Key Characters: Purslane is characterized by the fleshy, succulent stems and leaves, the long hairs in the leaf axils, and by the 2 sepals.

40. **Nevada bitterroot**   *Lewisia pygmaea*   Purslane family

Perennial herb from thick fleshy roots, the stems very short, leafless except for a pair of membranous, bractlike leaves. *Leaves* numerous, basal, linear to linear-oblanceolate, to 4 in. (10 cm) long and about 1/8 in. (2–3 mm) wide. *Flowers* usually borne singly at the apex of the stem, with 2–4 (usually 4) ovate sepals, 1/4–3/8 in. (7–10 mm) long, and with 5–9 pink to reddish petals, 3/8–5/8 in. (10–15 mm) long. *Fruit* ovoid, 1/4–3/8 in. (5–10 mm) long, with numerous seeds. This low plant is easily overlooked.

Range and Habitat: Colorado to Washington, southward to New Mexico, Arizona, and California. Found occasionally on open slopes in the mountains of northern to south-central New Mexico; 7,500–9,000 ft.

Key Characters: Nevada bitterroot is usually characterized by 4 sepals, conspicuous flowers with several petals, essentially no stem, and by the thick, fleshy roots.

Boerhaavia erecta

Portulaca parvula

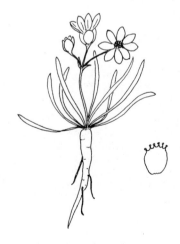

Lewisia pygmaea

41. **Yellow flame flower**   *Talinum angustissimum*   Purslane family

Glabrous perennial herb, the stems leafy, slender, often woody at the base, to 16 in. (40 cm) tall. *Leaves* alternate, linear, flattened, to about 2³/₈ in. (6 cm) long. *Flowers* borne singly in the leaf axils, on pedicels usually subtended by bracts, with 2 sepals and 5 yellow petals, ³/₈–¹/₂ in. (10–12 mm) long. *Fruit* a globose capsule about ³/₁₆ in. (4–5 mm) in diameter. Flame flower is usually very noticeable, owing to the brightly colored flowers.

Range and Habitat: Western Texas to southern Arizona and northern Mexico. Occasionally found on dry slopes, plains, and in arroyos in southern New Mexico; 3,500–6,500 ft.

Key Characters: Yellow flame flower may be recognized by the glabrous, somewhat fleshy stems, and by the showy yellow flowers.

Related Species: Common flame flower (*Talinum aurantiacum*) differs in the leaves being narrowly elliptic, widest near the middle, and in the orange to scarlet flowers.

42. **Western spring beauty**   *Claytonia lanceolata*   Purslane family

Perennial herb from fleshy taproots or tubers, the stems sometimes fleshy, 1 to several, to 8 in. (20 cm) tall. *Leaves* 1 or 2 at the base of the stem, these ovate to oblanceolate, 2–4 in. (5–10 cm) long, stalked, an additional pair of opposite leaves subtending the inflorescence, these linear to lanceolate or oblanceolate, sessile, to 3¹/₄ in. (8 cm) long. *Flowers* in loose clusters at the apex of the stems, with 2 ovate sepals, about ¹/₄ in. (6 mm) long, and 5 white or pink petals, to ¹/₂ in. (12 mm) long. *Fruit* ovoid, about ³/₁₆ in. (4 mm) long.

Range and Habitat: Alberta to British Columbia, southward to New Mexico and California. Occasionally found in moist ground in the mountains of New Mexico; 6,500–7,500 ft.

Key Characters: Western spring beauty is characterized by the 2 basal leaves and single pair of opposite stem leaves, and by the 2 sepals.

43. **Rock purslane**   *Calandrina ciliata*   Purslane family

Herbaceous plant with much-branched stems to about 12 in. (30 cm) tall. *Leaves* alternate, somewhat fleshy, narrowly oblong to spatulate or oblanceolate, to about 3¹/₄ in. (8 cm) long. *Flowers* in slender clusters subtended by leaflike bracts, the sepals 2, keeled, about ³/₁₆–¹/₄ in. (4–7 mm) long, the 3–7 (usually 5) rose red petals ³/₁₆–³/₈ in. (4–10 mm) long. *Fruit* ovoid, about ¹/₄ in. (5–6 mm) long.

Range and Habitat: New Mexico to British Columbia, California, Baja California, and Sonora. Found mostly in open grassy plains in extreme southwestern New Mexico; 4,000–6,000 ft.

Key Characters: Rock purslane may be identified by the 2 sepals, the alternate stem leaves, and by the usually more numerous (often as many as 14) stamens.

44. **Chickweed**   *Stellaria jamesiana*   Pink family

Slender perennial herb, the stems mostly erect or nearly so, branched, angled, 8–20 in. (20–50 cm) tall, with glandular hairs in the upper part. *Leaves* opposite, linear-lanceolate to lanceolate, sessile, 1¹/₄–4 in. (3–10 cm) long, without teeth. *Flowers* in loose clusters, with 4 or 5 sepals about ¹/₄ in. (5–6 mm) long having membranous margins, and 4 or 5 white, deeply 2-lobed petals, these longer than the calyx. Chickweed is a rather inconspicuous plant.

Range and Habitat: Idaho and Wyoming to Texas, New Mexico, and California. Common in damp, shaded places in mountains throughout New Mexico; 7,000–10,000 ft.

Key Characters: Chickweed is characterized by the deeply 2-lobed petals and the fruit opening by 6 valves.

Related Species: A similar chickweed, *S. longipes,* has flowers borne on ascending or erect pedicels and scarious bracts subtending the inflorescence, while the flowers of *S. jamesiana* are borne on reflexed pedicels, and the bracts are not scarious.

Talinum angustissimum

Claytonia lanceolata

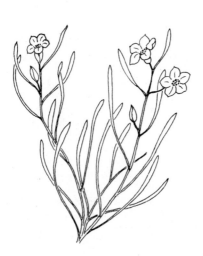

Calandrina ciliata

Stellaria jamesiana

45. Meadow chickweed   *Cerastium arvense*   Pink family

Perennial herb, the stems erect to ascending, with rough hairs, to 12 in. (30 cm) tall. *Leaves* opposite, linear to narrowly oblong or lanceolate, pointed at the apex, 3/8–1 3/8 in. (10–35 mm) long. *Flowers* few in loose clusters, on erect to nodding pedicels, subtended by scarious-margined bracts, with 5 sepals 3/16–3/8 in. (5–8 mm) long, and 5 white petals, usually twice as long as the sepals. *Fruit* straight, as long as or longer than the calyx.

Range and Habitat: North America. Commonly found in woods, on dry, open slopes or plains throughout New Mexico; 7,000–9,500 ft.

Key Characters: Meadow chickweed is characterized by having 5 styles, the capsules curved and splitting into 10 segments, and by the petals at least twice as long as the sepals.

46. Pond lily   *Nuphar polysepalum*   Water lily family

Aquatic perennial herb from rhizomes. *Leaves* floating or emersed, ovate with a deep narrow notch at the base, thus appearing as if the elongate petiole were attached near the center of the leaf, the leaf blades 8–16 in. (20–40 cm) long. *Flowers* solitary from the leaf axils, usually borne slightly above water, the 7–9 sepals green to greenish yellow on the outside, yellow on the inside, 3/4–2 in. (2–5 cm) long, the numerous petals much smaller than the sepals, scalelike, grading into the numerous stamens. *Fruit* ovoid, 1 1/4–1 5/8 in. (3–4 cm) in diameter. This close relative of the cultivated water lily is conspicuous in ponds, even when not in flower.

Range and Habitat: Montana to Alaska, southward to New Mexico and California. Found occasionally in ponds and lakes or sometimes in slow-moving streams, in northern New Mexico; 8,000–10,000 ft.

Key Characters: Pond lily is characterized by the round leaves with a deep, narrow notch, the petiole attached near the center of the blade, the water habitat, and by the conspicuous flowers.

47. Yellow columbine   *Aquilegia chrysantha*   Buttercup family

Perennial herb, the stems glabrous to hairy, sometimes sticky, to 32 in. (80 cm) tall. *Leaves* petioled, compound, to 1 3/4 in. (4–5 cm) long, divided into 2 or 3 leaflets, these 3-lobed, often hairy on the lower surface and stalked. *Flowers* mostly erect, showy, yellow, 2–3 1/4 in. (5–8 cm) long, with 5 yellow, spreading sepals 3/4–1 3/8 in. (20–35 mm) long and 5 yellow petals 3/8–5/8 in. (8–15 mm) long, each petal producing an elongated, hollow, yellow spur back from the sepals, 1 5/8–2 3/4 in. (4–7 cm) long. *Fruit* of slender-tipped follicles. Yellow columbine is an extremely interesting, as well as showy, part of the spring flora.

Range and Habitat: Colorado to Texas, Arizona, and Mexico. Common on moist slopes and canyons throughout New Mexico; 6,000–9,500 ft.

Key Characters: Yellow columbine may be identified by the 5 long yellow spurs on the bright yellow flower.

Related Species: A similar columbine, *A. chaplinei,* occasionally found in southeastern New Mexico, may be distinguished by the glabrous leaflets, the sepals about 1/2 in. (13 mm) long, and the spurs 1 3/8–1 5/8 in. (35–40 mm) long.

Cerastium arvense

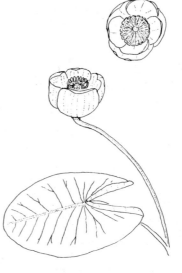

Nuphar polysepalum

Aquilegia chrysantha

48. **Rocky Mountain columbine**   *Aquilegia caerulea*   Buttercup family

Perennial herb, the stems glabrous or with glandular hairs above, to 32 in. (80 cm) tall.
Leaves compound, divided into 2 or 3 leaflets, these 3-lobed, glabrous to sparsely hairy, 1¼–
3¼ in. (3–8 cm) long. *Flowers* large, showy, erect, 2¼–3¼ in. (6–8 cm) long and about as
wide, with 5 blue or white sepals ¾–1½ in. (2–4 cm) long and 5 white petals ⅝–1 in.
(15–25 mm) long, the spurs usually blue, rarely white, 1⅛–2 in. (3–5 cm) long. *Fruit* of
slender-tipped follicles. Rocky Mountain columbine is one of our showiest flowers and is the
state flower of Colorado.
Range and Habitat: Montana to Idaho, southward to New Mexico and Arizona. Usually
found in woods and meadows in northern New Mexico; 7,000–12,000 ft.
Key Characters: Rocky Mountain columbine may be recognized by the elongated spurs, and
by the large, showy, blue and white flowers.

49. **Baneberry; Cohosh**   *Actaea arguta*   Buttercup family

Perennial herb, the stems glabrous or nearly so, to about 32 in. (80 cm) tall. *Leaves*
compound, long-petioled, divided into 2 or 3 ovate leaflets, these bearing teeth or with 3–5
lobes. *Flowers* in a narrow cluster at the apex of the stem, with 4 or 5 early-falling sepals and
4–10 small white petals. *Fruit* of red or white berries ¼–⅜ in. (6–8 mm) long, on stalks
½–¾ in. (10–20 mm) long. Baneberry is easily confused with certain elderberries, but
caution is urged as the baneberry is reputed to be very poisonous.
Range and Habitat: South Dakota to Alaska, southward to New Mexico, Arizona, and
California. Common in moist woods throughout New Mexico; 7,500–10,000 ft.
Key Characters: Baneberry may be recognized by the large, lobed leaves, and by the narrow
cluster of white flowers or red or white berries at the apex of the stem.

50. **Elk's lip**   *Caltha leptosepala*   Buttercup family

Perennial herb, the glabrous stems leafless or bearing a single leaf or bract, to about 8 in. (20
cm) tall. *Leaves* somewhat fleshy, mostly basal, glabrous, ovate to nearly orbicular, cordate at
the base, the margins bearing pointed or rounded teeth, palmately veined, 1⅝–3¼ in. (4–8
cm) long. *Flowers* 1 or 2 at the tip of each stem, conspicuous, white or yellow, the 6–12
sepals white, petallike, the petals absent. *Fruit* of follicles about ½ in. (12 mm) long. Elk's
lip is a low but conspicuous flower growing in patches in wet meadows.
Range and Habitat: Montana to Alaska and Washington, southward to New Mexico and
Arizona. Normally found in wet meadows or often in boggy areas in mountains of northern
New Mexico; 9,500–12,000 ft.
Key Characters: Elk's lip is characterized by the basal, long-petioled, cordate leaves and by
the flowering stem leafless or nearly so, bearing 1 or 2 conspicuous yellow or white flowers.

51. **Larkspur**   *Delphinium scaposum*   Buttercup family

Perennial herb, the stems unbranched, leafless, 12–18 in. (30–45 cm) tall. *Leaves* basal,
glabrous, palmately divided into cuneate-obovate, toothed or lobed segments. *Flowers*
irregular, in a narrow cluster at the apex of the stem, blue and white, about 1 in. (25 mm)
long, the 5 sepals ½–⅝ in. (13–15 mm) long, the upper petals white, tinged with blue,
prolonged into a short spur at the base, the lower petals blue. This larkspur is very poisonous
as are many other plants of the buttercup family.
Range and Habitat: Colorado and Utah to New Mexico and Arizona. Often found on open
ground in western New Mexico; 5,000–7,500 ft.
Key Characters: This plant may be identified by the typical larkspur flower with a single
spur, the leafless flowering stem, and by the petals having 2 colors.

Aquilegia caerulea

Actaea arguta

Caltha leptosepala

Delphinium scaposum

52. Nelson's larkspur
Delphinium nelsonii   Buttercup family

Perennial herb, the stems erect, unbranched, leafy, glabrous or often with a dense covering of white hairs in the inflorescence, 12–24 in. (30–60 cm) tall. *Leaves* few, alternate, 1¼–2 in. (3–5 cm) wide, palmately divided into broad, wedge-shaped divisions, these again 3-cleft into oblong, obtuse segments, the leaves on petioles 1¼–3½ in. (3–9 cm) long. *Flowers* in narrow clusters at the apex of the stems, blue to bluish purple, the sepals ovate, ¼–⅝ in. (11–15 mm) long, the spur ½–⅝ in. (12–15 mm) long. *Fruit* of follicles ½–¾ in. (13–19 mm) long, usually hairy when young. Nelson's larkspur is reputed to be highly poisonous.

Range and Habitat: South Dakota and Idaho to Nevada, Colorado, Arizona, and New Mexico. Usually found on dry plains in northern to western New Mexico; 6,500–8,000 ft.

Key Characters: Nelson's larkspur is characterized by the leafy stems 12–24 in. (30–60 cm) tall, the usually somewhat hairy leaves not exceeding 2 in. (5 cm) wide, and the blue to bluish purple flowers.

53. Plains larkspur
Delphinium virescens   Buttercup family

Perennial herb, the stems stout, erect, usually leafless, with curly hairs, to about 12 in. (30 cm) tall. *Leaves* usually basal, rarely scattered on the stem, pinnately divided into numerous segments, these pinnatifid into obtuse lobes, the leaves with curly hairs on both sides. *Flowers* in narrow clusters at the apex of the stems, bluish white, drying brownish, the sepals oblong, obtuse, about ½ in. (12–14 mm) long, the lower petals notched and marked with white hairs, the spurs ⅝–¾ in. (15–20 mm) long. *Fruit* ½–¾ in. (12–20 mm) long.

Range and Habitat: Colorado to Texas and Arizona. Common on dry plains and hills throughout New Mexico; 5,000–6,500 ft.

Key Characters: Plains larkspur is characterized by the low growth habit and the whitish flowers.

54. Western virgin's bower
Clematis ligusticifolia   Buttercup family

Perennial, the stems trailing along the ground or climbing. *Leaves* opposite, pinnately compound, the 3–7 leaflets lanceolate, oblong, or ovate, pointed at the apex, with pointed, coarse teeth or lobes. *Flowers* usually several in loose clusters on long, hairy peduncles, the sepals white, about ⅜ in. (10 mm) long, the petals absent, the styles narrowly featherlike, 1–2 in. (25–50 mm) long. The flowers are unisexual, with the staminate (male) flowers on one plant and the pistillate (female) flowers on another.

Range and Habitat: British Columbia to North Dakota, California, Texas, and Arizona. Commonly found on slopes and in canyons throughout New Mexico; 4,000–7,500 ft.

Key Characters: Western virgin's bower may be recognized by the densely vining habit, the white flowers, and the styles in fruit not exceeding 2 in. (5 cm) long.

Related Species: Drummond clematis, *C. drummondii*, differs in the leaves being densely covered with grayish hairs and the styles in fruit 2¼–4 in. (6–10 cm) long. It ranges from Texas to Arizona and Mexico at altitudes of 3,000–5,000 ft., and is usually found on slopes and in canyons of southern New Mexico.

New Mexico clematis, *C. neomexicana*, differs from western virgin's bower primarily in having blunt rather than pointed leaf divisions. It ranges through New Mexico and Arizona at altitudes of 5,000–7,000 ft. and is often found in canyons in west-central to southwestern New Mexico.

Delphinium nelsonii

Delphinium virescens

Clematis ligusticifolia

55. Rocky Mountain clematis   *Clematis pseudoalpina*   Buttercup family

Perennial with usually short stems, these either trailing on the ground or longer and climbing. *Leaves* compound, divided into 2 or 3 divisions, the leaflets 3-lobed, lanceolate or ovate, pointed at the apex, toothed on the margins, glabrous. *Flowers* perfect, solitary or in small clusters, the 4 sepals petallike, thin, purple to white or violet, lanceolate, 3/4–2 in. (2–5 cm) long, petals absent, the styles featherlike, 1–2 in. (25–50 mm) long. The conspicuous dark purple or violet flowers are striking when spotted on this low-growing plant. Each flower has functional staminate and pistillate parts.

Range and Habitat: South Dakota to New Mexico and Arizona. Commonly found in woods throughout New Mexico; 7,000–9,000 ft.

Key Characters: Rocky Mountain clematis may be recognized by the thin violet to white sepals, the perfect flowers, and the relatively short stems.

56. Pasqueflower   *Pulsatilla ludoviciana*   Buttercup family

Perennial herb, the stems with long, silky hairs, leafless except for a whorl of leaflike bracts on the upper half, to 16 in. (40 cm) tall. *Leaves* basal, long-stalked, palmately divided, the primary lateral divisions 2-parted, the terminal one 3-parted, each segment cleft into linear lobes. *Flowers* solitary at the apex of the stem, large, showy, whitish to purplish, the 5–7 sepals petallike, 3/4–1 1/2 in. (2–4 cm) long, the petals absent, the styles in fruit featherlike, about 1 1/4 in. (3 cm) long. Pasqueflower often occurs among low-growing vegetation, and thus is quite conspicuous even though short.

Range and Habitat: Illinois to Alaska and Washington, southward to Texas and New Mexico. Usually found in open meadows throughout New Mexico; 7,000–10,000 ft.

Key Characters: Pasqueflower is easily recognized by the solitary flower, the long, persistent, featherlike styles, and by the leaflike bracts on the upper part of the flowering stem.

57. Desert anemone   *Anemone tuberosa*   Buttercup family

Perennial herb from tuberous roots, the stems 4–12 in. (1–3 dm) tall. *Leaves* of 2 types, the basal ones on petioles 2–2 3/4 in. (5–7 cm) long, palmately divided, nearly glabrous, 1 1/8–2 in. (3–5 cm) wide, the divisions wedge-shaped, the stem (involucral) leaves whorled or opposite, sessile to short-petioled, similar to the basal ones. *Flowers* solitary or in clusters at the apex of the stem, conspicuous, the 8 sepals oblong, pink, 3/8–5/8 in. (10–14 mm) long, petals absent, the styles not featherlike and usually falling from the fruit.

Range and Habitat: Texas to New Mexico, Utah, and California. Occasionally found on rocky slopes in south-central to southwestern New Mexico; 4,000–5,000 ft.

Key Characters: Desert anemone may be recognized by the 8 sepals, the sessile, whorled, upper involucral leaves, and by the tuberous roots.

Clematis pseudoalpina

Pulsatilla ludoviciana

Anemone tuberosa

71

58. Candle anemone   *Anemone cylindrica*   Buttercup family

Perennial herb from thick rhizomes, the stems 12–24 in. (30–60 cm) tall. *Leaves* of 2 types, the basal ones with silky hairs, petioled, palmately divided into 3–5 toothed or incised divisions, the stem (or involucral) leaves similar but whorled in several series, petioled. *Flowers* solitary or in clusters at the apex of the stems, conspicuous, the 5 or 6 sepals greenish white, oblong, 1/4–3/8 in. (8–10 mm) long, petals none, the fruiting head cylindric, 3/4–1 1/2 in. (2–4 cm) long, the styles falling early.
Range and Habitat: New Brunswick to British Columbia, southward to New Jersey, Missouri, New Mexico, and Arizona. Commonly found in damp soil of meadows or along streams throughout New Mexico; 6,500–8,000 ft.
Key Characters: Candle anemone may be recognized by the cylindric fruiting head, the 5 or 6 greenish white sepals, and the stems arising from rhizomes.
Related Species: Meadow anemone, *Anemone canadensis,* differs in the stem or involucral leaves being sessile. It ranges from Labrador to Alberta, southward to Maryland, Colorado, and New Mexico, and may be found in woods or meadows, often along streams, at elevations of 7,000–8,500 ft. in northern to south-central New Mexico.

Another anemone, *Anemone globosa,* is similar to the candle anemone but has globose fruiting heads. It ranges from Saskatchewan to British Columbia, southward to New Mexico and California. It may be found in open woods or grassy meadows at altitudes of 7,000–12,500 ft. in northern New Mexico.

59. White water-crowfoot   *Ranunculus aquatilis*   Buttercup family

Aquatic perennial herb, the stems submersed, glabrous or nearly so. *Leaves* both basal and alternate, petioled, finely dissected into filiform divisions. *Flowers* solitary or in loose clusters, the 5 sepals falling early, about 1/8 in. (2–4 mm) long, the 5 petals white, about 1/8–1/4 in. (4–8 mm) long, the fruiting head globose. White water-crowfoot is unusual in that about all one sees are the small white flowers on the surface with shadows of herbage beneath.
Range and Habitat: Temperate North America and Eurasia. Common in ponds and streams throughout New Mexico; 5,000–9,000 ft.
Key Characters: White water-crowfoot is easily recognized by its aquatic habitat, by the small, white, floating flowers, and by the finely dissected leaves.
Related Species: Another white water-crowfoot, *R. circinatus,* is very similar but flowers about a month later.

60. Desert crowfoot   *Ranunculus cymbalaria*   Buttercup family

Glabrous perennial herb from stolons, to 12 in. (30 cm) tall. *Leaves* mostly basal, cordate at the base, shallowly crenately lobed, long-petioled. *Flowers* solitary or in loose clusters at the ends of the stems, the 5 sepals glabrous, about as long as the 5 yellow petals, 1/16–3/16 in. (3–8 mm) long, the fruiting heads cylindric, bearing 100 or more achenes (fruit).
Range and Habitat: Alaska through western North America to Mexico. Common in wet ground throughout most of New Mexico except for the extreme eastern part; 5,000–8,000 ft.
Key Characters: Desert crowfoot may be identified by the presence of stolons, by the mostly basal crenate or crenate-dentate leaves, and by the small yellow flowers.

Anemone cylindrica

Ranunculus aquatilis

Ranunculus cymbalaria

61. **Crowfoot** *Ranunculus inamoenus* Buttercup family

Perennial herb, nearly glabrous to bearing scattered stiff hairs, the stems leafy, not rooting at the nodes. *Leaves* of 2 kinds, the basal ones long-petioled, ovate to nearly orbicular, crenate or 3-lobed, the stem leaves sessile, deeply 3-lobed. *Flowers* solitary or in loose clusters, the 5 sepals spreading, hairy, nearly as long as the 5 petals, these yellow, $^1/_8$–$^1/_4$ in. (3–8 mm) long, the fruiting heads cylindric.
Range and Habitat: Alberta to New Mexico. Common in damp meadows throughout New Mexico; 7,000–10,000 ft.
Key Characters: This crowfoot may be identified by the absence of stolons, the deeply lobed stem leaves, the fruits (achenes) with beaks less than $^1/_{16}$ in. (1.0–1.5 mm) long, and the yellow petals $^1/_8$–$^1/_4$ in. (3–8 mm) long.

62. **Oregon grape; creeping barberry** *Berberis repens* Barberry family

Shrub with yellowish inner bark, the stems trailing or ascending, glabrous, not spiny, to about 8 in. (20 cm) long. *Leaves* alternate, pinnately compound, the 3–7 leaflets, glabrous, ovate to oblong, to $2^3/_8$ in. (6 cm) long, the margins usually with 10–20 slender, spiny teeth on each side. *Flowers* in short terminal clusters, yellow, the 6 sepals not united, the 6 petals yellow. *Fruit* an ovoid blue black berry about $^1/_4$ in. (6 mm) in diameter. Oregon grape has been used medicinally by various groups and is widely cultivated.
Range and Habitat: Wyoming to British Columbia, southward to New Mexico and California. Common on moist, shaded slopes throughout New Mexico; 6,500–10,000 ft.
Key Characters: Oregon grape may be easily recognized by the trailing stems with yellowish inner bark, the hollylike leaves with 10–20 spiny teeth on each side, and by the small blue black berries.

63. **Red barberry** *Berberis haematocarpa* Barberry family

Shrub with yellowish inner bark, the stems branched, erect to ascending, to 7 ft. (2 m) tall or taller. *Leaves* alternate, pinnately compound, leaflets 3–7, normally 5, lanceolate to oblong-lanceolate, long-pointed, the terminal leaflet usually more than twice as long as wide, to $2^3/_8$ in. (6 cm) long, the margins with coarse, spine-tipped teeth. *Flowers* yellow, in few-flowered clusters, the 6 sepals not united, the 6 petals yellow. *Fruit* a globose blood red berry about $^1/_4$ in. (6–7 mm) in diameter. Red barberry fruit makes an excellent jelly.
Range and Habitat: Western Texas to New Mexico and California, southward into Mexico. Often common on dry plains and slopes in central and southern New Mexico; 5,000–7,000 ft.
Key Characters: Red barberry may be recognized by the stems with yellowish inner bark, the blood red berries, and the terminal leaflet being about twice as long as wide.

64. **Colorado barberry; Fendler mahonia** *Berberis fendleri* Barberry family

Shrub with yellowish inner bark, the stems erect, smooth, to 39 in. (1 m) tall, bearing 3-parted spines at the nodes. *Leaves* in clusters at the nodes, elliptical to oblanceolate, to $^1/_4$ in. (6 mm) long, usually smooth but sometimes with weak spines on the margins. *Flowers* in short clusters at the tips of the lateral branches, the 6 sepals not united, the 6 petals yellow. *Fruit* an ellipsoid scarlet berry $^3/_{16}$–$^1/_4$ in. (4–6 mm) long. Fendler mahonia has been used for food and medicine.
Range and Habitat: Colorado and New Mexico. Found on open or partially shaded hillsides, sometimes in canyons or along streams in northern New Mexico; 6,000–8,500 ft.
Key Characters: Fendler mahonia may be recognized by the smooth stems with yellowish inner bark, the 3-parted spines at the nodes, and by the clustered leaves.

Ranunculus inamoenus

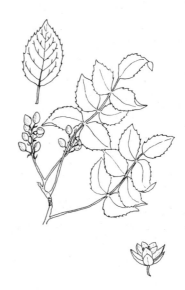

Berberis repens

Berberis haematocarpa

Berberis fendleri

65. **Prickly poppy**   *Argemone pleiacantha*   Poppy family

Perennial herb with colored sap, the stems sparsely spiny, erect, branched, to about 39 in. (1 m) tall. *Leaves* deeply pinnately lobed, usually spiny on the larger veins, the upper ones not clasping. *Flowers* solitary, large, showy, white, the 2 or 3 sepals ending in a horn bearing a sharp spine, the 6 petals in 2 whorls, thin, white, crumpled. *Fruit* a capsule. Prickly poppy is a conspicuous flower. The plant has been used for medicinal purposes.
Range and Habitat: New Mexico to southern Arizona and northern Mexico. Often found on dry plains and waste ground in southwestern New Mexico; 5,000–7,500 ft.
Key Characters: Prickly poppy can be recognized by the large, showy, white flowers to 2 in. (5 cm) across with an orange center, by the spiny stems and leaves, and by the colored sap.

66. **Mexican poppy**   *Eschscholzia mexicana*   Poppy family

Annual herb, the stems slender, glabrous, erect to spreading, to about 8 in. (20 cm) tall. *Leaves* dissected into narrow segments, smooth. *Flowers* solitary or in small terminal clusters, with 2 or 3 sepals and 4 bright yellow to orange petals $5/8–1 1/8$ in. (15–30 mm) long, the stamens numerous. *Fruit* a linear 10-ribbed capsule. Mexican poppy often grows in patches or covering large areas, offering a spectacular view.
Range and Habitat: Western Texas to southern Utah, southeastern California, and Mexico. Usually found on rocky slopes and mesas in west-central to southwestern New Mexico; 4,500–6,500 ft.
Key Characters: Mexican poppy is characterized by the relatively large, bright yellow to orange flowers on short, smooth plants.

67. **Scrambled eggs**   *Corydalis aurea*   Fumatory family

Annual or biennial herb, the stems much-branched, prostrate or nearly so, glabrous and glaucous, to 18 in. (45 cm) long. *Leaves* alternate, variously once- or twice-pinnatifid into elliptical, glabrous segments $1/8–3/8$ in. (3–8 mm) long. *Flowers* in few-flowered slender clusters, irregular, on pedicels that curve downward, the 2 sepals inconspicuous and falling early, the 4 petals yellow, $1/2–5/8$ in. (12–15 mm) long, one of the outer ones projected into a spur.
Range and Habitat: Nova Scotia to Alaska, southward to Pennsylvania, New Mexico, Arizona, and California. Often found on damp slopes in the mountains of New Mexico; 6,500–10,000 ft.
Key Characters: This plant may be recognized by the clusters of bright yellow flowers, each bearing a single spur, and by the smooth, bluish green, finely dissected leaves.

68. **Heartleaf bittercress**   *Cardamine cordifolia*   Mustard family

Perennial herb, the stems glabrous to hairy, branched, to about 28 in. (70 cm) tall. *Leaves* alternate, petioled, ovate-cordate, toothed on the margins, $3/4–2 3/8$ in. (2–6 cm) long. *Flowers* in clusters, with 4 sepals and 4 white petals $3/8–1/2$ in. (8–12 mm) long. *Fruit* linear, erect, $1 1/8–1 1/2$ in. (3–4 cm) long. Heartleaf bittercress usually grows along streams where the clusters of white flowers contrast with the dark green foliage.
Range and Habitat: Idaho to Wyoming, New Mexico, and Arizona. Commonly found in wet ground, usually along streams throughout New Mexico; 7,000–10,000 ft.
Key Characters: Heartleaf bittercress is characterized by the heart-shaped, dark green leaves, by the clusters of small white flowers, and by the moist habitat.

Argemone pleiacantha

Eschscholzia mexicana

Corydalis aurea

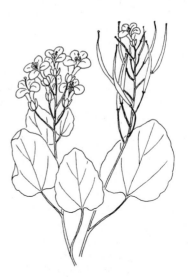

Cardamine cordifolia

69. **Greggia**   *Greggia camporum*   Mustard family

Perennial herb, the stems branching from near the base, covered with grayish, star-shaped hairs, to about 16 in. (40 cm) tall. *Leaves* alternate, oblanceolate or obovate, toothed or pinnatifid or sometimes the margins smooth, grayish, and hairy with starlike hairs. *Flowers* borne in slender clusters, the 4 sepals inconspicuous and falling early, the 4 petals white, tinged with purple, especially beneath, about ³/₈ in. (10 mm) long. *Fruit* oblong, obscurely 4-angled, ³/₈–³/₄ in. (1–2 cm) long.
Range and Habitat: Western Texas to New Mexico and Mexico. Normally found on dry plains and hills in central to southern New Mexico; 3,500–5,000 ft.
Key Characters: Greggia may be recognized by the star-shaped hairs, the 4 white petals that are purple-tinged beneath, and by the obscurely 4-angled fruits.

70. **Twistflower**   *Streptanthus cordatus*   Mustard family

Annual or biennial herb, the stems usually erect and unbranched, to 20 in. (50 cm) tall. *Leaves* alternate, of 2 kinds, the basal ones obovate to spatulate, toothed mostly toward the apex, the stem leaves not toothed, often clasping the stem, glabrous. *Flowers* in slender clusters, the 4 sepals brownish purple, ¹/₄–³/₈ in. (7–10 mm) long, the flask-shaped calyx closed or nearly so when blooming, the 4 petals recurved at the apex, purplish, ³/₈–⁵/₈ in. (10–15 mm) long. *Fruit* linear, spreading, 2–4 in. (5–10 cm) long and about ¹/₄ in. (6 mm) wide.
Range and Habitat: Wyoming to Oregon, southward to New Mexico, Arizona, and California. Usually found on dry plains and hills in northern New Mexico; 5,000–8,000 ft.
Key Characters: This twistflower is characterized by the flask-shaped calyx, by the toothed basal leaves, and by the brownish purple flowers.   •

71. **Twistflower**   *Streptanthus carinatus*   Mustard family

Annual or biennial herb, the stems mostly simple. *Leaves* alternate, glabrous, of 2 forms, the basal ones pinnatifid, about 4 in. (10 cm) long, the stem leaves lanceolate to oblong, often long-pointed at the apex, clasping the stem at the base, the margins smooth. *Flowers* in slender clusters, the 4 sepals purplish, the calyx flask-shaped and nearly closed when blooming, the 4 petals purple or white, twisted. *Fruit* linear, 1¹/₄–3¹/₈ in. (3–8 cm) long and about ¹/₈ in. (3–4 mm) wide.
Range and Habitat: Texas to southern Arizona and Mexico. Often found on dry plains and slopes, sometimes in canyons, in southern New Mexico; 4,000–5,000 ft.
Key Characters: This twistflower is characterized by the flask-shaped calyx, the pinnatifid basal leaves, and by the white petals.

72. **Twistflower**   *Streptanthus validus*   Mustard family

Annual or biennial herb, the stems mostly simple. *Leaves* alternate, glabrous, of 2 forms, the basal ones pinnatifid, those of the stem oblong and pointed at the apex. *Flowers* in slender clusters, the 4 sepals yellow, about ³/₈ in. (10 mm) long, the calyx flask-shaped and nearly closed when blooming, the 4 petals about twice as long as the sepals, yellow. *Fruit* linear, 1³/₈–2 in. (3.5–5.0 cm) long, about ¹/₈ in. (3–4 mm) wide.
Range and Habitat: Western Texas and New Mexico. Often found on dry hills in southern New Mexico; 4,000–6,500 ft.
Key Characters: This twistflower is characterized by the flask-shaped calyx, the pinnatifid basal leaves, and by the yellow flowers.

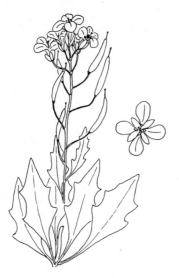

Greggia camporum

Streptanthus cordatus

Streptanthus carinatus

Streptanthus validus

73. **Rockcress**   *Arabis pulchra*   Mustard family

Perennial, the base sometimes shrubby, the stems erect or spreading, densely hairy, 8–20 in.
(20–50 cm) tall. *Leaves* alternate, mostly linear, sessile, densely hairy, entire, to 3¼ in. (8
cm) long. *Flowers* in slender terminal clusters, on hairy pedicels, the 4 sepals hairy, the 4
petals white or tinged with pink, ³/₈–³/₄ in. (10–20 mm) long. *Fruit* linear, hanging
downward, hairy, 1⁵/₈–2³/₄ in. (4–7 cm) long, about ⅛ in. (3 mm) wide.
Range and Habitat: Colorado and Utah to New Mexico and Arizona. Found occasionally on
open slopes in northwestern New Mexico; 5,000–6,500 ft.
Key Characters: This rockcress is characterized by the hanging or pendulous hairy fruit and
the white to pink-tinged petals.

74. **Fendler rockcress**   *Arabis fendleri*   Mustard family

Perennial, somewhat woody at the base, the stems erect to spreading, bearing branched hairs
near the base, glabrous above, to 24 in. (60 cm) tall. *Leaves* alternate, of 2 forms, the basal
ones oblanceolate, hairy, toothed on the margins, the stem leaves oblong to lanceolate, entire
or nearly so, often glabrous and clasping the stem. *Flowers* in slender terminal clusters on
glabrous pedicels, the 4 petals white to pink or purple, ³/₁₆–⁵/₁₆ in. (5–8 mm) long. *Fruit*
linear, glabrous, hanging downward, 1¼–2½ in. (3–6 cm) long. Fendler rockcress has been
utilized for medicinal purposes.
Range and Habitat: Wyoming to Colorado and Nevada, southward to Texas, New Mexico,
and Arizona. Common on open, rocky slopes or in open pine woods throughout New Mexico;
5,000–9,000 ft.
Key Characters: Fendler rockcress may be identified by the hanging or pendulous, glabrous
fruit, the hairy leaf margins, and the small white to purple petals.

75. **Hairy whitlowgrass**   *Draba rectifructa*   Mustard family

Annual herb, the stems hairy with simple and branching hairs, appearing grayish, to 16 in.
(40 cm) tall. *Leaves* alternate, ovate-lanceolate to obovate, covered with grayish hairs,
minutely toothed to smooth on the margins, ³/₈–1³/₁₆ in. (1–3 cm) long. *Flowers* in slender
clusters longer than the rest of the stem, the pedicels spreading or ascending, the 4 petals
yellow, about ⅛ in. (3–4 mm) long, less than ⅛ in. (2–2.5 mm) wide.
Range and Habitat: Colorado and Utah to New Mexico and Arizona. Usually found in open
woods in northern New Mexico; 8,000–9,500 ft.
Key Characters: Hairy whitlowgrass may be identified by its perennial nature, and by the
yellow flowers in a cluster longer than the rest of the stem.

76. **Smooth whitlowgrass**   *Draba reptans*   Mustard family

Annual herb, the stems erect or nearly so, sparsely hairy toward the base, glabrous in the
upper portion, 2–6 in. (5–15 cm) tall. *Leaves* alternate, ovate to narrowly obovate, to ⁵/₈ in.
(15 mm) long, bearing simple hairs on the upper surface and star-shaped hairs beneath, the
margins without teeth but ciliate. *Flowers* in slender, glabrous clusters on spreading or
ascending pedicels, the petals obovate, white, sometimes very small or absent. *Fruit* linear,
³/₁₆–³/₄ in. (5–20 mm) long.
Range and Habitat: Montana to Oregon, southward to Texas, New Mexico, and California.
Often found on dry slopes or sandy plains in northern New Mexico; 5,000–7,000 ft.
Key Characters: Smooth whitlowgrass is characterized by its annual nature, the white
petals, the short fruits, and by the glabrous inflorescence.

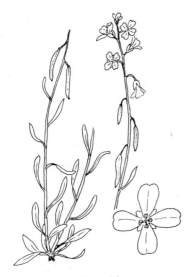

Arabis pulchra

Arabis fendleri

Draba rectifructa

Draba reptans

77. **Desert plume**   *Stanleya pinnata*   Mustard family

Perennial, usually woody at the base and glabrous throughout, the stems simple or branched, to 39 in. (1 m) tall. *Leaves* petioled, of 2 forms, the basal ones in a rosette, usually pinnatifid, the stem leaves alternate, sometimes entire, often clasping the stem. *Flowers* in slender clusters, yellow, with 4 sepals, and 4 petals about as long as the sepals, ³/₈–⁵/₈ in (10–15 mm) long. *Fruit* slender, 1¹/₄–3¹/₈ in. (3–8 cm) long, on a stipe ³/₈–1 in. (10–25 mm) long.

Range and Habitat: North Dakota to Idaho, southward to Texas, New Mexico, Arizona, and California. Found on dry plains and mesas in central to south-central and northwestern New Mexico; 4,500–6,500 ft.

Key Characters: Desert plume may be identified by the fruit borne on a stipe and the yellow flowers.

Related Species: A closely related desert plume (*Stanleya albescens*) differs in having whitish flowers, and is found on plains and in canyons in northwestern to west-central New Mexico at altitudes of 5,000–6,000 ft.

78. **Wright thelypodium**   *Thelypodium wrightii*   Mustard family

Glabrous biennial herb, the stems erect, much-branched, to 39 in. (1 m) tall or taller. *Leaves* simple, the basal ones lyrate-pinnatifid, 4–6 in. (10–15 cm) long, the stem leaves with smooth to toothed or pinnatifid margins, linear-lanceolate, becoming smaller upward. *Flowers* in loose clusters, on pedicels widely spreading or curving downward, the 4 sepals about ¹/₄ in. (6 mm) long, the 4 petals longer than the sepals, white or pale purple. *Fruit* linear, nearly erect, slender, 1⁵/₈–2³/₄ in. (4–7 cm) long, on slender, spreading pedicels. This plant is attractive even though it bears relatively small flowers.

Range and Habitat: Colorado to New Mexico, Arizona, and northern Mexico. Common on dry ground throughout New Mexico; 4,500–8,000 ft.

Key Characters: This plant may be recognized by the 4 rose purple, obovate petals, by the glabrous condition of the plant, and by the basal leaves being toothed.

79. **Western wallflower**   *Erysimum capitatum*   Mustard family

Coarse biennial, hairy herb, the stems erect, to 32 in. (80 cm) tall. *Leaves* hairy, the basal ones lanceolate, usually toothed, sometimes minutely so, pointed at the apex, 1⁵/₈–6 in. (4–15 cm) long, ¹/₈–³/₈ in. (3–10 mm) wide, the stem leaves alternate, some usually with branched hairs. *Flowers* in slender terminal clusters on stout pedicels about ¹/₄ in. (4–6 mm) long, the 4 sepals ¹/₄–¹/₂ in. (8–12 mm) long, the 4 petals yellow to orange or maroon, ¹/₂–³/₄ (12–20 mm) long. *Fruit* erect to ascending, 4-angled, 2–4 in. (5–10 cm) long, less than ¹/₈ in. (2 mm) wide. Western wallflower is a conspicuous plant, thriving in a wide range of altitudes. The plant has been used for a variety of medicinal purposes.

Range and Habitat: Saskatchewan to Washington, southward to New Mexico, Arizona, and California. A common plant on open slopes throughout New Mexico; 7,000–11,500 ft.

Key Characters: Western wallflower may be recognized by the larger petals and the 4-angled, erect, elongated fruit.

Stanleya pinnata

Thelypodium wrightii

Erysimum capitatum

80.   **Western tansy mustard**   *Descurainia pinnata*   Mustard family

Annual herb, the stems erect, simple or branched, grayish, to about 28 in. (70 cm) tall.
Leaves alternate, pinnate or twice-pinnate, densely covered with grayish hairs, oblanceolate to
obovate, the basal leaves in a rosette, often withering early. *Flowers* in elongate, terminal,
slender clusters, the 4 petals yellow, about 1/8 in. (2–3 mm) long. *Fruit* club-shaped, 5/8–3/4
in. (14–18 mm) long, borne on pedicels 5/8–7/8 in. (14–23 mm) long, these widely spreading
or ascending. Tansy mustard is one of the first flowers to appear in the spring.
Range and Habitat: Arkansas to Oregon, southward to Texas, Arizona, and Mexico. Found
on open slopes and plains, and in valleys throughout New Mexico; 4,000–7,500 ft.
Key Characters: Western tansy mustard may be recognized by the once- or twice-dissected
leaves, the grayish herbage, and the relatively short, club-shaped fruits.

81.   **Desert tansy mustard**   *Descurainia obtusa*   Mustard family

Annual, sometimes glandular herb with grayish hairs, the stems erect, simple, or branched,
to 39 in. (1 m) tall. *Leaves* alternate, the lower ones coarsely twice pinnatifid into obtuse
segments, the upper ones pinnate. *Flowers* in slender terminal clusters, the 4 petals pale
yellow, about 1/8 in. (2–3 mm) long, slightly longer than the 4 sepals. *Fruit* linear, sparsely
hairy to glabrous, 1/2–3/4 in. (12–20 mm) long, (only 1/4–3/8 in. [6–10 mm] long in one
variety), on spreading pedicels 3/8–3/4 in. (10–20 mm) long. Tansy mustard is one of the first
flowers to appear in the spring.
Range and Habitat: Southwestern Colorado to New Mexico, Arizona, and California.
Usually found in canyons and on streambanks, sometimes on open slopes and ridges, in
northern to central and western New Mexico; 5,000–7,500 ft.
Key Characters: Desert tansy mustard may be identified by the linear, not club-shaped,
fruit and the once- or twice-pinnatifid leaves.

82.   **Linear-leaved tansy mustard**   *Sisymbrium linearifolium*   Mustard family

Perennial glabrous herb, the stems simple or branched, erect to spreading, to 39 in. (1 m)
tall or taller. *Leaves* simple, the basal ones lanceolate to spatulate, toothed on the margins, 2–
4 in. (5–10 cm) long, the upper ones linear, entire. *Flowers* in loose clusters, the 4 sepals
about 1/4 in. (5–6 mm) long, the petals rose purple, 1/2–3/4 in. (12–20 mm) long. *Fruit*
nearly erect, slender, 1 5/8–2 3/4 in. (4–7 cm) long, on slender, spreading pedicels. This plant
is attractive even though it bears relatively small flowers.
Range and Habitat: Colorado to New Mexico, Arizona, and northern Mexico. Common on
dry ground throughout New Mexico; 4,500–8,000 ft.
Key Characters: This plant may be recognized by the 4 rose purple, obovate petals, by the
glabrous condition of the plant, and by the basal leaves being toothed.

83.   **Wintercress**   *Barbarea vulgaris*   Mustard family

Glabrous biennial or perennial herb, the stems erect, branching, angled. *Leaves* of 2 forms,
the basal ones lyrate-pinnatifid, in a rosette, the lower stem leaves unlobed or lyrate-
pinnatifid, the upper stem leaves variously toothed, rarely pinnatifid, usually clasping the
stem. *Flowers* in slender clusters, the 4 petals spatulate, yellow, 3/16–5/16 in. (5–8 mm) long.
Fruit linear, 4-angled, spreading, 3/4–1 1/8 in. (2–3 cm) long, bearing a slender beak to about
1/8 in. (1.5–2 mm) long.
Range and Habitat: Quebec to Illinois, southward to Virginia, Kentucky, Oklahoma, and
New Mexico. Occasionally found in wet meadows and waste places in northern New Mexico;
3,000–6,500 ft.
Key Characters: Wintercress may be recognized by the short beak on the 4-angled fruit, the
glabrous condition, and the lyrate-pinnatifid basal leaves.

Descurainia pinnata

Descurainia obtusa

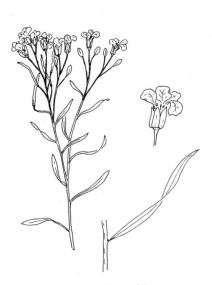

Sisymbrium linearifolium

Barbarea vulgaris

85

84. **Watercress**   *Rorippa nasturtium-aquaticum*   Mustard family

Glabrous, aquatic perennial herb, the stems decumbent, rooting at the nodes, to 16 in. (40 cm) long. *Leaves* pinnately compound or pinnately lobed, the leaflets or segments wavy, the terminal lobe larger than the lateral ones. *Flowers* in short, dense clusters, the 4 petals white, about twice as long as the sepals. *Fruit* sessile, linear, spreading, ³/₈–1¹/₈ in. (10–30 mm) long. Watercress has been used for food by various groups.
Range and Habitat: Introduced from Europe, now found throughout North America. Common in streams throughout New Mexico; 5,000–8,000 ft.
Key Characters: Watercress is easily recognized by its aquatic habitat, the divided leaves, and the 4 white petals.

85. **Yellow cress**   *Rorippa sinuata*   Mustard family

Perennial herb from creeping rhizomes, the stems hairy, to 20 in. (50 cm) tall. *Leaves* shallowly sinuate-pinnatifid, glabrous above, hairy beneath, sessile, sometimes clasping the stem, usually 1¹/₄–2¹/₂ in. (30–60 mm) long. *Flowers* in slender clusters, on pedicels ³/₁₆–¹/₂ in. (5–12 mm) long, ascending to drooping, the 4 sepals saclike at the base, somewhat hairy, about ¹/₈ in. (3 mm) long, the 4 petals yellow, ¹/₈–¹/₄ in. (3–6 mm) long. *Fruit* oblong to cylindric, ¹/₄–¹/₂ in. (6–12 mm) long.
Range and Habitat: Most of the states west of the Mississippi River, also in Illinois. Common in wet ground, usually near streams, throughout New Mexico; 5,000–8,000 ft.
Key Characters: Yellow cress may be identified by the wet habitat, the 4 yellow petals, and by the absence of a basal rosette of leaves.

86. **Twinpod**   *Physaria newberryi*   Mustard family

Perennial herb, bearing grayish scales or star-shaped hairs, the stems branched at the base and spreading. *Leaves* simple, mostly entire, the basal ones orbicular to spatulate, the stem leaves smaller, spatulate to nearly linear. *Flowers* in slender clusters, the 4 petals yellow, oblanceolate, ¹/₂–⁵/₈ in. (12–15 mm) long. *Fruit* membranous, inflated, globose, deeply notched at the apex, 2-celled.
Range and Habitat: Colorado to Utah, southward to New Mexico and Arizona. Occasionally found on dry ground in northwestern New Mexico; 5,000–7,000 ft.
Key Characters: Twinpod is easily recognized by the grayish, star-shaped hairs or silvery scales, and by the 2-celled, notched fruit.

87. **Spectacle-pod**   *Dithyrea wislizenii*   Mustard family

Erect annual herb, the stems simple or sparsely branched, 8–20 in. (20–50 cm) tall. *Leaves* simple, lanceolate, sinuate-toothed or nearly smooth, grayish to whitish. *Flowers* in elongate, slender terminal clusters, the 4 petals white, ³/₁₆–⁵/₁₆ in. (5–8 mm) long. *Fruit* resembling a pair of spectacles, each of the 2 cells about ¹/₄ in. (5–6 mm) wide. Spectacle-pod is an early-flowering, striking plant.
Range and Habitat: Colorado and Utah to Mexico. Common on dry hills, mesas, and streamsides, usually in sandy soil, throughout New Mexico; 3,500–6,500 ft.
Key Characters: Spectacle-pod is easily recognized by the 4 white petals, the grayish appearance of the plant, and by the unique, spectacle-shaped fruit.

Rorippa nasturtium-aquaticum

Rorippa sinuata

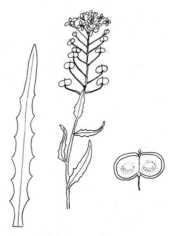

Physaria newberryi

Dithyrea wislizenii

88.   **Wild candytuft**   *Thlaspi alpestre*   Mustard family

Glabrous perennial herb, the stems usually not exceeding 12 in. (30 cm) tall. *Leaves* simple,
of 2 forms, the basal ones in a rosette, oval to spatulate, entire to somewhat toothed,
petioled, sometimes purple-tinged, the stem leaves oblong to ovate, often clasping the stem.
Flowers in slender clusters, white to purplish, on spreading pedicels. *Fruit* obovate to wedge-
shaped, shallowly notched or truncate at the apex, about 1/4 in. (6–7 mm) long and about as
wide. Wild candytuft is a low, inconspicuous plant.
Range and Habitat: Wyoming and Idaho to New Mexico and Arizona. Common in
meadows and canyons throughout New Mexico; 5,000–12,000 ft.
Key Characters: Wild candytuft is easily recognized by the short stems, the small 4-petaled
flowers, and the wedge-shaped fruits.
Related Species: Common pennycress, *Thlaspi arvense,* is an annual herb usually at least 12
in. (30 cm) tall, bearing fruit more than 1/4 in. (6 mm) wide. It is well established in the
United States and occurs in waste ground in northern to south-central and west-central New
Mexico at elevations of 4,500–9,000 ft.

89.   **Gordon bladderpod**   *Lesquerella gordonii*   Mustard family

Low annual herb, bearing few to numerous silvery gray hairs. *Leaves* alternate, lanceolate to
spatulate, mostly entire, the basal ones sometimes lyrate, often in rosettes. *Flowers* in slender
to loose clusters, pedicelled, the 4 petals bright yellow, 1/4–5/16 in. (6–8 mm) long. *Fruit*
inflated, globose, about 1/8 in. (3 mm) in diameter, borne on spreading, S-shaped pedicels.
Bladderpod is a low, early-flowering plant that often blankets an entire area with bright
yellow.
Range and Habitat: Oklahoma to Utah and California, southward to northern Mexico.
Common on dry plains and roadsides in east-central to southern New Mexico; 3,500–7,500
ft.
Key Characters: Gordon bladderpod may be recognized by the small, 4-petaled yellow
flowers and the inflated fruit on S-shaped pedicels. The fruit is glabrous, but a variety of the
species has hairy fruit.

90.   **Fendler bladderpod**   *Lesquerella fendleri*   Mustard family

Low perennial herb, covered with silvery, star-shaped hairs, the stems erect to spreading, 2–
12 in. (5–30 cm) tall. *Leaves* alternate, linear to linear-lanceolate, entire or toothed. *Flowers* in
narrow or loose clusters, pedicelled, the 4 petals yellow. *Fruit* inflated, globose or elongated,
1/8–5/16 in. (4–7 mm) long, on erect or ascending pedicels 3/16–1/2 in. (5–12 mm) long.
Fendler bladderpod is a low, early-flowering plant that often carpets large areas with bright
yellow flowers.
Range and Habitat: Kansas to Utah, southward to Texas, New Mexico, Arizona, and
Mexico. Common on rocky slopes and plains, often in sandy soils, throughout New Mexico;
3,500–7,000 ft.
Key Characters: Fendler bladderpod is characterized by the inflated, glabrous fruit on
curved but not S-shaped pedicels.

Thlaspi alpestre

Lesquerella gordonii

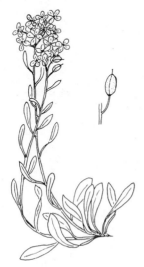

Lesquerella fendleri

91. Yellow bee-plant   *Cleome lutea*   Caper family

Coarse, annual, glabrous herb, the stems branching, to 39 in. (1 m) tall. *Leaves* alternate, with 3–5 leaflets, these lanceolate to oblanceolate, pointed at the apex, usually more than 3/4 in. (20 mm) long. *Flowers* in dense, slender clusters, the 4 sepals usually united at the base, the 4 petals yellow, 1/8–1/4 in. (4–7 mm) long, narrowed at the base, the staminal filaments exserted, not exceeding 5/8 in. (15 mm) in length. *Fruit* of slender capsules 5/8–1 1/2 in. (15–40 mm) long, circular in cross section, borne on a stipe 3/8–5/8 in. (10–15 mm) long. Yellow bee-plant is a fairly large and colorful plant.
Range and Habitat: Nebraska to Washington, New Mexico, Arizona, and California. Found on dry hills and plains or along streams in northwestern New Mexico; 4,500–6,500 ft.
Key Characters: Yellow bee-plant is characterized by the compound leaves with 3–5 leaflets, the 4 yellow petals, the exserted staminal filaments, and by the slender capsule borne on a stipe.

92. Clammyweed   *Polanisia trachysperma*   Caper family

Coarse, sticky, hairy herb, the stems erect, branched, 20–40 in. (5–10 dm) tall. *Leaves* alternate, with 3 oblanceolate to elliptic leaflets, these entire, blunt at the apex, 5/8–1 in. (15–25 mm) long, petioled. *Flowers* in crowded, slender, bracted, terminal clusters, the 4 petals white or yellowish white, 5/16–1/2 in. (8–12 mm) long, the stamens exserted, 5/8–3/4 in. (15–20 mm) long, purplish. *Fruit* of mostly sessile capsules, 1 1/8–2 in. (3–5 cm) long. Clammyweed is a conspicuous part of the spring flora but is unpleasant to the touch.
Range and Habitat: Canada to Missouri, Texas, New Mexico, and Arizona. Found on dry plains and hills, also in gravelly or sandy streambeds throughout New Mexico; 4,500–7,000 ft.
Key Characters: Clammyweed is characterized by the 3-foliolate leaves, the strongly sticky, hairy herbage, the white petals, the purplish staminal filaments, and the nonstipitate fruit.
Related Species: Another clammyweed, *P. uniglandulosa,* has yellow petals and longer staminal filaments. It occurs mostly on dry plains and hills in southern and southwestern New Mexico at altitudes of 4,000–6,500 ft.

93. Alumroot   *Heuchera versicolor*   Saxifrage family

Perennial herb, the stems 6–16 in. (15–40 cm) tall. *Leaves* mostly basal, orbicular to broadly ovate, cordate at the base, the petioles hairy. *Flowers* small, perfect, in open terminal clusters, the calyx 5-lobed, the 5 petals pink, much longer than the sepals, narrowed at the base, the perianth tube not more than 1.5 times longer than wide, the 5 stamens usually longer than the sepals. A variety of this species has a perianth tube about twice as long as broad.
Range and Habitat: Western Texas to Utah, Arizona, and California. Usually found in moist, rocky habitats in central to southern and western New Mexico; 7,000–12,000 ft.
Key Characters: This alumroot may be recognized by the densely hairy petioles, the stamens as long as or longer than the sepals, and by the pink petals.
Related Species: Another alumroot, *H. sanguinea,* differs in the stamens being shorter than the sepals, and the flowers deep pink to red. It ranges from New Mexico to Arizona and northern Mexico. It is found in moist, rocky habitats in southwestern New Mexico at altitudes of 7,000–12,000 ft.

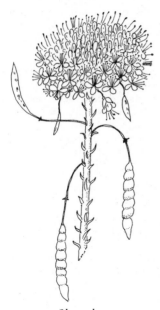

Cleome lutea

Polanisia trachysperma

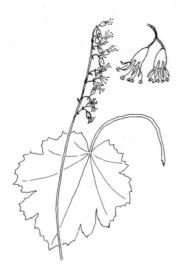

Heuchera versicolor

94. **Alumroot**   *Heuchera parvifolia*   Saxifrage family

Perennial herb, the stems bunched, mostly leafless, somewhat glandular, 4–16 in. (1–4 dm) tall. *Leaves* mostly basal, orbicular to broadly ovate, cordate at the base, with 7–9 lobes, the margins toothed and hairy, on mostly glabrous petioles. *Flowers* in loose terminal clusters, the 5 calyx lobes triangular, usually reflexed, the 5 petals greenish white, longer than the sepals, the perianth tube greenish white to yellowish, the 5 stamens shorter than the sepals.
Range and Habitat: Alberta to British Columbia, southward to New Mexico and Arizona. Common in damp woods and rocky places in northern to central New Mexico; 7,000–10,500 ft.
Key Characters: This alumroot may be identified by the stamens shorter than the sepals, the glabrous or nearly glabrous petioles, and by the greenish white flowers.

95. **Woodland star**   *Lithophragma tenella*   Saxifrage family

Perennial herb from bulblet-bearing roots, the stems unbranched, more or less glandular, 4–10 in. (10–25 cm) tall. *Leaves* mostly basal, round or kidney-shaped in outline, petioled, 3-cleft nearly to the base, the segments again cleft and toothed, the leaves 5/8–3/4 in. (15–20 mm) wide. *Flowers* in few-flowered, loose clusters, with calyx 5-lobed and about 1/8 in. (3–4 mm) long, 5 white petals strongly narrowed at the base, about as long as or slightly longer than the calyx, cleft into 3–7 linear segments, and with 10 stamens. Woodland star is an inconspicuous inhabitant of the forests.
Range and Habitat: Alberta to New Mexico, Arizona, and California. Usually found in open meadows in pine forests of northern New Mexico; 5,000–8,000 ft.
Key Characters: Woodland star may be identified by its herbaceous nature, the 10 stamens, and the cleft petals.

96. **Saxifrage**   *Saxifraga rhomboidea*   Saxifrage family

Perennial herb 4–12 in. (10–30 cm) tall. *Leaves* all basal, ovate, shallowly toothed, mostly glabrous, the margins and petioles ciliate, the petioles usually longer than the blades. *Flowers* borne in tight clusters at the tips of an often branched, leafless flowering stem bearing glandular hairs, with 5 oval or ovate calyx lobes, 5 oblong-ovate white petals about 1/8 in. (3–4 mm) long, narrowed at the base, and with 10 stamens. *Fruit* of follicles, 1/8–3/16 in. (3–5 mm) long, with usually spreading beaks.
Range and Habitat: Montana to Colorado and New Mexico. Usually found in moist areas in northern to central New Mexico; 7,000–13,000 ft.
Key Characters: This saxifrage may be recognized by the ovate basal leaves, the dense clusters of flowers, and the absence of reddish purple hairs on the leaves.
Related Species: Another saxifrage, *S. eriophora,* differs in bearing conspicuous reddish purple hairs on the petioles and lower leaf surfaces. Its range is New Mexico and southern Arizona, and it is found on rocky slopes in southern New Mexico at altitudes of 7,000–8,500 ft.

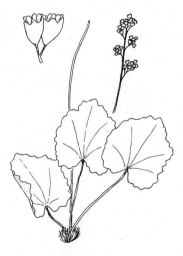

Heuchera parvifolia

Lithophragma tenella

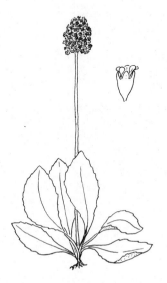

Saxifraga rhomboidea

97. Cliffbush
Jamesia americana
Saxifrage family

Large shrub to about 6½ ft. (2 m) tall, with reddish brown bark separating into shreddy fibers, the branches opposite and bearing grayish hairs. *Leaves* opposite, large, ovate, toothed, bright green above, with whitish hairs beneath, to about 4 in. (10 cm) long. *Flowers* large, in small, open clusters, the flowering branches and the 5 sepals bearing whitish hairs, the 5 white petals ¼–⁷/₁₆ in. (8–12 mm) long, 10 stamens, and 3 to 5 styles. *Fruit* a capsule about ³/₁₆ in. (4–5 mm) long. Cliffbush is a conspicuous flowering shrub. The fruits of this plant have been used for food in certain seasons.

Range and Habitat: Wyoming to New Mexico and Arizona. Common along streams and canyons throughout New Mexico; 7,000–9,500 ft.

Key Characters: Cliffbush may be recognized by its shrubby nature, the opposite leaves, the large white flowers in clusters with 5 petals and 10 stamens, and by the toothed, petiolate leaves.

98. Cliff fendlerbush
Fendlera rupicola
Saxifrage family

Much-branched shrub to about 6½ ft. (2 m) tall, with shreddy, grayish bark. *Leaves* opposite, ovate-lanceolate to oblong or elliptic, hairy, greenish, ³/₈–1⁵/₈ in. (1–4 cm) long. *Flowers* large, showy, solitary or in small clusters, usually many flowers per stem, with the calyx 4-lobed, the lobes longer than the tube, the 4 petals white, irregularly notched and narrowed at the base, ⁵/₈–³/₄ in. (16–20 mm) long, and with 8 stamens. *Fruit* a 4-celled capsule ³/₈–⁵/₈ in. (10–15 mm) long. Fendlerbush is one of the most conspicuous early-flowering shrubs, often almost covered with large white flowers.

Range and Habitat: Texas to Colorado, Utah, New Mexico, Arizona, and Mexico. Commonly found on rocky slopes throughout New Mexico; 6,000–7,500 ft.

Key Characters: Fendlerbush may be recognized by its shrubby nature, the many large, 4-petaled white flowers, the opposite leaves, and the 10 stamens.

Related Species: Other varieties of fendlerbush differ mostly in the color and density of hairs on the leaves, and the shape of the leaves. Their distribution is more limited in New Mexico.

99. Mock-orange
Philadelphus microphyllus
Saxifrage family

Much-branched shrub to 40 in. (1 m) tall, the young twigs sparsely hairy. *Leaves* opposite, entire, ciliate on the margins, mostly ovate-elliptic to elliptic, nearly glabrous above, hairy beneath, at least on the nerves, ³/₈–⁵/₈ in. (10–15 mm) long. *Flowers* usually solitary and terminal on the branches, with the calyx 4-lobed, about ³/₁₆ in. (5 mm) long, the 4 petals white, about ⁵/₈ in. (15 mm) long, and with 15–20 stamens. *Fruit* a 4-celled, globose capsule about ¼ in. (7 mm) in diameter. Mock-orange is a conspicuous flowering shrub on mountain slopes.

Range and Habitat: Colorado to Nevada, southward to Texas, New Mexico, and Arizona. Common on dry cliffs or in rocky canyons in the mountains of New Mexico; 7,000–9,500 ft.

Key Characters: Mock-orange may be recognized by its shrubby nature, the opposite leaves, the solitary flowers, and the 15–20 stamens.

Related Species: Several other species of mock-orange are present in New Mexico, most of them flowering in the spring. They are similar, differing mostly in the presence and density of hairs on the herbage, and in leaf size and shape.

Jamesia americana

Fendlera rupicola

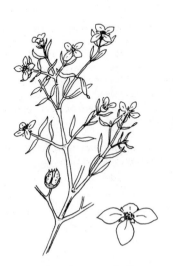

Philadelphus microphyllus

100.   Orange gooseberry   *Ribes pinetorum*   Saxifrage family

Spreading shrub, the stems to 6¹/₂ ft. (2 m) tall, bearing 1–3 spines at the nodes, the internodes not bristly. *Leaves* alternate, cordate at the base, with 5 irregularly toothed lobes, glabrous above, sparsely hairy beneath, 1–1.6 in. (25–40 mm) long, on hairy petioles not longer than the blades. *Flowers* solitary or in loose clusters, on pedicels that are not jointed, the calyx with 5 hairy lobes about twice as long as the perianth tube, reddish yellow, with 5 petals shorter than the sepals, and with 5 stamens. *Fruit* a reddish or purplish red berry ⁵/₁₆– ⁵/₈ in. (9–15 mm) in diameter, bearing sharp, stout yellow spines. The fruit is edible though usually bad-tasting.

Range and Habitat: New Mexico and Arizona. Common in open woods of west-central to south-central and southwestern New Mexico; 7,000–11,500 ft.

Key Characters: Orange gooseberry may be identified by the stems spiny at the nodes only, both the perianth tube and the fruit spiny, the petioles devoid of glands, and by the pedicels not jointed.

101.   Whitestem gooseberry   *Ribes inerme*   Saxifrage family

Shrub, the stems erect to spreading, to 10 ft. (3 m) tall, bearing 1–3 spines at the nodes, or spines sometimes absent. *Leaves* alternate, usually cordate at the base, glabrous above, glabrous or with glandular hairs beneath, ³/₈–2³/₈ in. (10–60 mm) in diameter, bearing 3–5 bluntly-toothed lobes, the petioles about as long as the blades or longer. *Flowers* solitary or in loose clusters, on pedicels that are not jointed, the perianth tube usually glabrous, about ¹/₈ in. (2–4 mm) long, the 5 calyx lobes greenish or greenish purple, reflexed, about as long as the perianth tube, with 5 petals and stamens. *Fruit* a glabrous, purplish red, smooth berry about ⁵/₁₆ in. (7–8 mm) in diameter. The fruit of this plant has been used for food but is not very tasty.

Range and Habitat: Montana to British Columbia, southward to New Mexico, Arizona, and California. Usually found in moist woods in northern to south-central and western New Mexico; 7,000–10,000 ft.

Key Characters: Whitestem gooseberry may be identified by the spiny stems, the pedicels not jointed, the glabrous perianth tube and berry, and the petioles as long or longer than the leaf blades.

102.   Trumpet gooseberry   *Ribes leptanthum*   Saxifrage family

Shrub to 6¹/₂ ft. (2 m) tall, the stems slender with 1 or 3 stout spines at the nodes. *Leaves* alternate, truncate or cordate at the base, ¹/₄–³/₄ in. (5–20 mm) wide, deeply 5-lobed, each lobe usually again lobed or toothed, the petioles not longer than the blade. *Flowers* solitary or in narrow clusters, on pedicels that are not jointed and often very short, the perianth tube cylindric, hairy, ¹/₄–³/₈ in. (5–8 mm) long, the 5 calyx lobes about as long as the perianth tube, longer than the 5 white or pink petals. *Fruit* of berries, these globose, usually glabrous, black, ¹/₄–³/₈ in. (6–8 mm) in diameter. This fruit has been used for food in times of famine.

Range and Habitat: Colorado and Utah to New Mexico and Arizona. Common in canyons and woods throughout New Mexico; 6,500–10,000 ft.

Key Characters: Trumpet gooseberry may be recognized by the spiny stem nodes, the perianth tube and fruit not bristly or spiny, and the leaves mostly less than ³/₄ in. (20 mm) wide.

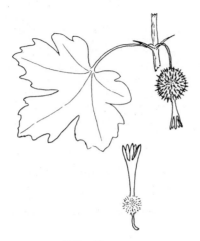

Ribes pinetorum

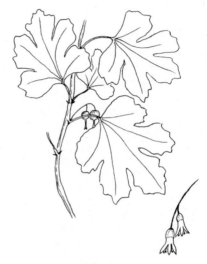

Ribes inerme

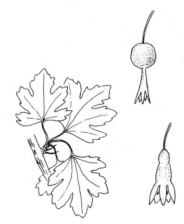

Ribes leptanthum

103. **Wax currant**   *Ribes cereum*   Saxifrage family

Shrub to 39 in. (1 m) tall, the stems not spiny, the young twigs finely hairy. *Leaves* alternate, truncate to cordate at the base, 5/8–1 1/2 in. (10–40 mm) wide, divided into 3–5 toothed lobes. *Flowers* solitary or in clusters on jointed pedicels, the perianth tube cylindric, 1/4–3/8 in. (6–8 mm) long, greenish white, the 5 sepals about 1/16 in. (2 mm) long, longer than the petals. *Fruit* of berries, these globose, bright red, 1/4–3/8 in. (6–8 mm) in diameter. These berries have been used for food.

Range and Habitat: Montana to British Columbia, southward to Oklahoma, New Mexico, and California. Common on open ridges, open slopes, or open pine forests throughout New Mexico; 6,500–9,000 ft.

Key Characters: Wax currant may be identified by the absence of spines, the perianth tube at least 1/8 in. (3 mm) long, the very short sepals, the red berries, and by the presence of a cup-shaped gland at the tip of the anthers.

Related Species: Rothrock currant, wild black currant, and golden currant are similar to wax currant, differing in length of the perianth tube, the length of the sepals, and the color of the flowers.

104. **Squaw apple**   *Peraphyllum ramosissimum*   Rose family

Much-branched shrub 3 1/4–6 1/2 ft. (1–2 m) tall, the branches rigid. *Leaves* bunched at the ends of the smaller branches, oblanceolate, the margins smooth or toothed. *Flowers* solitary or in 2- or 3-flowered umbels, with 5 reflexed, triangular sepals, hairy on the inner surface, 5 pink petals 1/4–3/8 in. (7–10 mm) long, and with about 20 stamens. *Fruit* globose, glabrous, yellowish brown, 3/8–1/2 in. (8–12 mm) in diameter. This plant is not common in New Mexico.

Range and Habitat: Colorado and New Mexico to Arizona, Utah, and Oregon. Found occasionally on dry hills in northwestern New Mexico; 5,500–6,500 ft.

Key Characters: Squaw apple may be recognized by the simple, sessile, bunched leaves and by the flowers that are solitary or in 2- or 3-flowered umbels.

105. **River hawthorn**   *Crataegus rivularis*   Rose family

Small tree to 17 ft. (5 m) tall, the branches bearing blackish spines to 1 in. (25 mm) long. *Leaves* alternate, mostly lanceolate or elliptic, about twice as long as wide, tapered at the base, the margins irregularly glandular-toothed. *Flowers* in loose clusters, white, with the calyx urn-shaped and with 5 reflexed lobes, the 5 petals mostly round, not more than 5/8 in. (15 mm) long, and with 10–20 stamens. *Fruit* nearly globose, 3/8–1/2 in. (8–12 mm) in diameter, dark red to nearly black, often white-spotted.

Range and Habitat: Idaho to Wyoming, Texas, New Mexico, and Arizona. Found in canyons and along streams in northern to central and western New Mexico; 7,000–8,000 ft.

Key Characters: River hawthorn may be identified by the size of the plant, by the small flowers, and by the blackish spines.

Related Species: Other hawthorns are similar, differing in length of spines, number of stamens, and shape of leaves.

Ribes cereum

Peraphyllum ramosissimum

Crataegus rivularis

106.   **Utah serviceberry**   *Amelanchier utahensis*   Rose family

Shrub or small tree, the stems spineless, the twigs slender, reddish brown when young, becoming gray. *Leaves* alternate, elliptic to ovate or obovate, rounded or truncate at the base, 1/4–1³/8 in. (8–35 mm) long, with finely toothed margins. *Flowers* in tight clusters at the ends of short branches, each cluster with 3–6 flowers, the pedicels hairy, the 5 calyx lobes tapering to a point, hairy, the 5 petals white. *Fruit* globose, orange or yellow.

Range and Habitat: Colorado to Nevada, southward to New Mexico and Arizona. Found on rocky slopes in northwestern to southwestern New Mexico; 6,000–7,500 ft.

Key Characters: Utah serviceberry may be recognized by the simple, petioled, leaves that are finely hairy beneath, the 5 white petals not more than ⁵/8 in. (15 mm) long, and the stems devoid of spines.

Related Species: Five other species of serviceberry occur in New Mexico, differing mostly in size, shape, hairiness of leaves, and color of fruit. They are found mostly in northern New Mexico at altitudes of 5,000–9,000 ft.

107.   **Western black chokecherry** *Prunus virginiana melanocarpa*   Rose family

Shrub or tree to 27 ft. (8 m) tall, with bitter, smooth, dark-colored bark, the twigs reddish brown, glabrous. *Leaves* alternate, simple, oblong to elliptic, rounded or cordate at the base, acute or pointed at the apex, glabrous, finely toothed on the margins, on glandular petioles. *Flowers* in narrow, glabrous clusters on short branches of the current year, with 5 sepals and 5 white or cream-colored petals ³/16–1/4 in. (4–6 mm) long. *Fruit* black or purplish black, 1/4–⁵/16 in. (6–8 mm) in diameter. The fruit, twigs, and bark of the western black chokecherry have been used for food and medicine, but the bark and other parts are known to be very toxic.

Range and Habitat: Alberta and British Columbia, southward to New Mexico and California. Common in moist canyons and on moist slopes, often along streams, throughout New Mexico; 6,000–8,000 ft.

Key Characters: Western black chokecherry may be recognized by the flowers present on the current year's growth, in narrow clusters, and the leaves rounded to cordate at the base.

108.   **Southwestern chokecherry**   *Prunus serotina*   Rose family

Small tree to 27 ft. (8 m) tall, the smooth, dark bark, as well as the leaves and seeds, bitter, the twigs reddish brown. *Leaves* alternate, petioled, ovate to elliptic, acute at the base and apex, finely toothed on the margins. *Flowers* in long, narrow clusters on short branches of the current year, with 5 sepals and 5 broadly obovate, white petals about 1/8 in. (3 mm) long. *Fruit* purplish black, 1/4–³/8 in. (6–10 mm) in diameter. Fruits of the southwestern chokecherry have been used for food.

Range and Habitat: Texas to Arizona and Mexico. Common along streams throughout New Mexico; 4,500–6,000 ft.

Key Characters: Southwestern chokecherry may be identified by the flowers borne on the current year's growth, and by the acute or pointed leaf bases.

Related Species: A variety of the southwestern chokecherry is distinguished by the hairy twigs, leaves, and inflorescence. It occurs in southern New Mexico.

Amelanchier utahensis

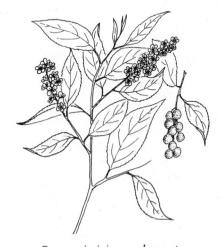

Prunus virginiana melanocarpa

Prunus serotina

109. **Wild plum** *Prunus americana* Rose family

Shrub or tree to 34 ft. (10 m) tall, the branches smooth and dark, the young twigs glabrous, the older bark grayish, the smaller branchlets often sharp-pointed. *Leaves* alternate, oblong to ovate, glabrous above, often sparsely hairy beneath, gradually tapering to a point at the apex, finely toothed on the margins, petioled. *Flowers* white, in small umbels, opening before the leaves appear, with 5 sepals and 5 white petals $3/8–5/8$ in. (8–15 mm) long. *Fruit* usually red with pale dots, $11/16–1$ in. (18–25 mm) in diameter. Wild plum is often used for food.
Range and Habitat: New York to southern Ontario, southward to Florida, Louisiana, and New Mexico. Common along streams, in valleys, and on slopes throughout New Mexico; 4,000–7,500 ft.
Key Characters: Wild plum is easily recognized by the clusters of white flowers appearing before the glabrous leaves, the glabrous pedicels, the grayish bark, and the white petals $3/8–5/8$ in. (8–15 mm) long.

110. **Burnet** *Sanguisorba annua* Rose family

Annual herb, glabrous, the stems 8–16 in. (20–40 cm) tall. *Leaves* pinnately compound with 7–15 leaflets, these $1/4–9/16$ in. (7–15 mm) long, pinnately parted into linear or oblong segments. *Flowers* in a crowded cylindrical spike, with the calyx greenish, 4-lobed, the lobes with membranous margins, the petals none, and with 4–12 stamens.
Range and Habitat: Arkansas to Kansas, Texas, and Arizona. Usually found on open, sandy plains in eastern to southern New Mexico; 4,000–5,500 ft.
Key Characters: Burnet may be recognized by its herbaceous nature, the 4-lobed calyx, the absence of petals, the dense, flowering spike, and the exserted stamens.

111. **Wild strawberry** *Fragaria americana* Rose family

Low perennial herb from short rootstocks, producing slender runners which root and produce new plants. *Leaves* basal, divided into 3 leaflets, these obovate to rhombic-ovate, usually sparsely hairy on both surfaces, the margins toothed from the apex to below the middle, the long petioles bearing spreading or reflexed hairs. *Flowers* in loose clusters at the top of a long, flowering stalk bearing spreading hairs, with 5 sepals alternating with 5 bractlets, with 5 white petals about twice as long as the sepals, and with 20 stamens. Wild strawberry is an excellent food plant, a favorite of many animals.
Range and Habitat: Widespread in North America except for the far-western part. Common in meadows of north-central to south-central New Mexico; 6,500–10,000 ft.
Key Characters: Wild strawberry may be recognized by its low nature, the presence of runners producing new plants, the basal leaves, the numerous stamens, and the red fleshy berry.
Related Species: California strawberry, *F. californica,* is similar except the lower surface of the leaves is densely covered with silky hairs. It ranges from New Mexico to California and Baja California and is common on shaded and open slopes in northern to central and western New Mexico at altitudes of 7,000–9,000 ft.

Prunus americana

Sanguisorba annua

Fragaria americana

103

112. **Rocky Mountain raspberry**   *Rubus deliciosus*   Rose family

Perennial with erect, woody stems to 5 ft. (1.5 m) tall, prickles or sharp bristles absent. *Leaves* simple, sometimes shallowly 5-lobed, mostly glabrous, 1$\frac{1}{8}$–2$\frac{1}{4}$ in. (3–6 cm) wide, petiolate. *Flowers* solitary, 1$\frac{3}{8}$–2$\frac{3}{8}$ in. (3.5–6 cm) in diameter, white to purple-tinged, the 5 sepals narrowed at the tip, hairy or often with glandular hairs, the 5 petals about $\frac{3}{4}$ in. (20 mm) long or longer. *Fruit* dark purple. The raspberry fruit is edible and favored by many wild animals, especially bears.
Range and Habitat: Wyoming to Oklahoma, Colorado, and New Mexico. Usually found in canyons and on rocky slopes in northern New Mexico; 5,500–8,500 ft.
Key Characters: Rocky Mountain raspberry can be recognized by the large flowers, the woody stems devoid of prickles or sharp bristles, the simple, often 5-lobed leaves, and by the dark purple, delicious fruit.
Related Species: New Mexico raspberry, *R. neomexicanus,* is similar but differs in having conspicuously 3-lobed leaves, petals usually less than $\frac{3}{4}$ in. (20 mm) long, and red fruit. It ranges from New Mexico to Arizona and Mexico, and is usually found in canyons of northeastern to central and southwestern New Mexico at altitudes of 5,000–8,000 ft.

113. **Red raspberry**   *Rubus strigosus arizonicus*   Rose family

Perennial, the stems erect, woody, to 6$\frac{1}{2}$ ft. (2 m) tall, bearing stiff, slender, sharp bristles, often also with stalked glands. *Leaves* pinnately compound, with 5–9 leaflets, these long-pointed at the apex, toothed on the margins, sparsely hairy beneath, the terminal leaflet 2$\frac{7}{8}$–4 in. (7–10 cm) long. *Flowers* in clusters of 4–7, or sometimes solitary in the axils, the 5 sepals long-pointed at the tip and with glandular hairs, the 5 petals white. *Fruit* red, about $\frac{3}{8}$ in. (10 mm) in diameter. The raspberry fruit is edible and is a favorite of many wild animals, especially bears.
Range and Habitat: Colorado to New Mexico and Arizona. Common in open woods throughout New Mexico; 6,500–12,000 ft.
Key Characters: Red raspberry is easily recognized by the numerous sharp bristles on the stem, the large terminal leaflet, and the red fruit.
Related Species: Arizona dewberry (*R. arizonensis*) and whitebark raspberry (*R. leucodermis*) are similar but have short, curved prickles on the stem, the stems widely spreading or trailing in the Arizona dewberry, and erect to somewhat spreading in the whitebark raspberry.

114. **Western thimbleberry**   *Rubus parviflorus*   Rose family

Perennial with stems erect or ascending, to 39 in. (1 m) tall, woody at the base, prickles or sharp bristles absent, the older bark shredding. *Leaves* simple, 2$\frac{3}{8}$–6$\frac{1}{2}$ in. (6–18 cm) wide, cordate at the base, unevenly toothed on the margins, palmately 3- to 5-lobed, the petioles glandular and hairy. *Flowers* white, 1–2 in. (25–50 mm) in diameter, with 5 ovate, spreading or reflexed sepals, slender-pointed at the apex, and 5 petals. *Fruit* red, $\frac{5}{8}$–$\frac{3}{4}$ in. (15–18 mm) wide. The fruit of the thimbleberry may be eaten by animals, but is not very palatable.
Range and Habitat: Ontario to Alaska, southward to Michigan, New Mexico, California, and Mexico. Common in woods throughout New Mexico; 7,000–9,500 ft.
Key Characters: Western thimbleberry is easily recognized by the large white flowers, these usually solitary, by the unarmed stems, and by the large, lobed leaves.

Rubus deliciosus

Rubus strigosus arizonicus

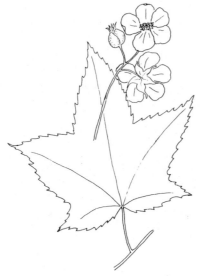

Rubus parviflorus

115. Silverweed · *Potentilla anserina* · · · · · · · · · · · · · · · Rose family

Perennial herb, the stems short, producing numerous slender runners bearing reduced leaves. *Leaves* mostly in a rosette, pinnately compound with large leaflets mixed with smaller leaflets, the leaflets 3/8–1 1/2 in. (10–40 mm) long, elliptic to oblanceolate, unevenly toothed on the margins, densely covered with whitish hairs beneath, sometimes also on the upper surface. *Flowers* solitary and axillary, with 5 sepals alternating with 5 bractlets, thus seemingly with 10 sepals, with 5 yellow petals, 3/16–3/8 in. (5–10 mm) long, and with 20–25 stamens. *Fruit* glabrous.

Range and Habitat: Newfoundland to Alaska, southward to New York, New Mexico, and California; also in Eurasia. Common in wet ground throughout New Mexico; 6,500–9,500 ft.

Key Characters: Silverweed may be recognized by its herbaceous nature, the solitary and axillary flowers, and by the dense, silky hairs on the lower surface or on both surfaces of the leaves.

Related Species: A cinquefoil, *P. glandulosa,* is found in wet meadows of northern and south-central New Mexico at altitudes of 7,000–9,000 ft., and differs in having flowers in loose terminal clusters.

116. Brook cinquefoil · · · · · · · · · · · · · · · · · · *Potentilla rivalis* · · · · · · · · · · · · · · · · Rose family

Annual or biennial herb, the stems erect or spreading, glandular and hairy, 8–24 in. (2–6 dm) tall. *Leaves* pinnately compound (digitately compound in one variety), with the lower ones having 5 leaflets and the upper ones with 3 leaflets, the leaflets toothed. *Flowers* on short pedicels borne in open clusters, with 5 sepals alternating with 5 bractlets, with 5 yellow petals, shorter than the sepals, and with 10 stamens.

Range and Habitat: Illinois to Washington, southward to New Mexico and California. Common in wet ground throughout New Mexico, more abundant in northern and western New Mexico; 5,500–7,500 ft.

Key Characters: Brook cinquefoil may be identified by its herbaceous nature, the styles attached to the top of the glabrous fruit, the leafy flower clusters, and the leaves with 3–11 leaflets.

117. Water avens · *Geum rivale* · · · · · · · · · · · · · · · · · · · Rose family

Perennial herb, the stems erect, hairy, 12–20 in. (3–5 dm) tall. *Leaves* of 2 kinds, the basal ones lyrately pinnately compound and toothed, the lateral leaflets obovate, the terminal leaflet rounded or kidney-shaped, the stem leaves with 3 lobes or 3 leaflets. *Flowers* in loose clusters, the 5 calyx lobes alternating with 5 bractlets, brownish purple, 1/4–1/2 in. (6–12 mm) long, the 5 petals pink or tinged with purple or yellow, obovate, narrowed at the base, the stamens numerous, the styles jointed.

Range and Habitat: Newfoundland to British Columbia, southward to New Jersey, Missouri, and New Mexico. Common in damp woods of northern New Mexico; 7,500–9,500 ft.

Key Characters: Water avens is characterized by the jointed styles with the upper segment about 3/16 in. (4–5 mm) long, the pinnate leaves, and by the pink or purple-tinged petals.

Related Species: Yellow avens (*G. strictum*) is similar but differs in having yellow petals, and the upper section of the style only about 1/16 in. (1–2 mm) long. It has about the same range, occurring mostly in northern and south-central New Mexico in damp woods at altitudes of 7,000–9,500 ft.

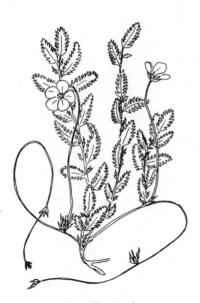

Potentilla anserina

Potentilla rivalis

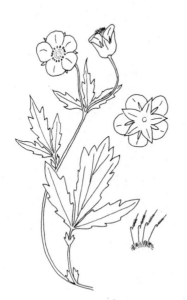

Geum rivale

118. **Cutleaf avens**   *Geum macrophyllum*   Rose family

Perennial herb, the stems erect to spreading, with bristly hairs, to 39 in.
(1 m) tall. *Leaves* pinnately compound with 5–11 leaflets, these usually again cleft, the
terminal leaflet much larger than the lateral ones. *Flowers* in loose clusters, the 5 calyx lobes
reflexed, $1/8$–$3/16$ in. (3–5 mm) long, the 5 petals yellow, obovate, longer than the calyx
lobes, the stamens numerous, the styles jointed, the lower segment about $3/16$ in. (4 mm)
long, the upper segment about half as long as the lower, hooked at the tip. The hooked styles
of the mature cutleaf avens fruit readily attach themselves to clothing.
Range and Habitat: Widespread in cool-temperate North America. Common in meadows of
northern and western New Mexico; 7,500–10,000 ft.
Key Characters: Cutleaf avens is characterized by the yellow flowers, the mixed larger and
smaller leaflets, and the jointed styles with the lower section about twice as long as the
hooked upper section.

119. **Wild rose**   *Rosa woodsii*   Rose family

Shrub to 39 in. (1 m) tall, the stems brown or gray, bearing scattered, straight, slender
prickles, also with 1 or 2 prickles adjacent to and below the nodes. *Leaves* pinnately
compound with 5–7 leaflets, stipulate, the leaflets oval to obovate or elliptic, $3/8$–$1 1/8$ in. (1–
3 cm) long. *Flowers* solitary or few in a loose cluster, the flowering branches often without
prickles, the 5 calyx lobes gradually tapering to a point, the 5 petals pink or rose purple,
about $5/8$–$3/4$ in. (15–20 mm) long. The *Rosa woodsii* complex in New Mexico is composed of
7 varieties, including Fendler rose, paleleaf rose, Macoun rose, New Mexico rose, Arizona
rose, and two varieties without common names. The description given is based on the Fendler
rose, *R. woodsii* var. *fendleri*.
Range and Habitat: Minnesota to British Columbia, southward to Mexico. Found on plains
and mountain slopes throughout New Mexico; 6,000–9,000 ft.
Key Characters: The wild rose is easily recognized by the large rose purple to pink flowers,
the stems with prickles between the nodes and 1 or 2 prickles next to the nodes, and the
gradually tapering calyx lobes arising from the globose perianth tube.
Related Species: The different varieties of *R. woodsii* are diverse in range, elevation, and
distribution in New Mexico, but all are similar in general description.

120. **Arkansas rose**   *Rosa arkansana*   Rose family

Shrub, the stems densely bristly between the nodes, 8–20 in. (2–5 dm) tall. *Leaves* pinnately
compound with 9 or 11 leaflets, these elliptic, acute at the base and apex, coarsely toothed on
the margins, the leaf rachis and petiole glabrous to sparsely hairy or glandular. *Flowers* in
loose terminal clusters, pink or rose purple, the 5 calyx lobes glandular on the back, the 5
petals obcordate, $3/4$–1 in. (20–25 mm) long, the perianth tube nearly globose, glabrous, $1/2$–
$5/8$ in. (12–15 mm) in diameter.
Range and Habitat: Wisconsin and Minnesota to Kansas, Colorado, and New Mexico.
Occasionally found on plains and hills in northern New Mexico; 6,500–8,000 ft.
Key Characters: Arkansas rose is characterized by the absence of prickles adjacent to the
nodes, the leaves with 9 or 11 leaflets, and the absence of hairs on the leaflets.
Related Species: Sunshine rose, a variety of *R. arkansana*, is similar except the leaves are
densely hairy. It ranges from Manitoba to Alberta, southward to Illinois, Texas, and New
Mexico. It occurs on plains and hills in northeastern to central and south-central New Mexico
at altitudes of 6,500–8,000 ft.

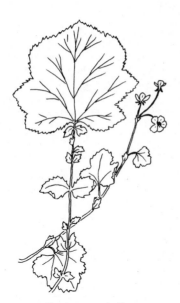

Geum macrophyllum

Rosa woodsii

Rosa arkansana

121. **Apache plume**   *Fallugia paradoxa*   Rose family

Much-branched shrub with slender, whitish branches. *Leaves* small, in bunches, pinnately lobed with 3–7 lobes, each lobe linear-oblong, obtuse, somewhat rolled up toward the lower surface. *Flowers* numerous, showy, white, the calyx tube hairy inside, the 5 lobes gradually tapering, alternating with 5 narrower bractlets, the 5 petals rounded or obovate, these easily knocked off, the stamens numerous. *Fruit* of numerous achenes, each bearing a long, twisted, hairy style that is persistent in fruit. Apache plume is so named because of the conspicuous reddish bundle of fruits. The plant has been used in several ways by native Americans.
Range and Habitat: Colorado and Utah to Texas, New Mexico, Arizona, and Mexico. Common, often abundant, on dry slopes and in arroyos throughout New Mexico; 5,000–7,500 ft.
Key Characters: Apache plume is easily recognized by the linear-lobed, small leaves borne in clusters or fascicles, the shrubby nature, the conspicuous, large white flowers, and by the fruit of numerous achenes with conspicuous, persistent, reddish styles to 2 in. (50 mm) long.

122. **Mountain mahogany**   *Cercocarpus montanus*   Rose family

Shrub or small tree to 13 ft. (4 m) tall, the branches upright to spreading. *Leaves* simple, ovate to obovate, rounded at the apex, more or less toothed on the margins, grayish green above, paler and hairy beneath, 3/4–1 1/2 in. (2–4 cm) long, borne in bundles or fascicles on petioles with spreading hairs. *Flowers* small, solitary in leaf axils, the calyx tube with spreading hairs, 1/4–3/8 in. (5–8 mm) long, the lobes yellowish white, spreading, the petals none, the stamens numerous, the perianth tube cylindrical. *Fruit* of hairy achenes, 5/16–3/8 in. (8–10 mm) long, bearing a long, slender, curved, featherlike tail. Mountain mahogany branches have had many uses among the native Americans.
Range and Habitat: South Dakota to Montana, Kansas, New Mexico, and Arizona. Common on dry hillsides and slopes throughout New Mexico; 6,000–8,500 ft.
Key Characters: Mountain mahogany is characterized by the fascicled, simple, toothed leaves, the absence of petals, and the long, featherlike tail on the achenes, these solitary from each flower.

123. **Antelope brush**   *Purshia tridentata*   Rose family

Low, much-branched shrub to 10 ft. (3 m) tall, the stems erect to spreading, hairy on the young branchlets. *Leaves* small, in bundles or fascicles, tapering to a narrow base, 3-lobed at the apex, 3/16–1 in. (5–25 mm) long, with whitish hairs beneath, on short petioles. *Flowers* solitary and terminal on the short branches, the calyx lobes ovate, the petals yellow, obovate, 3/16–3/8 in. (5–10 mm) long, longer than the calyx lobes, the stamens numerous. *Fruit* of 1 or 2 hairy achenes 5/16–1/2 in. (8–12 mm) long.
Range and Habitat: British Columbia to New Mexico and California. Usually found on dry slopes in northern New Mexico; 5,000–8,000 ft.
Key Characters: Antelope brush may be recognized by the small yellow petals and green sepals, and by the wedge-shaped, small, fascicled leaves that are 3-lobed at the apex.

Fallugia paradoxa

Cercocarpus montanus

Purshia tridentata

124. **Cliffrose**   *Cowania stansburiana*   Rose family

Much-branched, resinous shrub to 6¹/₂ ft. (2 m) tall, the stems with spreading branches. *Leaves* alternate, simple, ³/₈–⁵/₈ in. (10–15 mm) long, pinnately lobed into 5 or fewer linear or oblong lobes, glandular above and with matted hairs beneath. *Flowers* solitary, terminal on the branches, the calyx lobes 5, the 5 petals pale yellow, broadly obovate, ¹/₄–³/₈ in. (6–10 mm) long. *Fruit* of about 5 densely hairy achenes, bearing persistent, featherlike styles ⁵/₈–2 in. (15–50 mm) long.

Range and Habitat: Colorado to Utah, New Mexico, Arizona, and California. Normally found on dry slopes and mesas in northern to western and southwestern New Mexico; 5,000–7,500 ft.

Key Characters: Cliffrose is characterized by the glandular, lobed leaves, the small yellow flowers, and usually 5 achenes with long, featherlike, persistent tails (styles).

125. **Mesquitilla; fairy duster**   *Calliandra eriophylla*   Legume family

Low shrub, the stems to 12 in. (30 cm) tall, with numerous, stout, widely spreading branches, the young twigs somewhat hairy. *Leaves* bipinnate with 2–8 pinnae, each with 10–24 oblong leaflets ¹/₈–¹/₄ in. (3–6 mm) long and ¹/₁₆–¹/₈ in. (1–2 mm) wide, bearing grayish hairs. *Flowers* reddish purple, in dense, rounded axillary or terminal clusters, the calyx 5-lobed, ¹/₁₆–¹/₈ in. (1–2 mm) long, the corolla ³/₁₆–¹/₄ in. (4–6 mm) long, 20–25 stamens, long-exserted, united at the base. *Fruit* a densely hairy pod 1¹/₄–2¹/₂ in. (3–6 cm) long, about ³/₁₆ in. (5 mm) wide. Without flowers or fruit, the mesquitilla closely resembles a young mesquite without thorns.

Range and Habitat: Western Texas to southern California and Mexico. Common on gravelly slopes and mesas in southern New Mexico; 4,000–5,000 ft.

Key Characters: Mesquitilla may be recognized by the absence of thorns, the bipinnate leaves with small leaflets, and by the headlike clusters of reddish purple flowers with numerous exserted stamens.

Related Species: Another fairy duster, *C. reticulata,* differs in being entirely herbaceous, the leaflets longer, and the fruit glabrous. It is found in southwestern New Mexico at altitudes of 4,500–8,000 ft.

126. **Catclaw acacia; Devil's claw**   *Acacia greggii*   Legume family

Shrub or small tree, the stems usually armed with short, curved, pricklelike spines. *Leaves* bipinnate, 1¹/₈–2 in. (3–5 cm) long, with 2–6 pinnae, each with 4–14 oblong to obovate, prominently nerved leaflets, these oblique at the base, rounded or truncate at the apex. *Flowers* yellowish or white, borne in narrow, tight clusters (spikes) ³/₄–1¹/₂ in. (2–4 cm) long. *Fruit* a flat, linear pod, irregularly constricted between the seeds, 3¹/₄–4¹/₄ in. (8–12 cm) long. The spines of catclaw acacia can be devastating to clothing or skin.

Range and Habitat: Texas to Nevada, Arizona, and California, southward to New Mexico. Found along streams and washes in southern New Mexico; 3,500–5,000 ft.

Key Characters: Catclaw acacia may be recognized by the curved spines, the flowers borne in elongate spikes, and by the smaller leaflets.

Related Species: Roemer acacia, *A. roemeriana,* differs in the longer leaflets and in the flowers in dense, headlike clusters. It ranges from Texas to New Mexico and Mexico, occurring on dry plains in southeastern New Mexico at altitudes of 3,500–4,500 ft.

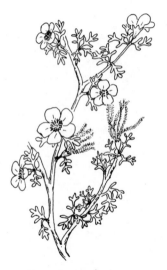

Cowania stansburiana

Calliandra eriophylla

Acacia greggii

127. **Whitethorn acacia; Mescat acacia** *Acacia constricta*   Legume family

Shrub, the branches armed with spreading, slender, straight or slightly curved spines. *Leaves*
1⅛–2¼ in. (3–6 cm) long, with 4–14 pinnae, each with 24–40 oblong, obtuse leaflets
about ¹/₁₂ in. (2 mm) long. *Flowers* yellow, borne in dense, headlike clusters, about ⅜ in.
(10 mm) in diameter. *Fruit* a linear, glabrous, pod, 2–5 in. (5–13 cm) long, more than 10
times longer than wide.
Range and Habitat: Texas to Arizona and Mexico. Common on dry plains and hills in
southern New Mexico; 4,500–5,500 ft.
Key Characters: Whitethorn acacia may be recognized by the straight or nearly straight,
slender spines, the flowers in dense yellow heads, and the herbage that is neither sticky nor
hairy.

128. **Viscid acacia**   *Acacia neovernicosa*   Legume family

Shrub bearing numerous sticky glands, the stems erect or spreading, armed with straight or
slightly curved spines. *Leaves* bipinnate, to 1 in. (25 mm) long, with 2–8 pinnae, each with
6–18 oblong or oval leaflets. *Flowers* yellow, in dense, headlike clusters, fragrant, on axillary
flowering stalks, the stamens numerous, exserted. *Fruit* a narrow pod, 1–2¾ in. (2.5–7.0
cm) long, curved, constricted between the seeds, covered with sticky glands.
Range and Habitat: Texas to New Mexico and Arizona, southward into Mexico. Found on
gravelly hillsides in southern New Mexico; 3,500–5,000 ft.
Key Characters: Viscid acacia may be identified by the straight or nearly straight spines,
constricted fruits bearing sticky glands, and the fragrant, dense heads of yellow flowers.
Related Species: Whiteball acacia, *A. angustissima,* is found in east-central and southern
New Mexico on rocky or grassy slopes at altitudes of 4,000–6,000 ft. It differs in having
long white heads of flowers, and lacking spines.

129. **Honey mesquite; Torrey mesquite**   *Prosopis glandulosa*   Legume family

Shrub to 10 ft. (3 m) tall, the stems rigid, tough, with many zigzag branches, armed with
stout, sharp spines to 2 in. (5 cm) long. *Leaves* bipinnate with 4–8 pinnae, each with 12–60
linear or oblong leaflets, these 1⅛–2 in. (3–5 cm) long in honey mesquite, ⅝–1 in. (15–25
mm) long in Torrey mesquite. *Flowers* yellow, in a dense, narrow, spikelike cluster 1½–3⅛
in. (4–8 cm) long. *Fruit* a narrow pod, straight or slightly curved, 4–8 in. (10–20 cm) long,
somewhat constricted between the seeds.
Range and Habitat: Kansas to Texas, westward to Arizona and Mexico. Common on plains
and prairies and in valleys of eastern to central, south-central, and southwestern New Mexico;
3,000–6,000 ft.
Key Characters: Honey and Torrey mesquite may be recognized by the glabrous leaflets and
twigs, and by the 16–24 leaflets on each pinna. Leaflet length distinguishes between these
two mesquites.
Related Species: Velvet mesquite, *P. velutina,* has finely hairy twigs and leaflets. It ranges
from western Texas to Arizona and occurs in eastern to southwestern New Mexico at altitudes
of 4,500–6,000 ft. Screwbean mesquite or tornillo (*P. pubescens*) differs from the above
mesquites in having only 10–16 leaflets per pinna and fruit that is tightly, spirally coiled. It
ranges from western Texas to southern Nevada and southern California, southward into
Mexico. It occurs along streams and washes in central to south-central and southwestern New
Mexico at altitudes of 3,500–4,500 ft.

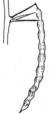

Acacia constricta

Acacia neovernicosa

Prosopis glandulosa

130. **Western sensitive briar**   *Schrankia occidentalis*   Legume family

Perennial herb, often shrubby, the stems mostly prostrate, 16–48 in. (40–120 cm) long,
armed with recurved prickles. *Leaves* bipinnate, sensitive (folding up when touched), with 4–
14 pinnae, each with 20–32 oblong or linear-oblong leaflets, these $^1/_8$–$^1/_4$ in. (4–6 mm) long.
Flowers pink, borne in dense, globose heads on stalks $1^1/_8$–$2^3/_4$ in. (3–7 cm) long. *Fruit* a
prickly, angled pod, $2^3/_8$–$3^1/_2$ in. (6–9 cm) long, about $^1/_8$ in. (2–3 mm) wide, beaked. The
sensitive briar is unusual in its ability to fold up its leaflets when touched.
Range and Habitat: Texas to southeastern Colorado and New Mexico. Usually found in deep
sand of plains in eastern New Mexico; 4,000–4,500 ft.
Key Characters: Western sensitive briar may be easily recognized by its sensitive leaflets,
the dense heads of pink flowers, and by its prostrate, prickly stems.

131. **Prairie bundleflower**   *Desmanthus illinoensis*   Legume family

Unarmed perennial, the stems often woody at the base, spreading to ascending, 12–40 in.
(30–100 cm) tall. *Leaves* bipinnate, with 16–30 pinnae, each with numerous, linear to oblong
leaflets, these about $^1/_8$ in. (2–3 mm) long, the petiole bearing a circular gland between the
pinnae of one or more pairs. *Flowers* greenish white, borne in dense, headlike axillary clusters,
the calyx about $^1/_{25}$ in. (1 mm) long, the petals about twice as long, the stamens 5. *Fruit*
borne in compact heads, the pods strongly curved and slightly twisted, $^1/_2$–1 in. (12–25 mm)
long, $^1/_6$–$^1/_4$ in. (4–7 mm) wide.
Range and Habitat: Ohio to South Dakota, southward to Florida, Texas, and New Mexico.
Common in valleys, along streambanks, roadsides, and on prairies throughout New Mexico;
3,000–6,500 ft.
Key Characters: Prairie bundleflower can be recognized by the bipinnate leaves, the lack of
spines or prickles, the greenish white heads of flowers, and the compact heads of strongly
curved fruits.

132. **Bundleflower**   *Desmanthus cooleyi*   Legume family

Unarmed perennial herb, the stems sometimes woody at the base, spreading to ascending,
angled, 8–20 in. (20–50 cm) tall. *Leaves* bipinnate, with 4–10 pinnae, each with numerous,
oblong to linear leaflets about $^1/_8$ in. (2.5–4.0 mm) long, these oblique at the base, the
petiole with a circular gland between the pinnae of the lowest pair. *Flowers* greenish white, in
dense, headlike clusters, the calyx about $^1/_{16}$ in. (1.5 mm) long, the petals about twice as
long, and with 10 stamens, the flowers borne on a stalk $^5/_8$–$^3/_4$ in. (1–2 cm) long. *Fruit*
solitary or few in a cluster, the pod linear, straight or nearly so, $1^1/_4$–$2^3/_4$ in. (3–7 cm) long,
and about $^1/_8$ in. (3 mm) wide.
Range and Habitat: Nebraska to Colorado, southward to Texas, New Mexico, Arizona, and
Mexico. Frequently found on dry plains and mesas throughout New Mexico; 3,500–7,000 ft.
Key Characters: Bundleflower may be recognized by the bipinnate leaves, the dense heads of
greenish white flowers, the absence of spines or prickles, and by the few, straight fruits.
Related Species: Other species of *Desmanthus* occur in various parts of New Mexico, and
differ in the size of the leaflets, the prominence of veins in the leaflets, the denseness of hairs
on the stems, and in the number and size of the glands between various pairs of pinnae.

Schrankia occidentalis

Desmanthus illinoensis

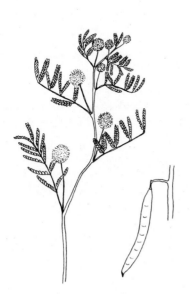

Desmanthus cooleyi

133. Fragrant mimosa — *Mimosa borealis* — Legume family

Shrub, ascending to spreading, to 6³/₄ ft. (2 m) tall, the branches armed with hooked prickles, these mostly solitary and opposite the petiole base. *Leaves* bipinnate, often sensitive, with 2–6 pinnae, each with 6–16 oblong to oval leaflets ¹/₈–¹/₄ in. (2–6 mm) long. *Flowers* pink, in dense, globose clusters, the calyx and corolla with 4 or 5 lobes, the 4–13 stamens exserted. *Fruit* a linear-oblong, glabrous pod, constricted between the seeds, unarmed, ³/₄–2 in. (2–5 cm) long, ¹/₄–⁵/₁₆ in. (6–8 mm) wide. The mimosas, like the acacias, can be very destructive to clothing and skin.

Range and Habitat: Oklahoma to Texas and New Mexico; southward into northern Mexico. Usually found in canyons and on rocky slopes of eastern to southern New Mexico; 4,000–6,000 ft.

Key Characters: Fragrant mimosa may be identified by the dense, globose heads of flowers, the armed branches, and leaves with 1–3 pairs of pinnae.

134. Graham mimosa — *Mimosa grahamii* — Legume family

Spreading to decumbent shrub to 32 in. (80 cm) tall, the branches somewhat angled, prickly. *Leaves* bipinnate, 2–4 in. (5–10 cm) long, with 8–16 pinnae, each with 16–30 oblong, distinctly veined leaflets about ¹/₆ in. (4–6 mm) long and ¹/₁₆–¹/₈ in. (1–2 mm) wide. *Flowers* white or pink, in round, headlike axillary clusters, the calyx and corolla with 4 or 5 lobes, the staminal filaments white. *Fruit* a linear to oblong, flat pod, glabrous or nearly so, ³/₄–1³/₁₆ in. (2–3 cm) long.

Range and Habitat: New Mexico and Arizona to Mexico. Found on dry slopes and mesas in southwestern New Mexico; 4,500–6,000 ft.

Key Characters: Graham mimosa may be identified by the flowers in globose heads, the leaves with 4–8 pairs of pinnae, the larger leaflets, and by the fruit not constricted between the seeds.

Related Species: A related variety, Lemmon mimosa, occupying the same range and a similar habitat, differs in having densely hairy leaves, flowers, and fruits.

135. Wait-a-bit — *Mimosa biuncifera* — Legume family

Shrub to 60 in. (1.5 m) tall, the branches armed with curved spines. *Leaves* bipinnate, with 8–20 pinnae, each with 10–24 linear to oblong leaflets, these strongly hairy, ¹/₁₆–¹/₆ in. (1–4 mm) long. *Flowers* white or pale pink, fragrant, borne in globose, headlike clusters, the calyx and corolla with 4 or 5 lobes, hairy. *Fruit* a linear pod, constricted between the seeds, ³/₄–1¹/₂ in. (2–4 cm) long, about ¹/₈ in. (3–4 mm) wide.

Range and Habitat: Central Texas to New Mexico, Arizona, and Mexico. Usually found on rocky slopes and mesas in central to southern New Mexico; 3,500–6,000 ft.

Key Characters: Wait-a-bit may be recognized by the globose heads of flowers, the 4–10 pairs of pinnae per leaf, the fruit constricted between the seeds, and the fruits glabrous or nearly so.

Related Species: Warnock mimosa (*M. warnockii*) is similar but differs in having short, stiff hairs on the fruit and is usually not as tall. It seems to be restricted to Texas and New Mexico, occurring on dry hills and plains in southern New Mexico at altitudes of 3,500–4,000 ft.

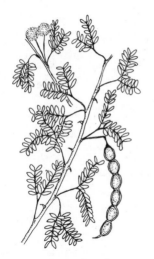

Mimosa borealis

Mimosa grahamii

Mimosa biuncifera

136. Prostrate ratany   *Krameria lanceolata*   Legume family

Perennial herb, sometimes woody only at the base, the stems prostrate or nearly so. *Leaves* alternate, simple, oblanceolate to narrowly oblong or linear, $^3/_8$–$1^1/_8$ in. (1–3 cm) long, not petioled. *Flowers* crimson, solitary on slender axillary stalks $^3/_4$–$1^1/_8$ in. (2–3 cm) long, the sepals 4 or 5, petallike, ovate-lanceolate, acute at the tip, $^3/_8$–$^7/_{16}$ in. (8–10 mm) long, with 5 petals shorter than the sepals, and with 4 stamens. *Fruit* a spiny, globose, single-seeded pod $^1/_4$–$^5/_{16}$ in. (7–9 mm) in diameter. Fruit of the prostrate ratany has been known as "sandbur" and will sometimes puncture the skin when stepped on with bare feet.

Range and Habitat: Arkansas and Kansas to Texas and Arizona, southward into Mexico. Commonly found in sandy soil of open plains in eastern to central and southern New Mexico; 4,000–6,500 ft.

Key Characters: Prostrate ratany is characterized by the prostrate, herbaceous nature, the simple leaves, and the spiny, globose fruit.

137. Sticky range ratany   *Krameria parvifolia*   Legume family

Low, much-branched shrub bearing silky hairs, the stems erect to spreading, to 28 in. (70 cm) tall, the young twigs bearing stalked glands. *Leaves* alternate, simple, linear, with grayish hairs, $^1/_8$–$^9/_{16}$ in. (5–15 mm) long. *Flowers* crimson, the calyx of 4 or 5 petallike sepals $^1/_4$–$^3/_8$ in. (7–9 mm) long, the 4 or 5 petals shorter than the sepals. *Fruit* a nearly spherical pod, $^1/_4$–$^3/_8$ in. (7–9 mm) long, densely covered with grayish hairs, with slender, barbed spines.

Range and Habitat: Western Texas to southern Nevada and California, southward into northern Mexico. Occasionally found on sandy hills, rocky ridges, and rocky slopes in eastern to central and southern New Mexico; 4,000–5,000 ft.

Key Characters: Sticky range ratany is characterized by its shrubby nature, the barbed spines on the fruit, and the branchlets devoid of spines.

138. Texas redbud   *Cercis canadensis*   Legume family

Small tree to $13^1/_2$ ft. (4 m) tall, with scaly bark, the twigs covered with brownish, feltlike hairs. *Leaves* alternate, simple, kidney-shaped, blunt at the apex, shiny green, on petioles $1^1/_8$–$4^3/_4$ in. (3–12 cm) long. *Flowers* usually pink or rose, irregular, borne in narrow axillary clusters, usually appearing before the leaves, the calyx bell-shaped, 5-lobed, swollen on one side, the 5 petals unequal in size, the 10 stamens separate. *Fruit* a pod, flat, leathery, linear-oblong, not constricted between the seeds, 2–4 in. (5–10 cm) long and about $^5/_8$ in. (15 mm) wide. Texas redbud is a conspicuous, striking tree when in flower. It is also known as "Judas tree."

Range and Habitat: Texas to New Mexico and Mexico. Uncommon on rocky slopes and near streams in extreme southeastern New Mexico; 4,500–6,000 ft.

Key Characters: Texas redbud may be recognized by the clusters of pinkish flowers appearing before or with the leaves, the branches unarmed, the simple leaves, and the 10 separate stamens.

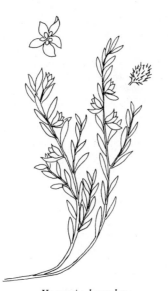

Krameria lanceolata

Krameria parvifolia

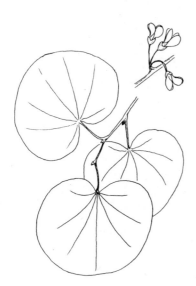

Cercis canadensis

139. Senna *Cassia bauhinioides* Legume family

Perennial herb to 17 in. (40 cm) tall, the stems branching, densely covered with spreading hairs. *Leaves* pinnate, with 2 oblong-ovate, obtuse leaflets, these oblique at the base, hairy on both surfaces, 3/8–1 1/2 in. (10–40 mm) long, and 5/16–5/8 in. (8–16 mm) wide. *Flowers* in axillary clusters of 2, borne near the ends of the branches, the calyx 5-toothed, the flower nearly regular, with 5 dark yellow petals 5/8–3/4 in. (15–18 mm) long, much longer than the sepals. *Fruit* a straight or slightly curved, somewhat flattened pod, 3/4–1 1/2 in. (2–4 cm) long. The dark yellow flowers of senna make it a very attractive plant.
Range and Habitat: Texas to Arizona and Mexico. Commonly found on rocky slopes and mesas in west-central to central, southern, and southwestern New Mexico; 4,000–5,500 ft.
Key Characters: This senna is easily recognized by the nearly regular, dark yellow flowers, and by the leaves with 2 leaflets.

140. Hairy senna *Cassia covesii* Legume family

Low perennial herb, the stems branching and brittle near the base, with densely matted white hairs, leafy, 12–24 in. (3–6 dm) tall. *Leaves* pinnate, with 4–6 obliquely oblong or elliptical leaflets 3/8–1 3/16 in. (1–3 cm) long. *Flowers* regular, in clusters, the calyx 5-toothed, the 5 petals yellow, oblong-ovate, 3/8–5/8 in. (10–15 mm) long, longer than the sepals. *Fruit* a straight or slightly curved, hairy pod, 3/4–1 3/16 in. (2–3 cm) long.
Range and Habitat: New Mexico to Arizona, southern Nevada, California, and northwestern Mexico. Usually occurring in dry, rocky ground in southwestern New Mexico; 4,000–4,500 ft.
Key Characters: Hairy senna may be recognized by the regular yellow flowers, the herbaceous nature, and by the leaves with 4–6 leaflets.

141. Rushpea *Hoffmanseggia jamesii* Legume family

Perennial herb, the stems branching at the base, erect or ascending, finely hairy with blackish glands, 4–16 in. (10–35 cm) long. *Leaves* bipinnate with 5–7 pinnae, each with 10–20 oblong to ovate-oblong leaflets about 1/8 in. (3–5 mm) long, these with blackish glands. *Flowers* somewhat irregular, with blackish glands, in narrow clusters, the calyx 5-lobed, the 5 petals dark yellow, glandular, less than twice as long as the calyx. *Fruit* a somewhat moon-shaped pod bearing blackish glands, 3/4–1 in. (20–25 mm) long, about 5/16 in. (8–9 mm) wide.
Range and Habitat: Kansas to Colorado, southward to Texas, New Mexico, and Arizona. Common on sandy hills and plains throughout New Mexico; 4,000–6,000 ft.
Key Characters: Rushpea is characterized by the bipinnate leaves with 10–20 leaflets per pinna, the moon-shaped fruit, and the blackish glands on leaflets, flowers, and fruits.

142. Sicklepod rushpea *Hoffmanseggia drepanocarpa* Legume family

Perennial herb from woody taproots, the stems finely hairy, without glands, 4–8 in. (1–2 dm) tall. *Leaves* bipinnate with 7–11 pinnae, each with 8–20 oblong, glandless leaflets with appressed hairs. *Flowers* somewhat irregular, in narrow clusters without glands, the calyx 5-toothed, the 5 petals dark yellow, slightly longer than the calyx. *Fruit* a strongly curved pod with appressed hairs, often forming a semicircle.
Range and Habitat: Texas to Colorado and Arizona, southward to Mexico. Common on dry slopes in central and southern New Mexico; 3,500–5,000 ft.
Key Characters: Sicklepod rushpea may be recognized by the bipinnate leaves, the narrow clusters of dark yellow, nonglandular flowers, and by the strongly curved fruit.
Related Species: Hog potato, *H. densiflora,* also occurs in central and southern New Mexico at altitudes of 3,500–6,000 ft., and differs in the stipitate-glandular (glands on stalks) flower clusters, and the slightly curved fruit.

Cassia bauhinioides

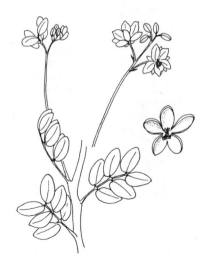

Cassia covesii

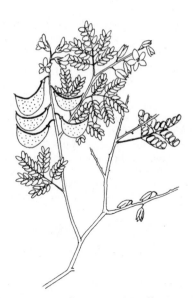

Hoffmanseggia jamesii

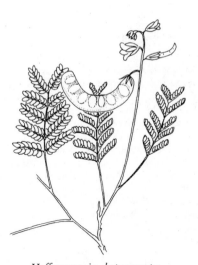

Hoffmanseggia drepanocarpa

143. **Big golden-pea**   *Thermopsis pinetorum*   Legume family

Perennial herb, the stems erect, branching, 12–24 in. (3–6 dm) tall, with ovate or ovate-lanceolate stipules subtending the petioles. *Leaves* palmate, with 3 ovate-oblong to elliptic leaflets 1 1/8–2 3/8 in. (3–6 cm) long. *Flowers* in often dense, narrow terminal clusters, the calyx 5-lobed, the 5 petals yellow, pealike. *Fruit* a pod, usually slightly curved, ascending to widely spreading, hairy when young, 1 1/2–3 1/8 in. (4–8 cm) long.
Range and Habitat: Wyoming to Colorado, Utah, New Mexico, and Arizona. Common in open woods and clearings in the mountains of New Mexico; 7,000–9,500 ft.
Key Characters: Big golden-pea may be recognized by the palmately 3-foliolate leaves, the bright yellow, pealike flowers in dense, narrow terminal clusters, and by the ascending to widely spreading fruit.

144. **Short-stemmed lupine**   *Lupinus breviculus*   Legume family

Annual herb covered with dense, soft hairs, the stems absent or not more than 3/8 in. (1 cm) long, the flowering stalks to 4 in. (10 cm) long. *Leaves* crowded, basal, on petioles 1 1/8–2 3/4 in. (3–7 cm) long, palmate, with 5–8 spatulate leaflets 1/4–5/8 in. (5–15 mm) long, the upper surface glabrous. *Flowers* in dense, headlike clusters about 3/4 in. (2 cm) wide, barely exserted above the leaves, each flower 1/4–3/8 in. (6–8 mm) long, the calyx densely hairy and soft, the upper lip 2-lobed, the lower one smooth or 3-lobed, about 1/4 in. (4–6 mm) long, the 5 petals blue, pealike. *Fruit* an ovoid, 2- or 3-seeded pod about 3/8 in. (10 mm) long.
Range and Habitat: Colorado to Oregon, southward to New Mexico, Arizona, and California. Frequently found on dry hills and in dry canyons and valleys in northern to western New Mexico; 5,000–7,000 ft.
Key Characters: Short-stemmed lupine is easily recognized by the short or absent stem, the dense, headlike clusters of flowers or fruit, and by the fruit only about 3/8 in. (10 mm) long.

145. **Annual lupine**   *Lupinus concinnus*   Legume family

Annual herb, the stems erect, branched, to 12 in. (30 cm) tall, the herbage with dense, spreading hairs. *Leaves* on slender petioles 1 1/2–3 in. (4–8 cm) long, longer than the leaflets, palmate with 5–8 oblanceolate leaflets, these obtuse to rounded at the apex, 3/8–3/4 in. (1–2 cm) long, 1/8–1/4 in. (3–6 mm) wide, dark green. *Flowers* in erect, narrow clusters 1 1/4–4 in. (3–10 cm) long, each flower pealike, 1/4–3/8 in. (7–9 mm) long, the calyx densely covered with soft hairs, the upper lip 2-lobed, the lower one 3-toothed, the 5 petals purple or bluish purple. *Fruit* a 2- to 4-seeded pod, 3/8–3/4 in. (10–18 mm) long.
Range and Habitat: New Mexico to California, southward to Sonora and Baja California. Found mostly on dry, open plains and slopes in southwestern New Mexico; 3,000–5,000 ft.
Key Characters: Annual lupine may be identified by the dense narrow clusters of flowers, the leaflets 3/8–3/4 in. (1–2 cm) long, and the fruit 3/8–3/4 in. (10–18 mm) long.
Related Species: Low lupine, *L. pusillus,* also occurs in northern to central and western New Mexico on dry slopes and sandy plains at altitudes of 5,000–7,000 ft., but differs in having leaflets and fruit 3/4–1 3/16 in. (2–3 cm) long.

146. **Few-flowered lupine**   *Lupinus sparsiflorus*   Legume family

Annual or biennial herb, with appressed or soft hairs, the stems 8–16 in. (2–4 dm) tall. *Leaves* long-petioled, palmate, with 5–9 linear to oblanceolate leaflets, these acute at the apex, about 1/8 in. (1.5–4.0 mm) wide. *Flowers* in loose, narrow clusters 3 1/8–7 7/8 in. (8–20 cm) long, the petals bright blue or purplish, with a yellow spot on the banner, 5/16–1/2 in. (8–13 mm) long, pealike. *Fruit* an ascending, 5- or 6-seeded pod 1/2–3/4 in. (12–20 mm) long.
Range and Habitat: California to southern Nevada, Arizona, and Baja California. Usually found in sandy soil in southwestern New Mexico; 4,500–5,000 ft.
Key Characters: Few-flowered lupine may be identified by the palmate leaves with 5–9 leaflets less than 1/6 in. (4 mm) wide, and by the banner (upper petal) with a yellow spot.

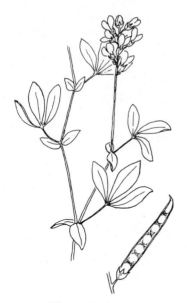

Thermopsis pinetorum

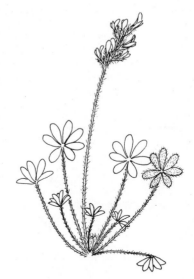

Lupinus breviculus

Lupinus concinnus

Lupinus sparsiflorus

147. **Palmer lupine**   *Lupinus palmeri*   Legume family

Perennial herb, usually 8–24 in. (2–6 dm) tall, the stems densely hairy with ascending or spreading hairs. *Leaves* palmate, with oblanceolate leaflets, these pointed at the apex, silky hairs on both surfaces. *Flowers* in loose, narrow clusters, usually violet, ⁵/₁₆–³/₈ in. (8–10 mm) long, pealike. *Fruit* a 4- to 6-seeded pod, ³/₄–1¹/₈ in. (2–3 cm) long.

Range and Habitat: New Mexico and Arizona. Usually found in wooded canyons and on wooded slopes in western and north-central New Mexico; 6,500–8,000 ft.

Key Characters: Palmer lupine may be identified by the perennial nature, the violet flowers ⁵/₁₆–³/₈ in. (8–10 mm) long, the ascending or spreading hairs on the stem, and by the silky hairs on the upper surface of the leaflets.

Related Species: Another lupine, *L. ammophilus*, ranges from Colorado to Utah and New Mexico. It occurs in sandy soil in northwestern New Mexico at altitudes of 6,000–8,000 ft. and differs mainly in the glabrous to sparsely hairy upper leaf surface.

148. **Narrowleaf bean**   *Phaseolus angustissimus*   Legume family

Perennial herb, the stems twining, usually at least 12 in. (30 cm) long. *Leaves* pinnate with 3 linear or linear-oblong, sometimes linear-lanceolate leaflets 1³/₁₆–2 in. (3–5 cm) long. *Flowers* several, in axillary, long-stalked, narrow clusters, the calyx 5-toothed, subtended by a pair of small bractlets, the petals purplish pink with a yellow keel, pealike, about ¹/₄–³/₈ in. (8–10 mm) long. *Fruit* a flat pod, ¹/₄–⁵/₁₆ in. (6–8 mm) wide, tipped with a beak (style) about ¹/₁₂ in. (2 mm) long.

Range and Habitat: New Mexico and Arizona. Commonly found on dry hills and plains in south-central to west-central and southwestern New Mexico; 4,000–7,000 ft.

Key Characters: Narrowleaf bean may be recognized by the perennial nature, the twining stems, the small bractlets subtending the calyx, and by the narrow leaflets.

149. **Feather indigobush**   *Dalea formosa*   Legume family

Shrub, the stems to 24 in. (6 dm) long, much-branched, the branches glabrous. *Leaves* pinnate, with 7–11 oblong or spatulate leaflets about ¹/₈ in. (2–3 mm) long, these glabrous and glandular-dotted beneath. *Flowers* 2–10 in narrow, somewhat dense clusters, each flower subtended by an ovate, glandular bract, the glandular calyx tube, about ¹/₈ to ³/₁₆ in. (3–4 mm) long, with long hairs, and 5 narrow, featherlike lobes longer than the tube, the petals pealike, mostly rose-colored, sometimes yellowish. *Fruit* a hairy, glandular-dotted pod.

Range and Habitat: Colorado to New Mexico, Arizona, and Mexico. Frequently found on dry plains and low hills, often among rocks, throughout New Mexico; 4,000–7,000 ft.

Key Characters: Feather indigobush is characterized by the usually rose-colored flowers, sometimes with yellowish markings, the shrubby, low, glabrous, much-branched habit, the hairy calyx tube, and by having 11 or fewer leaflets per leaf.

Related Species: Black indigobush, *D. frutescens*, is similar but has mostly simple or few-branched woody stems, and glabrous calyx tubes. It ranges from Texas to New Mexico and Mexico, occurring on dry soil of open slopes in southeastern and south-central New Mexico at altitudes of 6,500–8,000 ft.

150. **Gray indigobush**   *Dalea grayi*   Legume family

Perennial herb, the stems often woody at the base, branching, glabrous below the inflorescence. *Leaves* pinnate with 35–41 oblong or oval leaflets, these about ¹/₈ in. (2–5 mm) long, glandular-dotted beneath. *Flowers* in dense, spikelike clusters, the floral bracts glandular, the calyx tube hairy, the 5 lobes triangular with a long-pointed apex, the petals pealike, white when fresh.

Range and Habitat: New Mexico to southern Arizona and Mexico. Found on hills of southwestern New Mexico; 4,000–5,500 ft.

Key Characters: Gray indigobush is characterized by the hairy calyx tube, the triangular calyx lobes, numerous leaflets per leaf, and by the stems glabrous below the inflorescence.

Lupinus palmeri

Phaseolus angustissimus

Dalea formosa

Dalea grayi

151. **Bigtop dalea**   *Dalea enneandra*   Legume family

Perennial herb, the stems glabrous, erect, branched, to 40 in. (1 m) tall. *Leaves* pinnate with 5–11 linear-oblong or cuneate-lanceolate leaflets, these glabrous, glandular-dotted, $3/16$–$3/8$ in. (5–10 mm) long. *Flowers* in spreading clusters of narrow spikes, each flower subtended by an ovate to nearly round floral bract, having a silky haired calyx about $3/16$ in. (7 mm) long, with narrow, featherlike lobes longer than the tube, pealike white or pink-tinged petals, and 9 stamens. *Fruit* a hairy pod.

Range and Habitat: Iowa to Nebraska and Colorado, southward to Mississippi, Texas, and New Mexico. Found on dry plains in northern and eastern New Mexico; 5,000–6,500 ft.

Key Characters: Bigtop dalea is characterized by the featherlike calyx lobes, the hairy calyx tube, the glabrous lower stems and leaves, the 11 or fewer leaflets per leaf, the white petals, and by the 9 stamens.

152. **New Mexico indigobush**   *Dalea neomexicana*   Legume family

Perennial herb, the stems prostrate or nearly so, densely covered with silky hairs, and glandular-dotted, to about 16 in. (40 cm) long. *Leaves* pinnate with 11–15 cuneate-obovate leaflets, these sparsely hairy above, densely covered with soft hairs beneath, $3/16$–$5/16$ in. (5–8 mm) long. *Flowers* in dense, narrow clusters $3/4$–$2 3/8$ in. (2–6 cm) long, the calyx hairy, the tube about $1/8$ in. (3–4 mm) long, the lobes narrow, hairy, and featherlike, the corolla pealike, white to pink, not longer than the calyx. *Fruit* a hairy pod.

Range and Habitat: West Texas to southern Nevada and California, southward into Mexico. Occasionally found on sandy plains of southern New Mexico; 3,500–4,500 ft.

Key Characters: New Mexico indigobush may be recognized by the hairy stem and calyx, the prostrate habit, and by the cuneate-obovate leaflets.

153. **Spreading indigobush**   *Dalea terminalis*   Legume family

Perennial herb, the stems prostrate, densely hairy, to 24 in. (60 cm) long. *Leaves* pinnate with 7–15 obovate, hairy leaflets. *Flowers* in erect, slender spikes $1 1/8$–$3 1/8$ in. (3–8 cm) long, the floral bracts obovate, glandular dotted, the calyx tube glabrous with short, triangular lobes, the corolla pealike, reddish purple. *Fruit* a pod covered with short hairs.

Range and Habitat: West Texas to southern Utah, southward through Arizona and into Mexico. Common in dry fields and plains, usually in sandy soil throughout New Mexico; 4,000–5,500 ft.

Key Characters: Spreading indigobush may be recognized by its prostrate habit, the densely hairy stems and leaves, and by the glabrous calyx tube.

154. **Gregg dalea**   *Dalea greggii*   Legume family

Subshrub from a thick, woody base, the stems several-branched, prostrate, with matted hairs, glandular, often rooting at the nodes. *Leaves* pinnate with 5–11 obovate leaflets $1/8$–$1/4$ in. (3–6 mm) long. *Flowers* in dense, headlike terminal clusters $3/8$–$3/4$ in. (1–2 cm) long, the floral bracts densely hairy, ovate-lanceolate, the calyx tube hairy, about $1/8$ in. (2.5 mm) long, with inconspicuous glands, the lobes narrow and hairy, the corolla pealike, purple or reddish purple, sometimes marked with yellow. *Fruit* a densely hairy, glandular pod.

Range and Habitat: Texas to Arizona and Mexico. Found on limestone hills in southern New Mexico; 2,500–6,000 ft.

Key Characters: Gregg dalea may be recognized by the hairy stems and leaves, and by the prostrate, subshrubby habit.

Dalea enneandra

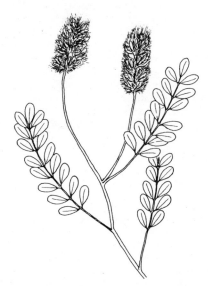

Dalea neomexicana

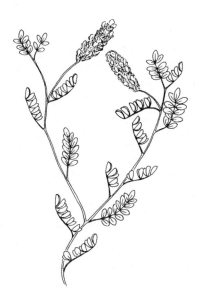

Dalea terminalis

Dalea greggii

155. **Western coralbean; chilicote**   *Erythrina flabelliformis*   Legume family

Shrub to 14 ft. (4 m) or more tail, the stems with scattered hooked prickles. *Leaves* pinnate
with 3 triangular to ovate-triangular leaflets, these cordate or rounded at the base, 1–3 in.
(25–75 mm) long, 1¹/₈–3³/₈ in. (30–85 mm) wide. *Flowers* borne in short, narrow terminal,
or axillary clusters (racemes), with the calyx ¹/₄–³/₈ in. (7–9 mm) long, bearing minute teeth,
the corolla pealike, scarlet, ⁵/₈–1 in. (15–25 mm) long, and with 10 stamens. *Fruit* a hard,
brown pod, 4–10 in. (10–25 cm) long and ⁵/₈–³/₄ in. (15–20 mm) wide, the seeds ³/₈–¹/₂ in.
(10–12 mm) long, bright scarlet. The attractive seeds are considered to be poisonous.
Range and Habitat: New Mexico and Arizona to northern Mexico. Occasionally found on
dry, rocky slopes in southwestern New Mexico; 4,500–5,500 ft.
Key Characters: Western coralbean may be recognized by the leaves with large, fan-shaped
leaflets, the hard brown fruit, the hooked prickles on the stems and petioles, and by the
scarlet flowers.

156. **Clover**   *Trifolium subacaulescens*   Legume family

Stemless perennial herb. *Leaves* basal, pinnate with 3 oval to elliptic-oblong, toothed leaflets,
these glabrous above and hairy beneath, ¹/₄–1 in. (5–25 mm) long. *Flowers* borne at the apex
of an erect or spreading, glabrous, leafless stalk 1¹/₈–4 in. (3–10 cm) long, in dense, globose,
5- to 12-flowered heads, the subtending bracts minute or absent, the calyx tube hairy, about
¹/₄ in. (4–6 mm) long with 5 lobes gradually tapering to a point, the corolla pealike,
yellowish white or pinkish, ¹/₄–¹/₂ in. (6–13 mm) long. *Fruit* a hairy 2-seeded pod.
Range and Habitat: Colorado to New Mexico and Arizona. Usually found on forested slopes
in north-central and northwestern New Mexico; 7,000–9,500 ft.
Key Characters: This clover may be identified by the absence of bracts subtending the
flowering heads, the absence of stems, the hairy calyx, and by the toothed leaflets.
Related Species: Other clovers (*T. lacerum*) and Fendler clover (*T. fendleri*) occur in damp
meadows in north-central to southwestern New Mexico at altitudes of 5,500–8,000 ft. They
differ from *T. subacaulescens* by bracts at least ¹/₁₂ in. (2 mm) long subtending the heads and
by the glabrous calyx. They differ from each other in that Fendler clover has larger heads and
flowers.

157. **Alfalfa**   *Medicago sativa*   Legume family

Perennial herb, the stems mostly erect, branched, glabrous or sparsely hairy, to 40 in. (1 m)
tall. *Leaves* pinnate with 3 oblong to obovate leaflets, these obtuse at the apex, minutely
toothed toward the apex, ³/₈–1¹/₈ in. (1–3 cm) long. *Flowers* borne in dense, narrow axillary
clusters ³/₈–2 in. (1–5 cm) long, the calyx tube bell-shaped with 5 equal lobes, the corolla
pealike, violet, about ⁵/₁₆ in. (7–9 mm) long. *Fruit* a hairy, coiled, several-seeded pod. Alfalfa
is commonly cultivated and often escapes from cultivation.
Range and Habitat: Introduced from Europe to temperate areas of North America.
Frequently found along roadsides and waste ground throughout New Mexico; 4,000–8,000 ft.
Key Characters: Alfalfa may be easily identified by the small clusters of violet flowers, the 3
leaflets minutely toothed above the middle, and by the coiled fruit.

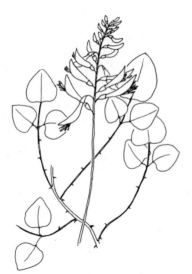

Erythrina flabelliformis

Trifolium subacaulescens

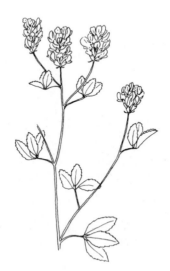

Medicago sativa

131

158. White sweet clover   *Melilotus albus*   Legume family

Biennial herb, the stems mostly erect, glabrous or nearly so, usually branched, to about 6½ ft. (2 m) tall. *Leaves* pinnate with 3 oblong to elliptic or oblanceolate leaflets, these obtuse at the apex, glabrous, toothed, ³/₈–1¹/₈ in. (1–3 cm) long. *Flowers* in elongated, slender axillary clusters (racemes) 1¹/₈–4⁵/₈ in. (3–12 cm) long, the corolla pealike, white, about ³/₁₆ in. (4–6 mm) long. *Fruit* a straight glabrous pod about ¹/₈ in. (3–4 mm) long.
Range and Habitat: Introduced from Europe and Asia throughout North America. Frequently found along roadsides and in waste and cultivated ground throughout New Mexico; 4,000–8,000 ft.
Key Characters: White sweet clover may be recognized by the slender clusters of small white flowers, the leaves with 3 toothed leaflets, and by the small, straight fruit.

159. Yellow sweet clover   *Melilotus officinalis*   Legume family

Biennial herb, the stems mostly erect, branched, usually glabrous, to about 6½ ft. (2 m) tall. *Leaves* pinnate with 3 oblong to oval, sharply toothed, glabrous leaflets ³/₈–1¹/₈ in. (1–3 cm) long. *Flowers* in elongated, slender axillary clusters (racemes) ³/₄–4³/₄ in. (2–12 cm) long, the corolla pealike, yellow, about ¹/₄ in. (5–6 mm) long. *Fruit* a straight, sparsely hairy pod about ¹/₈ in. (3–4 mm) long. Yellow sweet clover is very fragrant when cut or crushed.
Range and Habitat: Introduced from Europe throughout the United States. Frequently found along roadsides and in waste or cultivated ground throughout New Mexico; 4,000–8,000 ft.
Key Characters: Yellow sweet clover may be identified by the slender clusters of small yellow flowers, the leaves with 3 sharply toothed leaflets, and by the small, straight fruit.

160. Greene deervetch   *Lotus greenei*   Legume family

Perennial herb, the stems decumbent to prostrate, the herbage with dense, spreading hairs. *Leaves* pinnate with 4–7 linear-oblanceolate to cuneate-obovate leaflets, these ⁵/₁₆–⁹/₁₆ in. (8–15 mm) long and ¹/₈–¹/₄ in. (3–6 mm) wide. *Flowers* borne in 1- to 3-flowered axillary clusters on stalks exceeding the leaves, the calyx with soft hairs, the corolla pealike, yellow or orange, ¹/₂–⁵/₈ in. (12–18 mm) long. *Fruit* a linear, straight or curved pod densely covered with soft hairs, ³/₄–1¹/₈ in. (2–3 cm) long.
Range and Habitat: New Mexico and southern Arizona. Common on dry plains and hills in central to southern and southwestern New Mexico; 4,000–6,000 ft.
Key Characters: Greene deervetch may be identified by the leaves with 4–7 leaflets, the spreading hairs, and by the flowers in clusters of 1 to 3.

161. New Mexico deervetch   *Lotus neomexicanus*   Legume family

Perennial herb, the stems prostrate to ascending, the herbage sparsely hairy. *Leaves* pinnate with 3–6 oblanceolate leaflets, these usually obtuse at the apex, ¹/₄–⁵/₁₆ in. (5–8 mm) long, at least some of them ¹/₈ in. (3 mm) wide or wider. *Flowers* borne on 1- or 2-flowered axillary stalks, the calyx tube with appressed hairs, the corolla pealike, yellow to orange, ⁵/₁₆–⁵/₈ in. (8–15 mm) long. *Fruit* a curved, hairy pod ³/₄–1³/₈ in. (20–35 mm) long and about ¹/₈ in. (3–4 mm) wide.
Range and Habitat: New Mexico and eastern Arizona. Found on dry hills and mesas in southwestern New Mexico; 4,500–5,500 ft.
Key Characters: New Mexico deervetch is characterized by the leaves with 3–6 leaflets, some of them at least ¹/₈ in. (3 mm) wide, by the sparse, appressed hairs, and by the 1- or 2-flowered clusters.

Melilotus albus   *Melilotus officinalis*

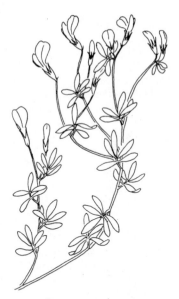

Lotus greenei   *Lotus neomexicanus*

162. **Missouri milkvetch**   *Astragalus missouriensis*   Legume family

Perennial herb, the stems prostrate, to about 6 in. (14 cm) long, both stems and leaves with appressed hairs. *Leaves* alternate, pinnately compound, the 9–17 leaflets elliptic or broadest above the middle, pointed or blunt at the tip. *Flowers* in small clusters at the summit of axillary flower stalks, pealike, pinkish purple, the upper (banner) petal about ⁵/₈–⁷/₈ in. (15–22 mm) long (smaller in one of the varieties). *Fruit* an oblong pod ⁵/₈–1 in. (15–25 mm) long, covered with appressed hairs. This plant is relatively common on prairies and plains and is reputed to be poisonous, especially at certain times.
Range and Habitat: Manitoba and Alberta to Texas and New Mexico. Mostly found on plains, prairies, and dry, open slopes throughout all but western New Mexico; 5,000–7,500 ft.
Key Characters: Missouri milkvetch is distinguished by the prostrate stems, the compound leaves with 9–17 leaflets, the pinkish purple flowers, and the straight pods.

163. **Torrey milkvetch**   *Astragalus scaposus*   Legume family

Perennial herb, essentially without stems, but with slender, leafless flower stalks. *Leaves* alternate, pinnately compound, with silvery appressed hairs, the 7–13 leaflets oval or broadest above the middle. *Flowers* in small terminal clusters, pealike, white to yellowish or purplish, the upper (banner) petal deeply notched, the lateral petals variously white or purple with white tips. *Fruit* a straight or curved pod ³/₈–⁵/₈ in. (10–15 mm) long, with silvery hairs.
Range and Habitat: Colorado to Nevada, southward to New Mexico and Arizona. Usually found in sandy or gravelly soils from central to northwestern New Mexico; 4,500–6,500 ft.
Key Characters: Torrey milkvetch is distinguished by its stemless nature, the silvery compound leaves with 7–13 leaflets, the often multicolored flowers, and the pod covered with silvery hairs.

164. **Torrance milkvetch**   *Astragalus siliceus*   Legume family

Perennial herb, the stems absent or always less than 4 in. (10 cm) long. *Leaves* alternate, pinnately compound, covered with silvery appressed hairs, the 5–9 leaflets mostly obtuse and broadest above the middle. *Flowers* in small clusters at the summit of curved, often arching flower stalks, pealike, pinkish purple, ³/₈–¹/₂ in. (10–12 mm) long, the upper (banner) petal deeply notched, the lateral petals white-tipped. *Fruit* an ovoid, greenish, hairy pod ¹/₄–⁵/₁₆ in. (5–8 mm) long.
Range and Habitat: Restricted to rocky areas of the plains of central New Mexico; 6,000–6,500 ft.
Key Characters: Torrance milkvetch is distinguished by the low-growing habit, the silvery leaves, and the pinkish purple flowers with some white-tipped petals and a deeply notched upper (banner) petal.

165. **Crescent milkvetch**   *Astragalus amphioxys*   Legume family

Perennial herb, the stems prostrate or sweeping upward somewhat at the tip, to about 4 in. (10 cm) long. *Leaves* alternate, pinnately compound, with appressed hairs, the 11–21 leaflets having silvery hairs on both sides and often blunt at the tip. *Flowers* in short clusters at the summit of flower stalks, pealike, pinkish purple, the upper petal (banner) ¹/₂–1¹/₈ in. (12–27 mm) long and notched at the tip, the calyx often with black hairs. *Fruit* a slender, usually crescent-shaped pod covered with short appressed hairs. This is a very conspicuous and attractive milkvetch. A variety of this species has been considered poisonous to livestock.
Range and Habitat: Colorado to Nevada, southward to Texas and Arizona. Usually associated with sandy or gravelly soils in valleys and on flats and slopes from north-central to south-central and western New Mexico; 4,000–6,000 ft.
Key Characters: Crescent milkvetch can be identified by the short prostrate stems, the silvery, pinnately compound leaves, the pinkish purple flowers, and the crescent-shaped pods.

Astragalus missouriensis

Astragalus scaposus

Astragalus siliceus

Astragalus amphioxys

166. Nuttall milkvetch   *Astragalus nuttallianus*   Legume family

Annual, the stems to 12 in. (30 cm) long, sparsely hairy. *Leaves* alternate, pinnately compound, the 7–23 leaflets often blunt or notched at the tip, the upper surface with few or no hairs. *Flowers* in small clusters, pealike, purple, the upper (banner) petal $1/4–5/16$ in. (6–8 mm) long, marked with a conspicuous pale "eye." *Fruit* a slender, usually curved pod about $1/2–1$ in. (12–25 mm) long. This plant is probably the most common of the desert milkvetches and is a very attractive wildflower. Four varieties of this plant occur in New Mexico.

Range and Habitat: Oklahoma to Utah, southward to Texas and Arizona. Dry streambeds in gravelly soils, on dry plains or slopes or sometimes in open woods, throughout New Mexico; 3,500–7,000 ft.

Key Characters: Nuttall milkvetch may be recognized by the sparsely hairy stems and leaves, the slender axillary stalks bearing purplish flowers with a pale "eye," and the slender, curved pods.

167. Woolly locoweed   *Astragalus mollissimus*   Legume family

Short-stemmed or stemless perennial herb, the stems usually less than 4 in. (10 cm) long, both stems and leaves woolly with silky hairs. *Leaves* alternate, pinnately compound, the 15–29 leaflets oval or broader above the middle, blunt at the tip, $3/8–3/4$ in. (10–20 mm) long. *Flowers* pealike, yellowish purple to pinkish purple, the upper (banner) petal mostly $1/2–7/8$ in. (14–22 mm) long. *Fruit* an ellipsoid, abruptly curved pod as long as the flowers. Although relatively unpalatable, this plant is poisonous to livestock. This description includes the six varieties of woolly locoweed found in New Mexico.

Range and Habitat: Nebraska and Wyoming to Texas and Arizona. Mostly on dry, open plains or slopes, sometimes in rocky areas throughout New Mexico; 4,000–8,500 ft.

Key Characters: Woolly locoweed is characterized by the very short stems or the lack of stems and the presence of elongate flower stalks, the yellowish purple to pinkish purple flowers, and the strongly curved pods.

168. Beaked milkvetch   *Astragalus nothoxys*   Legume family

Perennial herb, the stems to about 12 in. (30 cm) long, both stems and leaves with appressed hairs. *Leaves* alternate, pinnately compound, the 9–21 leaflets blunt and often notched at the tip. *Flowers* in short axillary clusters, pealike, pinkish purple, $5/16–1/2$ in. (8–12 mm) long, some of the petals often tipped with white. *Fruit* a slender brownish pod $5/8–7/8$ in. (15–22 mm) long.

Range and Habitat: New Mexico to Arizona and northern Mexico. Frequently associated with scrub oaks or junipers in sandy ground on open slopes in southwestern New Mexico; 5,000–7,000 ft.

Key Characters: Beaked milkvetch can be identified by the short stems, the compound leaves with leaflets hairy on both sides, the pinkish purple flowers, and the slender pods.

169. Ground plum   *Astragalus crassicarpus*   Legume family

Perennial herb, the stems curving upward from reclining bases, to 20 in. (50 cm) long, usually hairy. *Leaves* alternate, pinnately compound, the 15–29 leaflets broadest above the middle or elliptic. *Flowers* in dense axillary clusters, pealike, purple or lilac or occasionally white with purple spots, the upper (banner) petal $5/8–1$ in. (16–25 mm) long. *Fruit* a smooth, plumlike, fleshy pod $5/8–1$ in. (15–25 mm) long.

Range and Habitat: Manitoba and Alberta to Missouri, Texas, and New Mexico. Usually associated with open plains and waste ground, often along roadsides in eastern and southern New Mexico; 4,500–7,500 ft.

Key Characters: Ground plum may be identified by the curving stems, the compound leaves with 15 or more leaflets, the usually purple or lilac "pea flowers," and the fleshy, spongy fruits.

Astragalus nuttallianus

Astragalus mollissimus

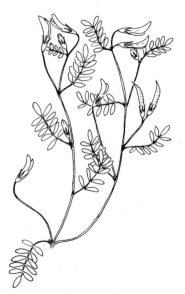

Astragalus nothoxys

Astragalus crassicarpus

170. **Beakpod milkvetch**   *Astragalus lentiginosus*   Legume family

Perennial herb, the stems curving upward, often from reclining bases, with usually appressed hairs. *Leaves* alternate, pinnately compound, the leaflets mostly 15–21 and notched at the tip, sometimes hairy beneath. *Flowers* pealike, in compound or loose clusters, pinkish purple or white, the upper petal (banner) 5/8–3/4 in. (15–20 mm) long. *Fruit* a rounded, often smooth and purplish pod 5/8–1 1/4 in. (15–30 mm) long, often with a recurved beak. This plant is considered to be poisonous to livestock.

Range and Habitat: Colorado and Utah to Mexico. Usually found in gravelly washes and canyons, or on rocky slopes and mesas from central to southern and western New Mexico; 4,000–7,500 ft.

Key Characters: Beakpod milkvetch is distinguished by the upward-curving stems, the compound leaves with leaflets notched at the tip, the purplish or whitish pealike corollas, and the rounded pod with an often curved beak.

171. **Mescal-bean**   *Sophora secundiflora*   Legume family

Evergreen shrub, to about 12 ft. (4 m) tall. *Leaves* alternate, pinnately compound, the 7–13 leaflets leathery and shiny, oblong or oval, mostly 3/4–2 in. (20–50 mm) long, notched or with a minute point at the apex. *Flowers* conspicuous, in densely flowered clusters, pealike, the corolla violet, the upper petal (banner) 3/8–1/2 in. (10–15 mm) long. *Fruit* a leathery pod constricted between the scarlet seeds. This plant is cultivated in southern areas for its beautiful foliage and attractive flowers. The seeds are considered to be poisonous.

Range and Habitat: Texas to New Mexico and northern Mexico. Found mostly along limestone cliffs and gravelly washes in southeastern New Mexico; 4,000–5,500 ft.

Key Characters: Mescal-bean can be identified easily by the shiny evergreen foliage, the conspicuous violet flowers, and the strongly constricted pods.

172. **Silky sophora**   *Sophora nuttalliana*   Legume family

Herbaceous perennial, the stems to 12 in. (30 cm) tall, both stems and leaves with silky hairs. *Leaves* alternate, pinnately compound, to 3 1/4 in. (8 cm) long, the 7–25 leaflets 1/4–1/2 in. (5–12 mm) long and blunt or notched at the tip. *Flowers* in dense, often short clusters, pealike, the corolla white, the blade of the upper petal about 10 mm long and rounded. *Fruit* a leathery pod, constricted between the seeds.

Range and Habitat: South Dakota to Texas and Arizona. Usually found on dry fields and plains throughout New Mexico; 4,000–6,500 ft.

Key Characters: Silky sophora can be identified by the stems and leaves with silky hairs, the white flowers, and the leathery fruits constricted between the seeds.

173. **Arizona peavine**   *Lathyrus arizonicus*   Legume family

Perennial herb, the stems climbing or trailing, to 16 in. (40 cm) long, often winged. *Leaves* alternate, pinnately compound, with unbranched tendrils at the tip, with 2–6 linear to oblong leaflets 1 5/8–3 in. (40–80 mm) long. *Flowers* in small clusters, pealike, with the corolla white to yellowish, 3/8–5/8 in. (11–15 mm) long, and with 10 stamens. *Fruit* a flattened pod.

Range and Habitat: Colorado and Utah to Mexico. Usually found in open coniferous forests throughout the mountains of New Mexico; 7,000–10,000 ft.

Key Characters: Arizona peavine is distinguished by the weak, often winged stems, the compound leaves with unbranched tendrils, and the white to yellowish flowers.

Astragalus lentiginosus

Sophora secundiflora

Sophora nuttalliana

Lathyrus arizonicus

174. **American vetch**   *Vicia americana*   Legume family

Perennial herb, the stems smooth, climbing or trailing, to 3 ft (1 m) long. *Leaves* pinnately compound, with 8–18 variable leaflets 5/8–13/8 in. (15–35 mm) long and 1/4–1/2 in. (6–14 mm) wide, the leaf rachis ending in a tendril. *Flowers* in small clusters, pealike, the corolla bluish purple, 5/8–3/4 in. (15–20 mm) long. *Fruit* a slender, flattened pod about 11/4 in. (30 mm) long.
Range and Habitat: Canada and Alaska to Virginia, New Mexico, and Arizona. Usually found on open or wooded slopes in the mountains of New Mexico; 5,000–10,000 ft.
Key Characters: American vetch may be recognized by the smooth, elongate stems, the pinnately compound tendrilled leaves with 8–18 leaflets, and the large bluish flowers about 3/4 in. (20 mm) long.

175. **Deer vetch**   *Vicia ludoviciana*   Legume family

Annual, glabrous throughout, the stems creeping or climbing, to 3 ft. (1 m) long. *Leaves* pinnately compound, 11/4–35/8 in. (3–9 cm) long, with 6–12 narrowly oblong or elliptic leaflets 1/4–1 in. (6–25 mm) long, these rounded or notched at the tip, the leaf rachis usually extended into a forked tendril. *Flowers* in slender clusters, pealike, the corolla blue to lavender, 1/4–5/16 in. (5–8 mm) long, the upper petal folded. *Fruit* a smooth flat pod about 1 in. (25 mm) long.
Range and Habitat: Florida to Missouri, Texas, and New Mexico. Usually found on dry plains and slopes in southern New Mexico; 3,500–6,000 ft.
Key Characters: Deer vetch can be identified by the smooth, creeping stems, the compound leaves with forked tendrils and leaflets rounded or notched at the tip, and bluish flowers with the upper petal folded.

176. **White prairie clover**   *Petalostemum candidum*   Legume family

Perennial herb, the stems to about 32 in. (80 cm) tall, smooth. *Leaves* alternate, pinnately compound, with 7–9 narrow gland-dotted leaflets to 3/4 in. (20 mm) long. *Flowers* pealike, in dense, terminal spikes to 2 in. (5 cm) long, the corolla white, the blade of the upper petal broadly heart-shaped. *Fruit* a smooth, 1- or 2-seeded pod about 1/8 in. (3 mm) long.
Range and Habitat: Saskatchewan to Mississippi, Arizona, and Mexico. Usually found on open, dry slopes and prairies throughout New Mexico; 4,500–8,000 ft.
Key Characters: White prairie clover can be identified by the slender, smooth stems, the pinnately compound leaves with gland-dotted leaflets, and the white flowers in dense, terminal spikes.

177. **Narrow-leaved false indigo**   *Amorpha fruticosa*   Legume family

Much-branched shrub, to about 10 ft. (3 m) tall. *Leaves* pinnately compound, to 8 in. (20 cm) long, with 9–25 gland-dotted leaflets 3/4–15/8 in. (20–40 mm) long, these acutely pointed or slightly notched at the tip. *Flowers* in groups of 1–4 dense spikes, each spike to 8 in. (20 cm) long, the corolla pealike, purplish, the upper petal about 1/4 in. (5 mm) long, the other petals missing. *Fruit* a curved, resin-dotted pod about 5/16 in. (8 mm) long.
Range and Habitat: Wisconsin to Saskatchewan, southward to Mexico. Mostly in canyons and along streams throughout much of New Mexico; 4,500–7,500 ft.
Key Characters: Narrow-leaved false indigo is distinguished by the pinnately compound leaves with gland-dotted leaflets, and the dense spikes of purplish flowers having only one petal.

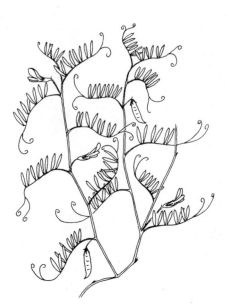

Vicia americana

Vicia ludoviciana

Petalostemum candidum

Amorpha fruticosa

178.   **New Mexico locust**   *Robinia neomexicana*   Legume family

Tree or large shrub, to about 25 ft. (8 m) tall, the twigs with straight or slightly curved
short spines. *Leaves* alternate, pinnately compound, with 9–19 oblong or elliptic leaflets,
these hairy, rounded at both ends, and with a tiny point at the tip. *Flowers* pealike, in
glandular, hairy clusters about 2–4 in. (5–10 cm) long, the corolla rose pink, about 3/4–1 in.
(20–25 mm) long, the upper petal recurved. *Fruit* a pod bearing gland-tipped hairs. This
plant is extremely attractive in flower and has much potential as a protective cover for
wildlife.
Range and Habitat: Colorado to Nevada, southward to northern Mexico. In canyons or
slopes in open or partially shaded areas in the mountains of New Mexico; 6,000–9,500 ft.
Key Characters: New Mexico locust can be identified by the tree or shrub habit, the twigs
with short spines, the compound leaves with leaflets rounded at both ends, and the rose pink
flowers.

179.   **Silvery locoweed**   *Oxytropis sericea*   Legume family

Perennial herb without true stems or stems very short, but with flowering stalks to 16 in. (40
cm) tall. *Leaves* basal, pinnately compound with 11–21 oblong or lance-shaped leaflets with
silvery hairs. *Flowers* many, in narrow clusters at the summit of the flower stalks, the corolla
showy, pealike, white but lower petals purple-tipped. *Fruit* an oblong pod, this beaked at the
tip. Like many other species of the locoweed genus, this plant is considered to be toxic to
foraging livestock.
Range and Habitat: Saskatchewan to British Columbia, southward to Colorado, Utah, and
New Mexico. Usually found on open slopes throughout New Mexico; 6,500–9,000 ft.
Key Characters: Silvery locoweed is distinguished by the grayish silvery stems and leaves in
a basal cluster, the leaves with 11–21 leaflets,and the showy, irregular white flowers at the
summit of the flower stalks.

180.   **Red bladderpod**   *Sphaerophysa salsula*   Legume family

Perennial herb, the stems erect, with grayish hairs. *Leaves* alternate, pinnately compound,
11/4–4 in. (3–10 cm) long, the 15–25 oblong leaflets mostly 1/8–3/4 in. (3–18 mm) long.
Flowers in loose, narrow clusters, the corolla showy, pealike, dull red, the upper petal about
1/2 in. (13 mm) long. *Fruit* an inflated, nearly spherical, papery-walled pod.
Range and Habitat: Native of Asia, now occasionally found in the western United States.
Occasionally found on moist streambanks or drainage ditches throughout New Mexico;
4,500–6,000 ft.
Key Characters: Red bladderpod can be identified by the compound leaves with 15 or more
leaflets and the conspicuous, dull red, irregular flowers.

181.   **Carolina geranium**   *Geranium carolinianum*   Geranium family

Annual or biennial herb, the stems not clustered, with glandular hairs. *Leaves* petioled, the
blades rounded in outline, palmately divided into several lobes, each lobe cleft into oblong
divisions. *Flowers* solitary or in loose clusters, the petals pink or white, 1/4–3/8 in. (6–10 mm)
long, about as long as the sepals, the stylar column covered with spreading hairs.
Range and Habitat: Canada and Alaska to the West Indies and Mexico. Occasionally found
in open fields and canyons throughout New Mexico; 5,000–7,500 ft.
Key Characters: Carolina geranium can be recognized by the annual or biennial habit, the
leaf lobes divided into oblong divisions, and the pink or white flowers with petals about as
long as the sepals.

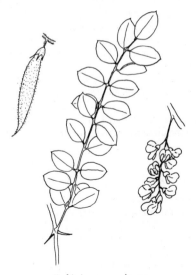

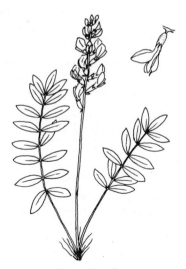

Robinia neomexicana

Oxytropis sericea

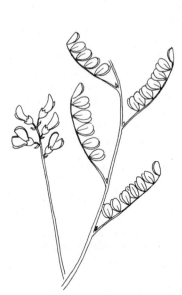

Sphaerophysa salsula

Geranium carolinianum

182. **Purple geranium** *Geranium caespitosum* Geranium family

Perennial herb, the stems clustered and branching, to 28 in. (70 cm) long, with backward-pointing hairs. *Leaves* usually long-petioled, the blades rounded in outline, palmately lobed, the lobes coarsely toothed. *Flowers* in loose apical clusters, the petals purple, oblong or broadest above the middle, 1/2–5/8 in. (12–17 mm) long, the sepals with a fringe of stiff hairs on the margins, the stylar column about 3/4 in. (20 mm) long. In addition to their aesthetic value, these plants provide good forage, especially for sheep.
Range and Habitat: Wyoming to Texas, Arizona, and Mexico. Usually associated with moist slopes, sometimes in partial shade in the mountains throughout New Mexico; 6,000–9,500 ft.
Key Characters: Purple geranium is easily identified by the clustered spindly stems with hairs pointing backward, the somewhat rounded, palmately lobed leaves, and the rose purple or purple flowers.

183. **Red-stemmed filaree** *Erodium cicutarium* Geranium family

Annual, with or without stems, mostly spreading to ascending. *Leaves* basal or opposite, with both typical hairs and gland-tipped hairs, pinnately lobed, the leaflets sharply toothed or lobed. *Flowers* in small terminal clusters, the petals rose purple, about 1/4–3/8 in. (5–9 mm) long, each sepal with 1 or 2 bristles at the tip, the style projecting as an elongate column. This plant is probably the most prolific of our weedy annuals.
Range and Habitat: Native of Europe, now widespread in North America. Typically found in waste ground nearly anywhere in New Mexico; 3,000–7,500 ft.
Key Characters: Red-stemmed filaree is easily recognized by the pinnately lobed leaves with sharply toothed leaflets, the rose purple flowers, and the greatly elongated stylar column.
Related Species: The closely related Texas heronbill, *E. texanum,* differs in having the leaves nearly as broad as long and 3- to 5-lobed, never pinnately lobed.

184. **Yellow woodsorrel** *Oxalis stricta* Woodsorrel family

Perennial herb, the stems to 20 in. (50 cm) tall, usually densely covered with short hairs. *Leaves* alternate, compound, the 3 leaflets broadest near the tip and notched, tapering to the base, 5/8–3/4 in. (15–20 mm) wide. *Flowers* in small, loose clusters, the petals yellow, 1/4–3/8 in. (5–10 mm) long, the stamen filaments without hairs.
Range and Habitat: Nova Scotia to Wyoming, southward to Florida, Texas, Arizona, and Mexico. Mostly in fields or on slopes, often in waste ground, in northern and western New Mexico; 4,500–9,000 ft.
Key Characters: Yellow woodsorrel is distinguished by the stems with short hairs, the shallowly notched leaflets, and the yellow flowers with smooth stamen filaments.

185. **Plains yellow flax** *Linum aristatum* Flax family

Annual, the stems erect, angled, to 12 in. (30 cm) tall, both stems and leaves without hairs. *Leaves* alternate, linear, 1/4–3/8 in. (6–10 mm) long, the margins rolling inward. *Flowers* in loose clusters, yellow, the petals about 1/2–3/4 in. (12–22 mm) long, the sepals with long, slender points, the styles united nearly to the summit.
Range and Habitat: Western Texas to Arizona and Mexico. Found mostly on sandy plains and mesas in southern New Mexico; 4,500–8,000 ft.
Key Characters: Plains yellow flax is distinguished by the erect angled stems, the linear leaves, and the yellow flowers with slender-pointed sepals.

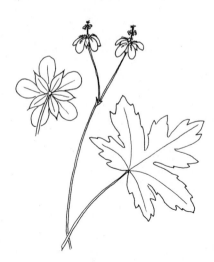

Geranium caespitosum

Erodium cicutarium

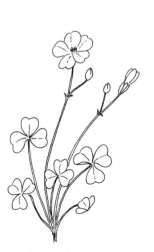

Oxalis stricta

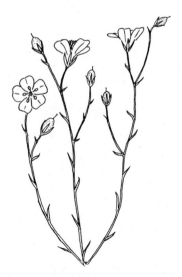

Linum aristatum

186. **Meadow flax**   *Linum pratense*   Flax family

Annual, the stems to about 18 in. (45 cm) tall, both stems and leaves without hairs. *Leaves* alternate, linear or narrowly lance-shaped, $3/8-3/4$ in. (10–20 mm) long, the margins without teeth, relatively few on the upper stem. *Flowers* conspicuous, blue or white, with 5 petals mostly $3/16-3/8$ in. (5–10 mm) long, and with 5 stamens, united at the base, the 5 styles separate. As is characteristic of most flaxes, the petals of this plant fall off at the slightest disturbance.

Range and Habitat: Southern Canada to central Mexico. Scattered on sandy plains in eastern New Mexico; 3,500–5,000 ft.

Key Characters: Meadow flax is distinguished by the annual habit, the narrow short leaves, and the conspicuous blue or white, 5-petaled flowers.

187. **Creosote bush**   *Larrea tridentata*   Caltrop family

Much-branched resinous shrub, the stems erect to spreading, to 6 ft. (2 m) long. *Leaves* compound, with 2 inequilateral, somewhat sticky, evergreen leaflets, these often united at the base. *Flowers* solitary and axillary, the petals yellow, broadest toward the tip, about $1/4$ in. (6–8 mm) long, twisted lengthwise. *Fruit* densely covered with white hairs. These plants often occur in nearly pure stands in our desert regions and give off a peculiar resinous aroma after a rain.

Range and Habitat: Western Texas to Utah, California, and Mexico. Typically found on dry mesas, plains, or slopes in central and southern New Mexico; 3,000–5,000 ft.

Key Characters: Creosote bush can be distinguished by the shrubby nature, the compound leaves with 2 leaflets, the yellow axillary flowers, and the fruits with numerous white hairs.

188. **Goathead**   *Tribulus terrestris*   Caltrop family

Prostrate annual, the stems often 20 in. (50 mm) or more long, forming extensive radiating mats. *Leaves* opposite, pinnate, with mostly 4–6 pairs of oblong leaflets about $3/16$ in. (5 mm) long, the members of a pair usually unequal. *Flowers* solitary, axillary, yellow, mostly with 5 petals about $1/8-3/16$ in. (2–5 mm) long and oblong, and with 10 stamens. *Fruit* mostly 5-angled, ultimately separating into as many triangular nutlets bearing a pair of sharp spines. Although the flowers are attractive, this is one of our more troublesome weeds.

Range and Habitat: Native of Europe and widely established in the United States. Common in disturbed ground throughout New Mexico; 3,500–7,000 ft.

Key Characters: The goathead is distinguished by the prostrate stems with pinnately compound leaves, the relatively small yellow flowers, and the spiny, bony fruits.

189. **Arizona poppy**   *Kallstroemia grandiflora*   Caltrop family

Prostrate annual, the stems hairy, often 12 in. (30 cm) long or longer. *Leaves* pinnately compound, with 5–9 pairs of leaflets, each $5/8-1$ in. (15–25 mm) long, the members of a pair usually unequal in size. *Flowers* solitary, axillary, orange, with petals $3/4-1 1/4$ in. (20–30 mm) long, and with 10–12 stamens. *Fruit* forming a slender beak at the summit. This plant closely resembles the much smaller goathead, *Tribulus terrestris*.

Range and Habitat: Texas to Arizona and Mexico. Typically found on dry flats, slopes, and hills in southern New Mexico; 4,000–5,000 ft.

Key Characters: Arizona poppy is easily recognized by the prostrate hairy stems, the pinnately compound leaves, and the large, solitary orange flowers.

146

Linum pratense

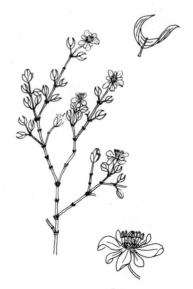

Larrea tridentata

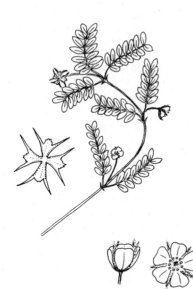

Tribulus terrestris

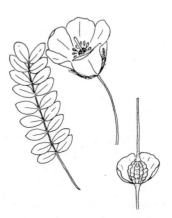

Kallstroemia grandiflora

190. **Mexican-orange**   *Choisya dumosa*   Rue family

Aromatic shrub, to about 6 ft. (2 m) tall. *Leaves* opposite, palmately compound with 5–10 narrow, coarsely toothed, gland-dotted leaflets, these mostly ¹/₂–2 in. (15–50 mm) long. *Flowers* solitary or in small clusters, white, about ⁵/₈–³/₄ in. (15–20 mm) wide, with 5 petals and 8–10 stamens. This beautiful shrub is one of the few members of the Rue family in southwestern United States.
Range and Habitat: Western Texas, New Mexico, and northeastern Mexico. Typically found in canyons and on rocky slopes in southern New Mexico; 4,500–5,500 ft.
Key Characters: Mexican-orange is easily recognized by the palmately compound leaves with slender, coarsely toothed leaflets and the conspicuous white flowers.

191. **White milkwort**   *Polygala alba*   Milkwort family

Perennial herb, the stems clustered, to about 14 in. (35 cm) tall, grooved and angled. *Leaves* alternate, linear to narrowly lance-shaped, sometimes in whorls at the base. *Flowers* numerous, in dense, spikelike clusters, the petals white with green centers, not spreading, irregular in shape, one of them forming a fringed, often purplish, keellike structure.
Range and Habitat: Kansas to Washington, southward to Mexico. Usually on dry plains and slopes throughout New Mexico; 5,000–7,500 ft.
Key Characters: White milkwort is distinguished by the clustered stems with slender leaves and the numerous whitish flowers in dense, spikelike, often somewhat lax clusters.

192. **Texas croton**   *Croton texensis*   Spurge family

Annual, the stems to 3 ft. (1 m) tall, both stems and leaves bearing numerous star-shaped hairs. *Leaves* linear to lance-shaped, mostly ³/₄–1⁵/₈ in. (20–40 mm) long, without teeth, bluntish or rounded at the tip. *Flowers* either male or female, the different sexes on separate plants, the petals absent, the male flowers with hairy stamens, the female flowers producing long-stalked 3-lobed capsules.
Range and Habitat: South Dakota to Alabama, Arizona, and Mexico. Found on dry, often sandy waste ground throughout New Mexico; 3,000–7,000 ft.
Key Characters: Texas croton is distinguished by the yellowish green leaves having star-shaped hairs, the hairy stamens of the male flowers, and the conspicuous 3-lobed capsules of the female flowers.

193. **Skunkbush**   *Rhus trilobata*   Sumac family

Much-branched shrub, to 6 ft. (2 m) tall, the twigs usually hairy. *Leaves* alternate, ill-scented when bruised, compound, usually with 3 lance-shaped or narrowly rhomboidal toothed or lobed leaflets. *Flowers* appearing before the leaves, in dense clusters, the petals yellowish, ¹/₈ in. (2–3 mm) long. *Fruit* berrylike, red to orange, bearing numerous short, gland-tipped hairs. This close relative of poison ivy (*R. radicans*) is also known as lemonade-berry because a drink similar to lemonade can be made from the berries.
Range and Habitat: Alberta to New Mexico, Arizona, and Mexico. Usually found on rocky slopes, often along watercourses throughout New Mexico; 5,000–7,500 ft.
Key Characters: Skunkbush is easily identified by the ill-scented compound leaves, the dense clusters of small yellowish flowers, and the red to orange sticky berries.

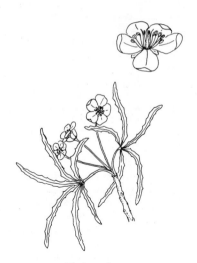

Choisya dumosa

Polygala alba

Croton texensis

Rhus trilobata

194. **New Mexico buckeye**   *Ungnádia speciosa*   Soapberry family

Branching shrub with reddish twigs, to 6 ft. (2 m) tall. *Leaves* alternate, pinnately compound, usually with 7 irregularly toothed, lance-shaped leaflets. *Flowers* in terminal clusters, bright pink, appearing before the leaves, the corolla asymmetrical, with 4 or 5 petals and conspicuous reddish or pinkish stamens. *Fruit* a leathery or woody 3-lobed capsule $1^{1}/_{4}$–2 in. (3–5 cm) wide. This is one of the most spectacular of all our desert shrubs.
Range and Habitat: Texas to New Mexico and Mexico. Found on rocky hills and slopes, usually on limestone, in south-central and southeastern New Mexico; 4,500–6,000 ft.
Key Characters: New Mexico buckeye is easily identified by the reddish twigs, the compound leaves with irregularly toothed leaflets, and the one-sided arrangement of the pink petals.

195. **Desert buckthorn**   *Ceanothus greggii*   Buckthorn family

Erect shrub with many rigid branches, to 6 ft. (2 m) tall. *Leaves* opposite, elliptic or often broadest above the middle, $^{3}/_{8}$–1 in. (10–25 mm) long, thickish, sometimes with a few tiny teeth, grayish green above, gray and hairy beneath. *Flowers* in masses of small axillary clusters, fragrant, white, but individual flowers very small, the 5 petals arched and hoodlike, the 5 stamens projecting well beyond the flowers. This is a lovely shrub when in flower and produces large amounts of nectar.
Range and Habitat: Western Texas to southern Arizona. Usually associated with rocky, often brushy slopes in southern New Mexico; 4,500–7,000 ft.
Key Characters: Desert buckthorn is easily recognized by the stiff branches, the opposite grayish green leaves, and the masses of tiny white flowers.

196. **Chinaberry**   *Melia azederach*   Mahogany family

Small tree, to about 32 ft. (10 m) tall, with a dense, rounded crown. *Leaves* twice pinnately compound, to about 24 in. (60 cm) long, the leaflets lance-shaped and toothed or lobed, smooth, $1^{1}/_{4}$–2 in. (3–5 cm) long. *Flowers* numerous, in conspicuous clusters, lavender, sweet-scented, the petals about $^{3}/_{8}$ in. (10 mm) long. Later in the season, the drooping clusters of purplish black berries are also very attractive.
Range and Habitat: Established here and there as an escape from cultivation in warmer areas of southern New Mexico; 3,500–5,500 ft.
Key Characters: Chinaberry can be identified by the dense crown, the twice-compound leaves with sharply toothed or lobed leaflets, and the clusters of pale lavender flowers.

197. **Paleface rosemallow**   *Hibiscus denudatus*   Mallow family

Perennial herb, the stems woolly. *Leaves* alternate, oval or nearly so, blunt to rounded at the tip, rounded or with a slight notch at the base, woolly. *Flowers* solitary and axillary, white to purplish with a reddish purple spot at the base inside, the petals $^{3}/_{8}$–$1^{1}/_{4}$ in. (10–30 mm) long, the calyx subtended by slender bristle-tipped bracts, the stamens numerous and united into a column.
Range and Habitat: Southern Texas to California and Mexico. Usually found on dry hills and mesas, sometimes in saline soils, in southern New Mexico; 3,500–5,000 ft.
Key Characters: Paleface rosemallow is distinguished by the woolly stems and leaves, the rounded-oval leaves, and the white to purplish flowers with a purplish basal spot.

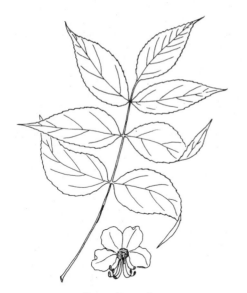

Ungnadia speciosa

Ceanothus greggii

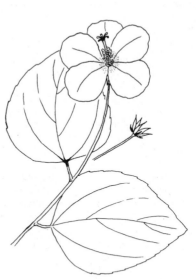

Melia azederach

Hibiscus denudatus

198. **Bird's-foot mallow** *Sphaeralcea digitata* Mallow family

Perennial herb, the stems often erect, both stems and leaves densely covered with star-shaped hairs. *Leaves* alternate, palmately divided into several often coarsely toothed lobes. *Flowers* 10–20 in a narrow cluster, orange red, the petals about $5/16$–$5/8$ in. (8–15 mm) long, the stamens numerous, united into a column, the anthers purplish red.

Range and Habitat: Western Texas to Utah, Arizona, and Mexico. Mostly on dry, rocky slopes in southern and western New Mexico; 3,500–7,000 ft.

Key Characters: Bird's-foot mallow is distinguished by the palmately divided leaves and the narrow clusters of orange red flowers with purplish stamens.

199. **Red globemallow** *Sphaeralcea coccinea* Mallow family

Perennial herb, the stems often prostrate at the base, to 20 in. (50 cm) long, both stems and leaves covered with star-shaped hairs. *Leaves* alternate, divided into several lobes, these often toothed or parted as well. *Flowers* in a narrow cluster, orange red, the petals $3/8$–$3/4$ in. (10–20 mm) long, the stamens numerous, united into a column.

Range and Habitat: Southern Canada to Texas, New Mexico, and Arizona. Mostly found on open hills and plains throughout New Mexico; 5,000–8,000 ft.

Key Characters: Red globemallow is distinguished by the stems and leaves covered with scalelike hairs, the leaves divided into several lobes, and the orange red flowers.

200. **Scurfy mallow** *Sida leprosa* Mallow family

Perennial herb, the stems often prostrate, to 16 in. (40 cm) long, both stems and leaves densely covered with star-shaped hairs. *Leaves* alternate, somewhat triangular, $3/4$–$1^5/8$ in. (20–40 mm) long, toothed on the margins. *Flowers* solitary or in small clusters, white to pale yellow, the petals $3/8$–$1/2$ in. (10–12 mm) long.

Range and Habitat: Western Texas to Arizona. Usually found in dry fields and plains in southern New Mexico; 3,500–4,000 ft.

Key Characters: Scurfy mallow is distinguished by the prostrate stems covered with scalelike hairs, the somewhat triangular leaves, and the white to pale yellow flowers.

201. **Tamarisk** *Tamarix pentandra* Tamarisk family

Large shrub or small tree, to 20 ft. (6 m) or more tall, the branches slender, flexible, and green. *Leaves* very small and scalelike, triangular. *Flowers* pinkish, numerous, in slender-branched or unbranched clusters, the petals about $1/16$ in. (2 mm) long. This plant is also known as "salt-cedar" because of its superficial resemblance to the juniper; introduced from the Old World.

Range and Habitat: Established throughout much of southwestern United States. Mostly along watercourses, often in saline conditions over much of New Mexico; 3,000–6,500 ft.

Key Characters: Tamarisk is distinguished by the slender, flexible green branches with tiny, scalelike leaves and the clusters of small pinkish flowers.

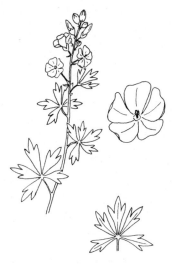

Sphaeralcea digitata

Sphaeralcea coccinea

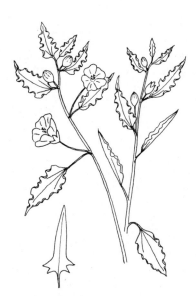

Sida leprosa

Tamarix pentandra

202. Bird's-foot violet   *Viola pedatifida*   Violet family

Stemless perennial with flowering stalks 4–8 in. (10–20 cm) tall. *Leaves* in a basal cluster, palmately parted into narrow, blunt divisions. *Flowers* solitary, showy, irregular, nodding, the petals violet, $3/8–3/4$ in. (10–20 mm) long, the lower petal with a short, thick spur, the lateral ones bearded.

Range and Habitat: Ohio to Saskatchewan, southward to New Mexico and Arizona. Usually found in open fields and on open plains and hills in northern New Mexico; 5,500–7,500 ft.

Key Characters: Bird's-foot violet can be identified by the leaves in a basal cluster and parted into narrow divisions, and by the flowers with violet, bearded petals.

203. Missouri violet   *Viola missouriensis*   Violet family

Stemless perennial with smooth, flowering stalks to 6 in. (15 cm) tall. *Leaves* in a basal cluster, smooth, broadly oval to rounded-triangular, finely toothed, $3/4–1 1/2$ in. (20–40 mm) long, usually flattened or notched at the base. *Flowers* solitary, showy, irregular, nodding, the petals violet, $3/8–5/8$ in. (10–15 mm) long, the lower petal notched at the tip and spurred, the lateral petals hairy.

Range and Habitat: Illinois to Colorado, southward to Texas and New Mexico. Typically associated with shady places near streams from northeastern to southern New Mexico; 5,000–6,500 ft.

Key Characters: Missouri violet is distinguished by the broadly rounded-triangular or heart-shaped leaves in a basal cluster, and the violet, hairy petals.

204. Nuttall violet   *Viola nuttallii*   Violet family

Perennial herb, the stems to 10 in. (25 cm) tall. *Leaves* alternate, lance-shaped, to $2 3/4$ in. (7 cm) long, often minutely toothed on the margins. *Flowers* solitary, showy, irregular, nodding, the petals yellow or tinged with purple, $5/16–1/2$ in. long, sparsely hairy, the lower petal bearing a short spur.

Range and Habitat: Canada to Kansas, New Mexico, and Arizona. Found on plains and hills of northern New Mexico; 6,000–7,500 ft.

Key Characters: Nuttall violet can be identified by the short stems, the lance-shaped leaves, and the yellow flowers.

205. Wavyleaf cevallia   *Cevallia sinuata*   Loasa family

Perennial herb, the stems to 24 in. (60 cm) tall, both stems and leaves with typical hairs and some stinging hairs. *Leaves* alternate, sessile, pinnately wavy-lobed. *Flowers* small, in dense terminal heads, with the petals and sepals similar, feathery, somewhat yellowish, $1/4–5/16$ in. (5–8 mm) long, and with 5 stamens.

Range and Habitat: Western Texas to Arizona and Mexico. Usually in dry soil on mesas and plains, or along roadsides in central and southern New Mexico; 3,500–6,500 ft.

Key Characters: Wavyleaf cevallia can be identified by the wavy-lobed leaves and flowers in dense terminal heads.

Viola pedatifida

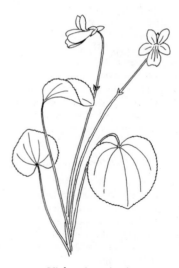

Viola missouriensis

Viola nuttallii

Cevallia sinuata

206. **Common stickleaf**   *Mentzelia pumila*   Loasa family

Biennial herb, the stems stout, often more than 24 in. (60 cm) tall, grayish or yellowish.
Leaves alternate, lance-shaped, 1³/₈–4 in. (3–10 cm) long, with minutely barbed hairs, wavy-
toothed or wavy-lobed. *Flowers* in small clusters, bright yellow, the petals pointed, ³/₈–⁵/₈ in.
(10–15 mm) long, with a few hairs at the tip, the stamens numerous, the outer series of
filaments flattened and petallike, thus flowers appear to have more than 5 petals.
Range and Habitat: Wyoming to Texas, westward to California. Usually associated with
sandy or gravelly soils throughout New Mexico; 4,500–8,000 ft.
Key Characters: Common stickleaf can be identified by the stout grayish or yellowish
stems, the wavy-toothed leaves, and the bright yellow flowers with the outer staminal
filaments appearing somewhat petallike.

207. **Tufted stickleaf**   *Mentzelia perennis*   Loasa family

Perennial herb, the stems erect to spreading, to 12 in. (30 cm) long, whitish, usually both
stems and leaves with minute barbed hairs. *Leaves* alternate, linear, 1¹/₄–4 in. (3–10 cm)
long, often toothed or with a few rounded lobes. *Flowers* terminal or axillary, pale lemon
yellow, the 5 petals about ³/₄ in. (20 mm) long, the stamens numerous, the outer filaments
broader than the inner ones.
Range and Habitat: Restricted to south-central New Mexico, often in damp soils near
streams; 5,000–6,500 ft.
Key Characters: Tufted stickleaf is distinguished by the whitish, often barbed stems, the
linear leaves, and the pale, lemon yellow flowers.

208. **Whitestem blazing star**   *Mentzelia albicaulis*   Loasa family

Annual, the stems prostrate at the base, then ascending, to 16 in. (40 cm) long, whitish and
shiny. *Leaves* alternate, linear to lance-shaped, with minute barbed hairs, to 2 in. (5 cm)
long, the lower ones often toothed, the midstem leaves pinnately lobed. *Flowers* in the leaf
axils, yellow, the 5 petals broadest toward the tip and tapering to the base, notched, the
stamens numerous, the filaments all filiform.
Range and Habitat: Nebraska to Texas, westward to California. Usually found in dry, often
sandy ground throughout New Mexico; 5,000–7,000 ft.
Key Characters: Whitestem blazing star is distinguished by the whitish, shiny stems, the
yellow flowers with 5 notched petals, and the numerous stamens.

209. **Tasajo cholla; cane cholla**   *Opuntia spinosior*   Cactus family

Large perennial, the stems erect, to 6¹/₂ ft. (2 m) or more tall, the joints cylindrical, 4³/₄–12
in. (12–30 cm) long and not more than ³/₄ in. (20 mm) thick, with numerous rounded
tubercles. *Spines* 10–20 per cluster, pinkish, to about ³/₈ in. (10 mm) long. *Flowers* funnel-
shaped, purplish, to 2 in. (5 cm) wide. *Fruit* yellowish.
Range and Habitat: New Mexico to Arizona and Mexico. Usually associated with plains,
slopes, and valleys, often in gravelly soils, in western New Mexico; 4,000–6,000 ft.
Key Characters: Cane cholla can be identified by the tall, erect stems with cylindrical
joints, the 10–20 pinkish spines per cluster, and the purplish, funnel-shaped flowers.

Mentzelia pumila

Mentzelia perennis

Mentzelia albicaulis

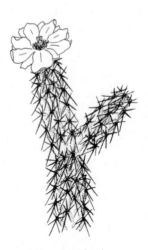

Opuntia spinosior

210. Club cholla   *Opuntia clavata*   Cactus family

Low perennial, the stems matted, to about 4 in. (10 cm) high, the joints club-shaped, about 2 in. (5 cm) long and half as wide, with conspicuous tubercles about ¹/₂ in. (15 mm) long. *Spines* 10–20 per cluster, grayish, strongly recurved, to 1 in. (25 mm) long, 1 in each cluster flattened. *Flowers* funnel-shaped, yellow, about 1¹/₄–2 in. (30–50 mm) wide. *Fruit* a yellow berry.

Range and Habitat: New Mexico and Arizona. Associated with dry plains and valleys from northern to south-central New Mexico; 6,000–8,000 ft.

Key Characters: Club cholla is distinguished by the club-shaped joints with conspicuous tubercles, the grayish recurved spines, and the yellow flowers.

Related Species: The devil cholla (*O. stanlyi*) differs in having much longer joints and 18–21 spines per cluster.

211. Desert Christmas cactus   *Opuntia leptocaulis*   Cactus family

Stems slender, erect or spreading, to 3 ft. (1 m) or more long and about ¹/₄ in. (5 mm) thick, nearly smooth. *Spines* solitary, never in clusters, grayish or pinkish, spreading somewhat downward, mostly 1–2 in. (25–50 mm) long. *Flowers* usually yellowish, funnel-shaped, about ³/₈–⁵/₈ in. (10–15 mm) wide. *Fruit* a red fleshy berry. The bright red fruits provide bright splashes of color in the winter desert landscape.

Range and Habitat: Oklahoma and Texas to Arizona and northern Mexico. Usually found on mesas, plains, and flats, often growing among shrubs from northeastern to west-central and southern New Mexico; 3,000–5,500 ft.

Key Characters: Christmas cactus is identified by the very slender stems, the solitary spines, the small yellowish flowers, and the bright red berry.

Related Species: A similar species, *O. kleiniae,* differs in having thicker stems with prominent tubercles, the flowers purplish and nearly three times as wide.

212. Plains prickly pear   *Opuntia polyacantha*   Cactus family

Low perennial, the stems usually clumped but spreading, to about 6 in. (15 cm) high, with flattened joints, these broadest above the middle, 2–4 in. (5–10 cm) long. *Spines* mostly 6–10 per cluster, whitish to reddish brown, very variable in length. *Flowers* funnelform, yellow, mostly 1⁵/₈–2 in. (40–50 mm) wide. *Fruit* an often densely spiny berry. At least four varieties of this species exist in our area.

Range and Habitat: Southern Canada to Texas, Arizona, and California. Typically associated with dry, sandy plains and hills throughout New Mexico; 5,000–8,500 ft.

Key Characters: Plains prickly pear is distinguished by the small, flattened joints, the whitish to reddish brown spines, the yellow flowers, and the spiny fruits.

Related Species: Another prickly pear of the plains habitat is *O. macrorhiza,* which differs in having a larger flower, about 2–2³/₈ in. (50–60 mm) wide and reddish purple fruits. A larger species, *O. violacea,* differs in having purplish-tinged joints, 0–3 spines per cluster, and smooth red fruits.

213. Whitespine prickly pear   •   *Opuntia erinacea*   Cactus family

Low perennial, the stems clumped, to about 12 in. (30 cm) high, with flattened joints, these mostly oval to nearly round, about 4–6 in. (10–15 cm) long. *Spines* whitish, often 1³/₈–4 in. (40–100 mm) long, very slender. *Flowers* funnel-shaped, pink or yellow, about 1³/₈–2³/₈ in. (40–60 mm) wide. *Fruit* densely spiny.

Range and Habitat: Colorado and New Mexico to California. Found mostly in sandy or gravelly slopes or in canyons or valleys in northern and western New Mexico; 4,000–7,000 ft.

Key Characters: Whitespine prickly pear can be identified by the oval to nearly round joints and the slender, very long whitish spines.

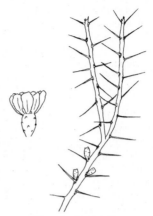

Opuntia clavata

Opuntia leptocaulis

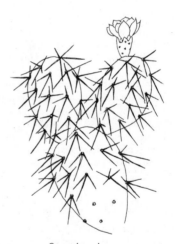

Opuntia polyacantha

Opuntia erinacea

214. **Sprawling prickly pear**   *Opuntia phaeacantha*   Cactus family

Spreading perennial, the stems mostly prostrate to sprawling, to about 3 ft. (1 m) tall, with flat joints broadest toward the top, the joints mostly 4–16 in. (10–40 cm) long and 4–8 in. (10–20 cm) wide. *Spines* 1–8 per cluster, usually dark brown but sometimes grayish, about ³/₄–2 in. (20–50 mm) long. *Flowers* funnel-shaped, yellow, 2–2³/₄ in. (50–70 mm) wide. *Fruit* a fleshy berry. There are several very similar varieties of this species in our area.
Range and Habitat: Oklahoma, Kansas, and Texas to California. Usually found on rocky, sandy, or gravelly slopes or plains throughout New Mexico; 4,000–8,000 ft.
Key Characters: Sprawling prickly pear is distinguished by the large, flat joints, the relatively few but elongate dark brown spines, and the large yellow flowers.

215. **Green pitaya**   *Echinocereus viridiflorus*   Cactus family

Fleshy perennial, the stems mostly ovoid, to about 8 in. (20 cm) tall and about 3 in. (7.5 cm) thick, with 10–14 parallel ribs. *Spines* about 12–18 per cluster, reddish or brownish or white. *Flowers* funnel-shaped, green or sometimes purplish, about ³/₄–1 in. (20–25 mm) wide. *Fruit* a green berry.
Range and Habitat: South Dakota to Texas and New Mexico. Usually found on rocky or sandy slopes or mesas or in draws in all but western New Mexico; 4,000–8,000 ft.
Key Characters: Green pitaya is distinguished by the ovoid stems with 10–14 parallel ribs and the usually green flowers and fruit.

216. **Strawberry hedgehog cactus;**
claret-cup cactus   *Echinocereus triglochidiatus*   Cactus family

Fleshy perennial, the stems in small clusters, cylindrical, to about 12 in. (30 cm) tall and 2³/₄ in. (7 cm) thick, with 5–12 parallel ribs. *Spines* mostly 3–15 per cluster, usually pink, gray, or tan. *Flowers* red, funnel-shaped, about 1⁵/₈–2 in. (4–5 cm) wide. *Fruit* a red, fleshy berry, usually spiny when young. This species is represented by several similar varieties in New Mexico.
Range and Habitat: Colorado to Nevada, southward to Mexico. Found on rocky or gravelly slopes or grasslands, often among pinyon and juniper trees throughout New Mexico; 4,500–7,000 ft.
Key Characters: Strawberry hedgehog cactus can be identified by the cylindrical stems with 5–12 parallel ribs, 3–15 spines per cluster, and the red or scarlet funnel-shaped flowers.
Related Species: Two related species include *E. enneacanthus,* which differs in the stems often forming large mounded clusters and in the flowers being purplish, and *E. fasciculatus* which has larger purplish flowers.

217. **Fendler hedgehog cactus**   *Echinocereus fendleri*   Cactus family

Fleshy perennial, the stems cylindrical or ovoid, to about 10 in. (25 cm) tall and 2³/₈ in. (6 cm) wide, with 8–10 parallel ribs. *Spines* mostly 8–12 per cluster, white to gray or yellow. *Flowers* reddish purple, funnel-shaped, about 2–3 in. (5–7 cm) wide. *Fruit* a greenish or reddish berry.
Range and Habitat: Texas to Arizona and northern Mexico. Usually found on open, sandy or gravelly plains or slopes throughout New Mexico; 6,000–8,000 ft.
Key Characters: Fendler hedgehog cactus is distinguished by the mostly cylindrical stems with 8–10 parallel ribs, the spines 8–12 per cluster, and the reddish purple flowers.

Opuntia phaeacantha

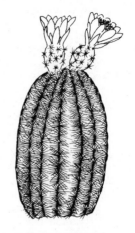

Echinocereus viridiflorus

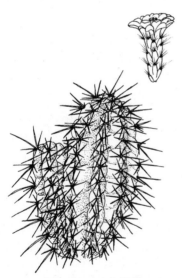

Echinocereus triglochidiatus

Echinocereus fendleri

218. Pectinate hedgehog cactus   *Echinocereus pectinatus*   Cactus family

Fleshy perennial, the stems solitary or clustered, to about 12 in. (30 cm) long and 4 in. (10 cm) wide, with 15–22 parallel ribs. *Spines* mostly 18–29 per cluster and spreading, red to white or pink. *Flowers* funnel-shaped, reddish purple or yellow, about 3¼–4¾ in. (8–12 cm) wide. *Fruit* a greenish or purplish berry.

Range and Habitat: Texas to Arizona and Mexico. Scattered on grassy slopes and flats, usually on limestone, in central and southern New Mexico; 4,000–5,000 ft.

Key Characters: Pectinate hedgehog cactus can be recognized by the cylindrical stems with 15–22 parallel ribs, the mostly spreading spines, and the reddish purple or yellow flowers, these more than 3 in. (8 cm) wide.

Related Species: The green-flowered hedgehog cactus differs in having stems with 14–17 ribs and small greenish flowers, about 1 in. (25 mm) wide.

219. Turk's head   *Echinocactus horizonthalonius*   Cactus family

Stems solitary, ribbed, rounded or ovoid, to about 12 in. (30 cm) tall, mostly with 8–10 ribs. *Spines* 6–9 per cluster, stout, recurved, transversely ridged. *Flowers* funnel-shaped, pink, about 2–2⅜ in. (5–6 cm) wide. *Fruit* a red, fleshy, woolly berry.

Range and Habitat: Texas to New Mexico and Mexico. Typically found on open, rocky slopes, often on limestone, in southern New Mexico; 3,000–5,000 ft.

Key Characters: Turk's head can be identified by the rounded to ovoid stems with usually 8–10 ribs, the stout transversely ridged spines, and the funnel-shaped pink flowers.

220. Horse crippler   *Echinocactus texensis*   Cactus family

Stems solitary, ribbed, hemispherical, to about 6 in. (15 cm) high and 12 in. (30 cm) wide, with 13–21 ribs. *Spines* 6–8 per cluster, stout, somewhat flattened and curved, transversely ridged. *Flowers* funnel-shaped, pinkish or purplish, about 2–2⅜ in. (50–60 mm) wide. *Fruit* a red, fleshy, woolly berry.

Range and Habitat: Western Texas and New Mexico to Mexico. Usually found on rocky slopes, often on limestone, in southeastern New Mexico; 3,000–4,000 ft.

Key Characters: Horse crippler is distinguished by the broadly hemispherical stems hidden among other vegetation, the small clusters of stout, transversely ridged spines, and the funnel-shaped pinkish or purplish flowers.

221. Heyder pincushion cactus   *Mammillaria heyderi*   Cactus family

Very short, spiny perennial, the stems rounded or flattened, sometimes concave at the summit, about 1⅝–2⅜ in. (4–6 cm) in diameter, covered with spirally arranged tubercles, each bearing at the tip 10–22 reddish brown to white spines to about ⅜ in. (10 mm) long. *Flowers* borne below the summit of the stems, white to yellowish, about ¾–1⅜ in. (20–30 mm) wide.

Range and Habitat: Texas to Arizona and northern Mexico. Found mostly in rocky or gravelly soils of central and southern New Mexico; 4,000–5,000 ft.

Key Characters: Heyder pincushion cactus is easily recognized by the very short, often flattish, but somewhat rounded stems with numerous reddish brown to white spines and small white to yellowish flowers.

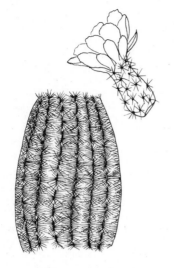

Echinocereus pectinatus

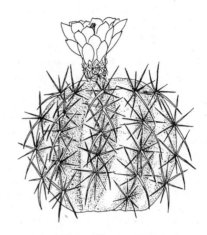

Echinocactus horizonthalonius

Echinocactus texensis

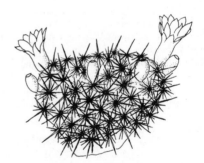

Mammillaria heyderi

222. **Graham pincushion cactus**   *Mammillaria grahamii*   Cactus family

Short, fleshy, very spiny perennial, the stems rounded to ovoid, to 3¹/₄ in. (8 cm) tall and 2³/₈ in. (6 cm) thick, covered with spirally arranged tubercles, each bearing at the tip 15–30 reddish to brownish or blackish spines to 1 in. (25 mm) long, the longer ones often hooked. *Flowers* borne below the summit of the stems, white or pale pink, about ³/₄–1³/₈ in. (20–30 mm) wide.

Range and Habitat: Texas to Arizona. Usually found on gravelly hills and in washes in southern New Mexico; 3,000–5,000 ft.

Key Characters: Graham pincushion is distinguished by the short, usually rounded stems, the numerous reddish or brownish spines with the longer ones often hooked, and the white or pale pink flowers.

223. **Plains pincushion cactus**   *Coryphantha vivipara*   Cactus family

Short, fleshy, very spiny perennial, the stems rounded to ovoid, usually clustered, mostly less than 4 in. (10 cm) tall and 2¹/₄ in. (6 cm) wide, covered with spirally arranged tubercles, each bearing at the tip 16–45 straight reddish or pinkish spines ³/₈–⁵/₈ in. (10–15 mm) long. *Flowers* borne at the summit of the stem, pink to purple, funnel-shaped, about 1³/₈ to 2 in. (30–50 mm) wide. *Fruit* a greenish, smooth, fleshy berry. There are several varieties of this plant in our area.

Range and Habitat: Southern Canada to Texas and New Mexico. Usually found on open plains, grasslands, or sandy or rocky slopes throughout New Mexico; 4,500–9,000 ft.

Key Characters: Plains pincushion cactus may be recognized by the short, broad, fleshy stems with numerous reddish or pinkish spines and the pink to purple funnel-shaped flowers, usually less than 2 in. (50 mm) wide.

224. **Pincushion cactus**   *Coryphantha macromeris*   Cactus family

Short, fleshy, very spiny perennial, the stems often clustered, to about 6 in. (15 cm) tall and 2 in. (5 cm) thick, covered with spirally arranged tubercles, each bearing at the tip 12–17 straight spines to about 2 in. (50 mm) long. *Flowers* borne at the summit of the stems, purplish, funnel-shaped, about 1¹/₄–1³/₄ in. (30–45 mm) wide. *Fruit* a greenish berry bearing woolly scales.

Range and Habitat: Western Texas and New Mexico to Mexico. Usually associated with open mesas and rocky slopes in southern New Mexico; 4,000–6,500 ft.

Key Characters: Pincushion cactus can be identified by the short stems bearing spiny tubercles and purplish funnel-shaped flowers less than 2 in. (50 mm) wide.

225. **Small-flowered gaura**   *Gaura parviflora*   Evening primrose family

Annual or biennial herb, stems with both long, soft hairs and gland-tipped hairs. *Leaves* alternate, hairy, 1¹/₄–6 in. (3–15 cm) long, the basal ones broadest above the middle and tapering to the base, wavy-toothed, the upper leaves lance-shaped. *Flowers* in slender, spikelike, often nodding clusters, the petals pink, broadest toward the tip, about ¹/₁₆ in. (2 mm) long, the sepals ¹/₁₆ in. (2–3 mm) long, recurved in flower.

Range and Habitat: Indiana to Washington, southward to Texas, California, Mexico, and Argentina. Usually found in waste ground or on open plains throughout New Mexico; 4,000–7,500 ft.

Key Characters: Small-flowered gaura is identified by the coarse stems with soft hairs and the flowers in slender spikes which nod at the tip.

Related Species: New Mexico gaura (*G. neomexicana*) differs in having much larger flowers, and petals about ³/₈–¹/₂ in. (8–12 mm) long.

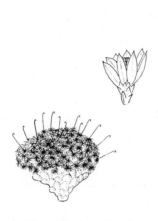

Mammillaria grahamii

Coryphantha vivipara

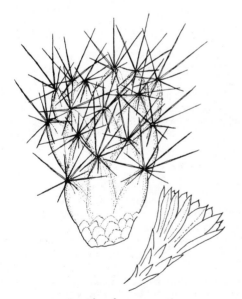

Coryphantha macromeris

Gaura parviflora

226. **Scarlet gaura**   *Gaura coccinea*   Evening primrose family

Perennial herb, the stems spreading or ascending, to 16 in. (40 cm) long. *Leaves* alternate, linear to lance-shaped or oblong, to 2³/₈ in. (6 cm) long, wavy-toothed or without teeth. *Flowers* in slender, spikelike clusters, the petals white to pink or red, elliptic, about ¹/₄ in. (3–6 mm) long, the sepals ¹/₄–³/₈ in. (5–10 mm) long, recurved in flower. This is a weedy plant with flowers often appearing as irregular.

Range and Habitat: Southern Canada to Texas, California, and Mexico. Usually found on open plains and hills throughout New Mexico; 3,500–7,500 ft.

Key Characters: Scarlet gaura is distinguished by the narrow, often wavy-toothed leaves and the white to red flowers in slender, spikelike clusters.

227. **Yellow evening primrose**   *Oenothera primiveris*   Evening primrose family

Annual, without stems or with very short stems. *Leaves* alternate, usually hairy, mostly 1¹/₄–4³/₄ in. (3–12 cm) long, usually regularly and deeply pinnately lobed, the lance-shaped lobes with teeth or lobes. *Flowers* opening in the evening, scattered, yellow but reddish in age, the petals ³/₄–1¹/₄ in. (20–30 mm) long, notched at the tip, the floral tube ³/₄–2³/₈ in. (20–60 mm) long, the 4 stigmas slender.

Range and Habitat: Texas to Nevada, Arizona, and California. Mostly inhabiting dry plains and open slopes in southern New Mexico; 4,000–5,000 ft.

Key Characters: Yellow evening primrose is recognized by the stems absent or nearly so, the regularly pinnately lobed leaves, and the notched yellow petals.

228. **Rose sundrops**   *Oenothera rosea*   Evening primrose family

Stout perennial, the stems widely spreading, to 24 in. (60 cm) long, both stems and leaves with long or short hairs. *Leaves* alternate, lance-shaped, ³/₄–2 in. (2–5 cm) long, wavy-toothed or without teeth. *Flowers* scattered, rose purple, the petals ³/₈–³/₄ in. (10–18 mm) long, the floral tube ¹/₄–⁵/₁₆ in. (5–8 mm) long, shorter than the ovary. This is an unusually attractive evening primrose, perfectly fitting its name.

Range and Habitat: Texas and New Mexico to Mexico and South America. Usually found on plains and prairies and in canyons of northern New Mexico; 4,000–6,000 ft.

Key Characters: Rose sundrops is easily recognized by the spreading stems, the rose purple flowers on a short floral tube, and the 4 slender stigmas.

229. **Stemless evening primrose**   *Oenothera caespitosa*   Evening primrose family

Perennial herb without stems (except in one variety). *Leaves* clustered at ground level, variously hairy, mostly lance-shaped or broadest above the middle and 1¹/₄–4 in. (3–10 cm) long, usually wavy-lobed or sometimes merely toothed. *Flowers* very large and conspicuous, fragrant, white, becoming pink on drying, notched at the tip, mostly 1–1⁵/₈ in. (25–40 mm) long, the floral tube mostly 2–3³/₈ in. (5–8 cm) long, the sepals about 1¹/₄ in. (30 mm) long. This very attractive plant is represented by four varieties in our area; the flowers open in the evening.

Range and Habitat: Montana to Washington, southward to New Mexico and California. Usually found on dryish, open, often rocky slopes throughout all but extreme eastern New Mexico; 4,000–8,000 ft.

Key Characters: Stemless evening primrose is identified by the leaves wavy-margined and clustered at ground level, the huge white flowers on long floral tubes, and the 4 slender stigmas.

Gaura coccinea

Oenothera primiveris

Oenothera rosea

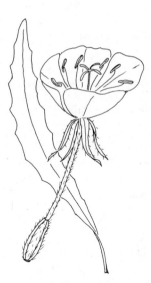

Oenothera caespitosa

230. **Hartweg evening primrose**   *Calylophus hartwegii*   Evening primrose family

Perennial herb, the stems to about 16 in. (40 cm) tall. *Leaves* narrow, to 2 in. (50 mm) long and ⁵/₁₆ in. (8 mm) wide. *Flowers* scattered, conspicuous, yellow or turning red when dry, the flower tube narrowly funnel-shaped or tube-shaped, ³/₄–2 in. (20–50 mm) long, the petals rhomboidal or rounded, ⁵/₈–1¹/₄ in. (15–30 mm) long, the sepals about ³/₈–⁵/₈ in. (10–15 mm) long, yellowish but often spotted with red. There are at least six varieties of this plant in New Mexico.
Range and Habitat: South Dakota to Texas and Arizona. Usually associated with dryish, often sandy soils on open plains and slopes in much of New Mexico; 4,500–8,000 ft.
Key Characters: Hartweg evening primrose is distinguished by the conspicuous yellow, somewhat funnel-shaped flowers, the large petals, and the disk-shaped stigma.
Related Species: The related *C. serrulatus,* of about the same range, differs in that the leaves are often toothed and the petals are shorter.

231. **Chimaya**   *Cymopterus fendleri*   Carrot family

Stemless perennial herb. *Leaves* pinnately compound, the final divisions oblong and entire or lobed, smooth. *Flowers* in terminal compound umbels, the cluster of stalks attached to the flowers subtended by small bracts united at the base, the main rays of the umbel unequal in length, the 5 petals yellow.
Range and Habitat: Colorado and Utah to Mexico. Mostly in gravelly soils in central, northwestern, and southern New Mexico; 4,500–6,500 ft.
Key Characters: Chimaya is characterized by the pinnate leaves with oblong divisions, and yellow flowers in terminal compound umbels.

232. **Mountain parsley**   *Pseudocymopterus montanus*   Carrot family

Perennial herb, the stems longitudinally ridged, usually 8–32 in. (20–80 cm) tall or nearly absent. *Leaves* successively divided into 3-parted units, the final divisions linear to oval, on petioles often having papery or purplish margins. *Flowers* in a conspicuously hairy umbel, the cluster of stalks attached to the flowers subtended by a series of slender, small bracts, the 5 petals yellowish or purplish.
Range and Habitat: Wyoming to Texas, Arizona, and Mexico. Usually found in open meadows or coniferous woods in the mountains of New Mexico; 6,000–12,000 ft.
Key Characters: Mountain parsley is distinguished by the leaves divided into many divisions and the small yellowish to purple flowers in umbels.

233. **Dwarf cornel**   *Cornus canadensis*   Dogwood family

Low herb from a woody base, the stems to 10 in. (25 cm) tall. *Leaves* 4–6 in a whorl near the apex of the stem, oval or broadest above the middle, pointed at the tip, tapered at the base, 1¹/₄–2³/₈ in. (30–60 mm) long, stiffly hairy above, smooth beneath. *Flowers* in a headlike cluster subtended by 4 petallike bracts ³/₈–⁵/₈ in. (10–15 mm) long, petals tiny, yellow to purple.
Range and Habitat: Greenland to Alaska, southward to West Virginia, New Mexico, and California. Associated with wooded slopes in northern New Mexico; 7,500–11,000 ft.
Key Characters: Dwarf cornel is easily identified by the whorled leaves near the stem tip and the headlike cluster of small flowers subtended by petallike bracts.

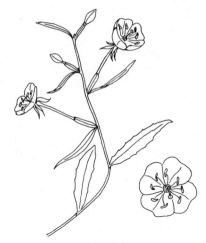

Calylophus hartwegii

Cymopterus fendleri

Pseudocymopterus montanus

Cornus canadensis

234. Arizona madrone — *Arbutus árizonica* — Heath family

Evergreen tree, to 48 ft. (15 m) tall, the branches spreading from a short, stout trunk, the younger bark smooth and reddish brown. *Leaves* alternate, lance-shaped, sometimes toothed, pointed at the tip. *Flowers* in terminal clusters, white or pink, urn-shaped with 5 short, recurved teeth at the top.

Range and Habitat: New Mexico to southern Arizona and northern Mexico. Usually associated with rocky or gravelly slopes in southwestern New Mexico; 4,500–8,000 ft.

Key Characters: Arizona madrone is distinguished by the smooth and reddish brown younger bark, the pointed leaves, and the clusters of pinkish, urn-shaped flowers.

235. Texas madrone — *Arbutus texana* — Heath family

Evergreen tree, to 32 ft. (10 m) tall, with branches spreading from a short, gnarled trunk, the younger bark white or pink. *Leaves* alternate, oval, 1¼–3⅛ in. (3–8 cm) long, blunt, the margins with small teeth. *Flowers* in loose, woolly clusters, white or pink, urn-shaped with 5 short, recurved teeth at the top.

Range and Habitat: Texas and New Mexico to Central America. Rocky slopes or canyon walls in the desert mountains of southeastern New Mexico; 4,500–6,500 ft.

Key Characters: Texas madrone can be recognized by the white or pink younger bark, the leaves blunt at the tip, and the woolly clusters of urn-shaped, pinkish flowers.

236. Pointleaf manzanita — *Arctostaphylos pungens* — Heath family

Erect or spreading shrub, to about 6 ft. (2 m) tall, the bark usually reddish brown. *Leaves* alternate, evergreen, lance-shaped or elliptic, sharply pointed, mostly ½–1⅜ in. (12–35 mm) long. *Flowers* in terminal clusters, pinkish, urn-shaped, with 5 small, recurved teeth, and with about 10 stamens.

Range and Habitat: New Mexico to Utah, Arizona, and California, southward to Mexico. Usually on dry, rocky slopes, often in extensively brushy thickets from central to southern and western New Mexico; 5,000–8,000 ft.

Key Characters: Pointleaf manzanita is distinguished by the reddish brown bark, the sharply pointed evergreen leaves, and the pink, urn-shaped flowers.

Related Species: The bearberry (*A. uva-ursi*) differs in being a trailing or creeping shrub with blunt or notched leaf tips.

237. Rusby primrose — *Primula rusbyi* — Primrose family

Perennial herb without true stems, but with leafless flowering stalks about 6–10 in. (15–25 cm) tall. *Leaves* in basal clusters, usually broader above the middle and tapering to the base, to about 4¾ in. (12 cm) long. *Flowers* in terminal clusters, pinkish purple but yellowish in the throat, narrowly funnel-shaped, ⅜–¾ in. (10–20 mm) wide, the lobes spreading and notched, the calyx with whitish, meallike particles.

Range and Habitat: New Mexico and Arizona. Mostly on damp, rocky slopes and ledges in the mountains of New Mexico; 7,500–10,000 ft.

Key Characters: Rusby primrose is distinguished by the basal leaves and the funnel-shaped flowers in clusters at the summit of a leafless flower stalk.

Arbutus arizonica

Arbutus texana

Arctostaphylos pungens

Primula rusbyi

238. **Ocotillo**   *Fouquieria splendens*   Ocotillo family

Arching shrub, the stems canelike, usually unbranched, to 10 ft. (3 m) tall, darkly furrowed. *Leaves* in clusters subtended by a spreading stout spine, broadest above the middle and tapering to the base, the margins without teeth, often short-lived. *Flowers* in terminal clusters, scarlet, tube-shaped, about ⁵/₈ in. (15 mm) long, the 5 lobes short, spreading downward, the 10–15 stamens projecting beyond the flowers. This is one of the most conspicuous of our desert plants, especially attractive in flower but not particularly so when both leaves and flowers are missing.

Range and Habitat: Western Texas to Arizona and Mexico. Usually confined to mesas and open, often rocky slopes in southern New Mexico; 4,000–6,500 ft.

Key Characters: Ocotillo is easily identified by the slender, canelike stems with spreading spines and frequently small clusters of leaves above the spines, and by the conspicuous scarlet tube-shaped flowers.

239. **Rough menodora**   *Menodora scabra*   Olive family

Perennial herb, usually woody at the base, the stems mostly 6–12 in. (15–30 cm) tall, both stems and leaves usually rough to the touch. *Leaves* usually alternate, broader above the middle, ³/₈–1 in. (10–25 mm) long. *Flowers* scattered, showy, bright yellow, with the corolla 5- or 6-lobed and about ⁵/₈ in. (15 mm) wide, the calyx having 7–15 slender lobes, the stamens 2 or 3.

Range and Habitat: Western Texas to Arizona and Mexico. Usually found on dry hills and mesas, often in rocky soils, throughout New Mexico; 4,000–7,000 ft.

Key Characters: Rough menodora is characterized by the rough stems and leaves, the showy yellow flowers, and the many-lobed calyx.

240. **Flowering ash**   *Fraxinus cuspidata*   Olive family

Large shrub or small tree, to about 20 ft. (6 m) tall, the twigs smooth. *Leaves* pinnately compound, with 5–7 smooth, lance-shaped leaflets 1¹/₄–2³/₈ in. (30–60 mm) long, these slender-pointed at the tip and toothed on the margins. *Flowers* in loose, drooping clusters, the 4 petals greenish white, very fragrant, and ³/₈–⁵/₈ in. (10–15 mm) long.

Range and Habitat: Texas to Arizona and Mexico. Found in dryish, often rocky slopes of south-central and western New Mexico; 5,000–7,000 ft.

Key Characters: Flowering ash is distinguished by the compound leaves with 5–7 smooth lance-shaped leaflets and the fragrant, relatively large greenish white flowers.

241. **Marsh centaury**   *Centaurium calycosum*   Gentian family

Branching annual, the stems mostly 8–20 in. (20–50 cm) tall. *Leaves* opposite, lance-shaped to elliptic, ³/₄–2 in. (20–50 mm) long, usually 7 or more pairs per stem. *Flowers* in loose terminal clusters, few, pink, the corolla tube-shaped, about ³/₈ in. (10 mm) long, the lobes spreading, ¹/₄–³/₈ in. (7–9 mm) long, the 5 stamens with twisted anthers.

Range and Habitat: Texas to Nevada, southward to Mexico. Typically found in moist, often marshy ground, in scattered populations throughout New Mexico; 4,000–6,500 ft.

Key Characters: Marsh centaury is easily recognized by the narrow opposite leaves and the pinkish tube-shaped flowers with lobes nearly as long as the tube.

Fouquieria splendens

Menodora scabra

Fraxinus cuspidata

Centaurium calycosum

242. **Butterflyweed**   *Asclepias tuberosa*   Milkweed family

Perennial herb, the stems mostly 12–32 in. (30–80 cm) tall, usually hairy. *Leaves* alternate, numerous, lance-shaped, mostly 1¼–3⅝ in. (30–90 mm) long. *Flowers* in groups of umbellike clusters, the corolla yellow to reddish orange, about ¼–⅜ in. (5–9 mm) long, with 5 yellow to bright orange hoodlike structures, the 5 calyx lobes recurved. Few plants in our flora can match the butterflyweed for beauty and showiness.
Range and Habitat: Ohio to Utah, southward to Texas and Arizona. Found in scattered populations, usually in gravelly canyons throughout New Mexico; 4,000–8,000 ft.
Key Characters: Butterflyweed is easily identified by the relatively tall, usually hairy stems and the yellow to reddish orange flowers.

243. **Plains milkweed**   *Asclepias brachystephana*   Milkweed family

Perennial herb, the stems mostly 6–10 in. (15–25 cm) tall. *Leaves* opposite, the younger ones sometimes woolly, linear to lance-shaped, the larger ones 2–3½ in. (5–8 cm) long and ¼–½ in. (6–15 mm) wide. *Flowers* in umbellike clusters, 3- to 8-flowered, the corolla purplish or tinged with green, about ³⁄₁₆ in. (4 mm) long, the 5 hoodlike appendages within having conspicuous teeth on the margins, the 5 calyx lobes recurved.
Range and Habitat: Kansas to Wyoming, southward to Texas, Arizona, and Mexico. Associated with dry, often sandy soils, on plains and mesas throughout New Mexico; 3,500–7,000 ft.
Key Characters: Plains milkweed is distinguished by the short stems, the 3- to 8-flowered clusters, and the purplish flowers.

244. **Silky bindweed**   *Convolvulus incanus*   Morning-glory family

Creeping perennial herb, the stems prostrate or somewhat climbing, both stems and leaves with silky hairs. *Leaves* mostly narrowly oblong, often deeply notched at the base or with a pair of basal lobes, ¾–2 in. (20–50 mm) long. *Flowers* scattered, sometimes 2 or 3 in a cluster, white or tinged with pink, funnel-shaped, ⅜–¾ in. (10–20 mm) long, 5-angled at the top, each angle slender-pointed. This plant is usually considered to be a noxious weed.
Range and Habitat: Nebraska and Colorado to Texas and Arizona. Usually found on dry hills and plains throughout New Mexico; 3,500–6,000 ft.
Key Characters: Silky bindweed is distinguished by the prostrate stems, these and the leaves with silky hairs, the oblong leaves, and the white or pinkish funnel-shaped, angle-lobed flowers.
Related Species: Field bindweed (*C. arvensis*) common in disturbed areas, differs in the stems and leaves being only sparsely hairy.

245. **Dwarf gilia**   *Ipomopsis pumila*   Phlox family

Dwarf annual, the stems to 8 in. (20 cm) tall, somewhat woolly. *Leaves* alternate, linear and unlobed or with 2–4 spreading, sharply pointed segments. *Flowers* in headlike, leafy clusters, white to pink or bluish, tube-shaped, mostly ⁵⁄₆–⅜ in. (8–10 mm) long, the lobes spreading, about ¹⁄₁₆ in. (2 mm) long, the stamens projecting.
Range and Habitat: Kansas to Wyoming, southward to New Mexico and Arizona. Mostly found on dry plains and slopes, often among shrubs, throughout New Mexico; 4,000–6,500 ft.
Key Characters: Dwarf gilia is easily recognized by the short, woolly stems, the sharply pointed leaf segments, and the leafy, headlike clusters of tube-shaped flowers.

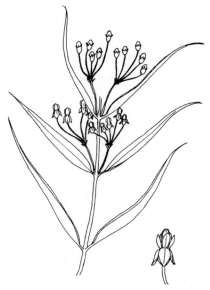

Asclepias tuberosa

Asclepias brachystephana

Convolvulus incanus

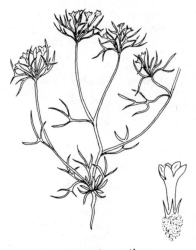

Ipomopsis pumila

246. **White desert gilia**   *Ipomopsis polycladon*   Phlox family

Low annual, the stems few leaved, 4–8 in. (10–20 cm) tall. *Leaves* alternate, pinnately lobed or deeply toothed, the lobes or teeth spine-tipped. *Flowers* in dense, leafy clusters, white, tube-shaped, about 1/8–3/16 in. (3–6 mm) long, the lobes spreading, to 1/16 in. (1.5 mm) long, the stamens not projecting beyond the flowers.
Range and Habitat: Texas to California. Usually found on dry, often sandy or gravelly plains, slopes, or mesas throughout New Mexico; 4,500–5,500 ft.
Key Characters: White desert gilia is distinguished by the spine-tipped leaf lobes and the white, tube-shaped flowers in dense, leafy clusters.

247. **Red rocket**   *Ipomopsis aggregata*   Phlox family

Biennial herb, the stems often solitary, to 24 in. (60 cm) tall, hairy and usually glandular. *Leaves* alternate, pinnately divided into linear lobes with a short, sharp point at the tip. *Flowers* in small clusters along the upper stem, red to pink or white, often spotted with yellow, tube-shaped to narrowly funnel-shaped, the tube 3/4–1 3/4 in. (20–45 mm) long, the lobes lance-shaped, spreading or somewhat recurved. There are several very similar subspecies of this plant in our area, all with a long flowering period.
Range and Habitat: Montana to British Columbia, southward to New Mexico, California, and Mexico. Usually associated with dry ground on open plains and slopes, often scattered in open coniferous forests, throughout New Mexico; 5,000–9,500 ft.
Key Characters: Red rocket is easily recognized by the usually tall stems, the leaves divided into several linear lobes, and the conspicuous, tube-shaped flowers with spreading lobes.

248. **Stiffleaf gilia**   *Gilia rigidula*   Phlox family

Perennial herb, the stems and branches spreading, to about 10 in. (25 cm) long, both stems and leaves with gland-tipped hairs. *Leaves* alternate, the basal ones divided into several flattened segments or sometimes the segments very slender and sharply pointed. The upper leaves always have needlelike segments or are merely needlelike and unsegmented. *Flowers* scattered, blue to purple with a yellow center, the corolla funnel-shaped, 5/16–1/2 in. (8–12 mm) long, the lobes spreading, oval, longer than the tube, the stamens projecting.
Range and Habitat: Texas to Colorado, New Mexico, and Arizona. Usually associated with dry, sandy plains and hills in southern New Mexico; 4,500–6,500 ft.
Key Characters: Stiffleaf gilia is easily recognized by the very slender, spine-tipped leaf segments, the flowers blue or purple with a yellow "eye," and the corolla lobes that are longer than the tube.

249. **Mexican gilia**   *Gilia mexicana*   Phlox family

Small annual, the stems mostly 4–12 in. (10–30 cm) tall, bearing cobwebby hairs at the base. *Leaves* grayish, covered with cobwebby hairs, pinnately or twice-pinnately divided into narrow lobes, the upper leaves becoming greatly reduced in size. *Flowers* in small clusters, funnel-shaped, blue with a yellowish center, the stamens not projecting.
Range and Habitat: New Mexico and Arizona to Mexico. Usually found on dry slopes and plains in southwestern New Mexico; 5,000–6,500 ft.
Key Characters: Mexican gilia is distinguished by the grayish stems and leaves bearing cobwebby hairs and the blue flowers with a yellowish "eye."

Ipomopsis polycladon

Ipomopsis aggregata

Gilia rigidula

Gilia mexicana

250. **Wavyleaf gilia**   *Gilia sinuata*   Phlox family

Short annual, the stems mostly 4–8 in. (10–30 cm) tall. *Leaves* mostly basal, bearing cobwebby hairs, pinnately divided into usually toothed lobes, the upper leaves greatly reduced and clasping the stem at the base. *Flowers* in an open cluster, whitish to purplish with a yellowish center, funnel-shaped, about 1/4–3/8 in. (7–10 mm) long, the corolla lobes spreading, the stamens projecting.
Range and Habitat: Wyoming to Washington, southward to New Mexico and California. Usually associated with sandy areas on open hills and mesas in western New Mexico; 4,500–7,000 ft.
Key Characters: Wavyleaf gilia is recognized by the webby-haired basal leaves, the stem leaves with clasping bases, and the flowers with a yellow "eye."

251. **Great Basin gilia**   *Gilia leptomeria*   Phlox family

Small annual, the stems mostly 4–8 in. (10–20 cm) tall, with short gland-tipped hairs. *Leaves* alternate and basal, the basal leaves toothed or pinnately lobed, the upper leaves often greatly reduced in size. *Flowers* in small clusters, white to pink, narrowly funnel-shaped, about 1/4 in. (4–6 mm) long, the stamens projecting.
Range and Habitat: Wyoming to Washington, southward to New Mexico and California. Usually found on dry, rocky slopes in northern New Mexico; 5,000–7,500 ft.
Key Characters: Great Basin gilia is distinguished by the small, glandular stems, the toothed or lobed basal leaves, and the white to pink, very small, funnel-shaped flowers.

252. **Prickly phlox**   *Leptodactylon pungens*   Phlox family

Perennial, woody toward the base, the stems to about 32 in. (80 cm) tall. *Leaves* alternate or sometimes opposite, divided into 3 or more very slender spiny-pointed segments. *Flowers* solitary or few in a cluster, white to pale yellowish or pinkish, funnel-shaped, 3/8–3/4 in. (10–20 mm) long, the lobes spreading and about 1/4 in. (6–8 mm) long.
Range and Habitat: Montana and Washington to New Mexico and California. Usually found in rocky or sandy plains or hills in northern New Mexico; 6,000–7,500 ft.
Key Characters: Prickly phlox can be identified by the woody lower stem, the leaves divided into needlelike, spiny-pointed segments, and the funnel-shaped flowers.

253. **Brandegee Jacob's ladder**   *Polemonium brandegei*   Phlox family

Perennial herb, the stems clustered, to 12 in. (30 cm) tall, both stems and leaves aromatic with glandular hairs. *Leaves* alternate, pinnately compound with numerous oblong to oval leaflets. *Flowers* in short, narrow clusters, the corolla yellow to white, narrowly funnel-shaped, 3/4–1 in. (20–25 mm) long, the lobes spreading, shorter than the tube. This is one of the most attractive of the Jacob's ladder species; the white form is called variety *mellitum*.
Range and Habitat: Montana to Wyoming, Nevada, and New Mexico. Usually found in open areas and meadows in the mountains of northern and central New Mexico; 8,000–12,000 ft.
Key Characters: Brandegee Jacob's ladder is characterized by the glandular aromatic stems and leaves, the leaves with numerous leaflets, and the yellow to white, funnel-shaped corolla.

Gilia sinuata

Gilia leptomeria

Leptodactylon pungens

Polemonium brandegei

254. Yellow trumpet — *Linanthus aureus* — Phlox family

Erect or spreading annual, the stems to about 4 in. (10 cm) long. *Leaves* opposite, cleft into 3 narrow segments. *Flowers* clustered, on slender stalks, funnel-shaped, $1/4$–$1/2$ in. (6–12 mm) long, yellow, often purplish inside the throat along with a ring of hairs. This is an exceedingly charming little plant.

Range and Habitat: Western Texas to Nevada, Arizona, and California. Sometimes abundant on dry plains and slopes in southern New Mexico; 3,000–6,000 ft.

Key Characters: Yellow trumpet is easily recognized by dwarf stems, the leaves divided into narrow segments, and the yellow, trumpetlike flowers.

255. Painted trumpet — *Linanthus bigelovii* — Phlox family

Erect annual, the stems to 12 in. (30 cm) tall, both stems and leaves without hairs. *Leaves* opposite, narrowly linear or cleft into 2 or 3 slender segments. *Flowers* clustered, sessile, funnel-shaped, $3/8$–$5/8$ in. (10–15 mm) long, white but the 5 lobes usually marked with purple or red. The splotches of color on the lobes of this flower have prompted the common name.

Range and Habitat: Texas to California and Baja California. Often common on dry slopes or mesas in central or southern New Mexico; 3,500–5,000 ft.

Key Characters: Painted trumpet can be identified by the funnel-shaped flowers with purplish or reddish markings on the lobes.

256. Woolly phlox — *Phlox hoodii canescens* — Phlox family

Perennial herb, the stems often matted, 2–4 in. (5–10 cm) long, often woolly. *Leaves* opposite, often woolly, linear, $1/4$–$1/2$ in. (5–12 mm) long, stiffly pointed at the tip. *Flowers* mostly solitary, white to lilac, tube-shaped, $5/16$–$1/2$ in. (8–12 mm) long, longer than the slender-pointed sepals, the lobes spreading abruptly and about $1/4$ in. (4–6 mm) long. This is a charming little creeper and has a very delicate aroma. It is similar to some alpine forms.

Range and Habitat: Saskatchewan to New Mexico and California. Usually found on dry, sandy plains of northwestern New Mexico; 5,000–7,000 ft.

Key Characters: Woolly phlox can be identified by the matted stems, the narrow, slender-pointed leaves, and the white to lilac flowers.

257. Santa Fe phlox — *Phlox nana* — Phlox family

Perennial herb, the stems mostly 4–10 in. (10–25 cm) long, with numerous gland-tipped hairs especially on the upper stem and in the flower cluster. *Leaves* opposite, narrowly lanceolate, $1/2$–$1 5/8$ in. (12–40 mm) long and $1/8$–$3/16$ in. (2–5 mm) wide, the margins without teeth. *Flowers* scattered, pink, tube-shaped, $1/2$–$3/4$ in. (13–18 mm) long, the lobes spreading abruptly, mostly $1/2$–$3/4$ in. (12–20 mm) long, irregularly toothed on the margins. This is one of our more common phloxes in New Mexico, often occurring in dense populations.

Range and Habitat: Western Texas to Arizona and Mexico. Often associated with grassy areas of plains, hills, and mountain slopes throughout all but northern New Mexico; 5,000–7,500 ft.

Key Characters: Santa Fe phlox may be recognized by the somewhat stiffish, narrowly lance-shaped leaves, the glandular nature of the upper stems and flower bases, and the large pink flowers with irregularly toothed lobe margins.

Related Species: Several related species include *P. cluteana,* differing in having evergreen, elliptic leaves and very few glands on the upper stem; *P. grayi,* differing in having the corolla tube at least twice as long as the calyx and the corolla lobes without teeth; and *P. stansburyi,* differing in having the corolla lobes only about $1/4$ in. (6–8 mm) long.

Linanthus aureus

Linanthus bigelovii

Phlox hoodii canescens

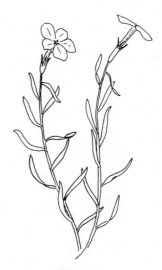

Phlox nana

258.   **Big-flowered collomia**   *Collomia grandiflora*   Phlox family

Erect annual, the stems 6–32 in. (15–80 cm) tall. *Leaves* alternate, linear to narrowly lance-shaped, 1¼–2¾ in. (30–70 mm) long, the margins without teeth. *Flowers* in dense clusters, each flower subtended by large floral bracts, the corolla white to pinkish, funnel-shaped, ³/₄–1¼ in. (20–30 mm) long, the lobes short, spreading, and blunt, the calyx much shorter than the corolla tube, and with 5 stamens. This plant has strikingly attractive flowers, made unusual by their often salmon pink color.

Range and Habitat: British Columbia to Arizona and California. Usually associated with open, rocky slopes or wooded areas, probably in the northwestern part of New Mexico; 7,000–8,000 ft.

Key Characters: Big-flowered collomia is identified by the narrowly lance-shaped leaves and the flowers in dense clusters, each flower elongate and narrowly funnel-shaped.

259.   **Purple nama**   *Nama hispidum*   Waterleaf family

Low annual, the stems branching from the base, to 6 in. (15 cm) tall, both stems and leaves stiffly hairy. *Leaves* narrow and linear or tapering from near the tip to the base, ³/₈–1 in. (10–25 mm) long and about ¹/₈ in. (1–4 mm) wide, the margins rolled under. *Flowers* in terminal leafy clusters, reddish purple, with the corolla funnel-shaped, ³/₈–¹/₂ in. (10–12 mm) long, the 5 rounded lobes spreading, and with 5 stamens. The lovely little plants are a spectacular sight when growing in a group.

Range and Habitat: Oklahoma to Colorado, Texas, and New Mexico. Scattered on dry plains and hills throughout New Mexico; 4,000–7,000 ft.

Key Characters: Purple nama is distinguished by the short, stiffly hairy stems, the narrow leaves with rolled margins, and the reddish purple, funnel-shaped corolla.

Related Species: The perennial *N. carnosum* is found in gypsum soils of southern New Mexico; it differs from purple nama in that the leaves are not more than ¹/₁₆ in. (1 mm) wide and the lobes of the corolla are recurved.

260.   **Mesa scorpionweed**   *Phacelia crenulata*   Waterleaf family

Annual, the stems to 24 in. (60 cm) tall, greenish, with numerous glandular hairs, odoriferous. *Leaves* alternate, the lower leaves petioled, often pinnately lobed with rounded teeth, to 4¾ in. (12 cm) long, the upper ones merely with rounded teeth. *Flowers* in dense, one-sided, often incurled spikes, the corolla bell-shaped, violet to purple but white in the throat, about ¹/₄–³/₈ in. (6–10 mm) long, with 5 round-toothed lobes. This is one of our most attractive scorpionweeds but is closely related to several hard-to-separate species.

Range and Habitat: New Mexico to Utah, Arizona, California, and Baja California. Usually associated with dry soils on mesas and foothills or along roadsides in central and western New Mexico; 4,000–5,000 ft.

Key Characters: Mesa scorpionweed is characterized by the pinnately lobed, wavy, or round-toothed leaves, and the violet to purple, bell-shaped flowers with toothed lobes.

Related Species: The varieties of *P. popei* differ in having few or no gland-tipped hairs and in the lobes of the corolla not being toothed.

Collomia grandiflora

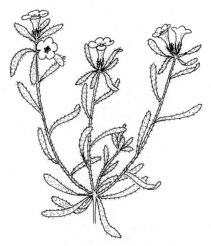

Nama hispidum

Phacelia crenulata

261. **Blue scorpionweed**   *Phacelia caerulea*   Waterleaf family

Annual, the stems purplish, 6–16 in. (15–40 cm) tall, both stems and leaves with gland-tipped hairs. *Leaves* alternate, about 3/4–3 1/8 in. (20–80 mm) long, pinnately divided, the lobes with rounded teeth, on petioles about as long as the blades. *Flowers* in one-sided spikes, white or blue, the corolla bell-shaped, 5-lobed, about 1/8 in. (3–4 mm) long.
Range and Habitat: Western Texas to California and Mexico. Typically found on dry plains and rocky slopes in central and southern New Mexico; 3,500–6,000 ft.
Key Characters: Blue scorpionweed is distinguished by the purplish stems, the leaves pinnately divided with rounded lobes and teeth, and the small, bell-shaped flowers.
Related Species: The closely related *P. ivesiana* differs in having the leaves pinnately divided nearly to the midrib into narrow lobes and the corolla white with yellowish tube.

262. **Western waterleaf**   *Hydrophyllum fendleri*   Waterleaf family

Perennial herb, the stems mostly 8–24 in. (20–60 cm) tall. *Leaves* alternate, to 12 in. (30 cm) long, pinnately divided nearly to the middle into several coarsely toothed lobes. *Flowers* bell-shaped or funnel-shaped, white or pale blue, about 1/4–3/8 in. (6–10 mm) long, the lobes rounded, not spreading, about half as long as the tube, each lobe with a slender appendage at the base.
Range and Habitat: Wyoming to Washington, southward to New Mexico and Utah. Associated with wet areas, often along streams in the mountains throughout New Mexico; 7,000–9,500 ft.
Key Characters: Western waterleaf is distinguished by the large, pinnately divided, coarsely toothed leaves and the somewhat bell-shaped blue or white flowers.

263. **Bindweed heliotrope**   *Heliotropium convolvulaceum*   Borage family

Annual herb, the stems with many spreading branches, both stems and leaves stiffly hairy. *Leaves* alternate, lance-shaped or sometimes linear, not fleshy, 3/8–1 5/8 in. (10–40 mm) long, without teeth. *Flowers* in the axils of upper leaves, conspicuous, the corolla white, funnel-shaped, about 3/8–5/8 in. (10–15 mm) wide, essentially unlobed, the tube stiffly hairy. This relative of the garden heliotropes has pleasantly scented flowers which open in the afternoon.
Range and Habitat: Nebraska to Utah, southward to Mexico. Usually found in dry, sandy, open ground, often along roadsides throughout New Mexico; 4,000–6,000 ft.
Key Characters: Bindweed heliotrope is distinguished by its low-spreading growth habit and the broadly funnel-shaped white flowers.

264. **Quailplant**   *Heliotropium curassavicum*   Borage family

Annual or perennial herb, the stems with many spreading branches, smooth. *Leaves* alternate, fleshy, narrowly oblong or broader toward the tip and tapering to the base, to 2 3/8 in. (6 cm) long, without hairs. *Flowers* in usually paired, incurved, one-sided spikes, the corolla white or with a tinge of blue, funnel-shaped, about 1/4–3/8 in. (6–9 mm) wide, the lobes appearing as angles. This attractive plant is made more attractive by its pleasing fragrance.
Range and Habitat: Florida to New Mexico, southward into tropical America. Widely distributed in alkaline soils in New Mexico; 4,000–5,000 ft.
Key Characters: Quailplant is easily recognized by the smooth, fleshy leaves and the usually white, funnel-shaped flowers with the corolla appearing unlobed.

Phacelia caerulea

Hydrophyllum fendleri

Heliotropium convolvulaceum

Heliotropium curassavicum

Abronia fragrans

Aquilegia caerulea

Aquilegia chrysantha

Arbutus texana

Argemone pleiacantha

Asclepias brachystephana

Berberis haematocarpa

Berberis repens

Bouvardia glaberrima

Calochortus gunnisonii

Caltha leptosepala

Cardamine cordifolia

Cercocarpus montanus

Chilopsis linearis

Clematis ligusticifolia

Commelina erecta

Convolvulus arvensis   Dalea formosa

Delphinium nelsonii

Delphinium virescens

Dithyrea wislizenii

Echinocactus horizonthalonius

Echinocereus triglochidiatus

Epipactis gigantea

Erigeron philadelphicus   Erodium cicutarium

Erysimum capitatum

Eschscholzia mexicana

Fallugia paradoxa

Fendlera rupicola

Fouquieria splendens

Fragaria americana

Gaura coccinea

Gilia rigidula

Heliotropium convolvulaceum

Ipomopsis aggregata

Iris missouriensis

Kallstroemia grandiflora

Larrea tridentata

Lesquerella fendleri

Lewisia pygmaea

Lithospermum incisum

Lonicera albiflora

Melampodium leucanthum

Mentzelia pumila

Mimulus glabratus

Nicotiana trigonophylla

Opuntia phaeacantha

Phlox nana

Prosopis glandulosa

Psilostrophe tagetina

Robinia neomexicana

Rosa woodsii

Rumex hymenosepalus

Schrankia occidentalis

Solanum elaeagnifolium

Stenandrium barbatum

Stephanomeria pauciflora

Thermopsis pinetorum

Verbena goodingii

Verbesina nana

Yucca glauca

Yucca elata

Zinnia grandiflora

265. **Common hound's tongue**   *Cynoglossum officinale*   Borage fai

Coarse biennial or perennial herb, the stems to 24 in. (60 cm) tall, hairy. *Leaves* alternate, mostly lance-shaped, to 12 in. (30 cm) long, becoming much smaller upward, the lower o petioled, the upper ones sessile. *Flowers* in elongate terminal clusters, usually purplish, the corolla with a short tube and 5 usually spreading lobes, about 1/4–3/8 in. (6–9 mm) wide. *Fruit* a cluster of 4 flattened nutlets bearing short, barbed prickles.
Range and Habitat: Although introduced from Europe, this plant is established here and there in North America. Usually associated with waste ground from northern to south-central New Mexico; 5,000–8,000 ft.
Key Characters: Common hound's tongue is identified by the coarse, hairy stems, the large, usually lance-shaped leaves, the purplish flowers, and the barbed fruits.

266. **Rocky Mountain bluebell**   *Mertensia lanceolata*   Borage family

Perennial herb, the stems erect, 8–16 in. (20–40 cm) tall. *Leaves* alternate, mostly lance-shaped or nearly so, variously hairy, 1 1/4–2 in. (30–50 mm) long, the upper ones gradually reduced in size and sessile. *Flowers* in terminal clusters, funnel-shaped, 5-lobed, bluish, the tube 1/8–3/8 in. (3–10 mm) long, hairy inside toward the base. There are several varieties of this species in our area.
Range and Habitat: Saskatchewan to North Dakota, Montana, and New Mexico. Usually on mountain slopes or in dryish soils on open plains and hills in northern New Mexico; 6,500–9,500 ft.
Key Characters: Rocky Mountain bluebell is distinguished by the short, smooth stems, the lance-shaped leaves, and the cluster of bluish, funnel-shaped flowers with hairs inside the tube.

267. **Cutflower puccoon**   *Lithospermum incisum*   Borage family

Perennial herb, the stems often clustered, to 16 in. (40 cm) tall, both stems and leaves with bristly hairs. *Leaves* alternate, linear, mostly 3/8–2 in. (10–50 mm) long, without teeth. *Flowers* yellow, tubular, 3/8–1 1/4 in. (10–30 mm) long, with 5 spreading, variously and irregularly toothed lobes at the top, a crestlike appendage in the throat, older plants often with very small, closed flowers. Although individually conspicuous, these plants are often obscured by the grasses and shrubs with which they are usually associated.
Range and Habitat: Canada to Texas and Arizona. Open grassy areas or brushy slopes throughout New Mexico; 4,000–7,000 ft.
Key Characters: Cutflower puccoon is recognized by the foliage with bristly hairs and the conspicuous yellow flowers with lobes variously toothed at the margin.

268. **Western false gromwell**   *Onosmodium occidentale*   Borage family

Coarse perennial, the stems mostly 16–32 in. (40–80 cm) tall, both stems and leaves with bristly hairs. *Leaves* alternate, lance-shaped to elliptic, 1 5/8–2 3/8 in. (40–60 mm) long, conspicuously veined. *Flowers* in one-sided, incurved, conspicuously bracted spikes, the corolla dull greenish yellow, narrowly funnel-shaped, 1/2–3/4 in. (12–20 mm) long, the 5 lobes not spreading.
Range and Habitat: Southern Canada to Texas, Utah, and New Mexico. Usually on open plains and slopes in northeastern New Mexico; 4,500–7,000 ft.
Key Characters: Western false gromwell is characterized by the coarse stems and leaves with bristly hairs, the leaves with conspicuous veins, and the strongly bracted, one-sided incurved spikes.

Cynoglossum officinale

Mertensia lanceolata

Lithospermum incisum

Onosmodium occidentale

269. **Dakota vervain**   *Verbena bipinnatifida*   Vervain family

Perennial herb, the stems ascending or spreading from the base, to 12 in. (30 cm) long,
hairy. *Leaves* opposite, mostly 1 1/4–3 1/2 in. (30–90 mm) long, divided into 3 main divisions,
each division pinnately lobed. *Flowers* pinkish purple, in somewhat flattened, headlike spikes,
with the floral bracts about as long as the flowers, the corolla tubular, 3/8–1/2 in. (8–12 mm)
long, with the lobes spreading and the top about 3/8 in. (8–10 mm) wide, each lobe notched.
This is a beautiful and showy plant, especially in large populations.
Range and Habitat: South Dakota to Alabama and Arizona. Found on plains and slopes,
often in open pine forests throughout most of New Mexico; 4,000–6,000 ft.
Key Characters: Dakota vervain can be identified by the strongly divided leaves and the
showy pinkish purple flowers in flattened, headlike spikes.

270. **Prostrate vervain**   *Verbena bracteata*   Vervain family

Annual or perennial herb, the stems prostrate to somewhat ascending, to 16 in. (40 cm)
long, both stems and leaves hairy. *Leaves* opposite, mostly 3/8–1 5/8 in. (10–40 mm) long,
cleft into 3 lobes, each lobe sharply toothed, the middle lobe larger than the others. *Flowers*
bluish or purplish, in elongated spikes at least 3/8 in. (10 mm) wide, the floral bracts about
twice as long as the flowers, the corolla tubular, about 3/16 in. (4–5 mm) long, with the lobes
spreading and the top about 1/8 in. (3 mm) wide.
Range and Habitat: Widely distributed in North America. Found mostly in open fields,
plains, and waste ground throughout New Mexico; 3,500–7,500 ft.
Key Characters: Prostrate vervain is distinguished by the mostly prostrate stems, the 3-
lobed leaves, and the small bluish or purplish flowers in elongate spikes.

271. **Southwestern vervain**   *Verbena gooddingii*   Vervain family

Perennial herb, the stems several, ascending, to 16 in. (40 cm) long, with long hairs and a
few glands. *Leaves* opposite, mostly 5/8–2 in. (15–50 mm) long, divided into 3 major lobes,
each lobe sharply toothed. *Flowers* pinkish purple, in dense, headlike spikes, with floral bracts
about as long as the flowers, the corolla tubular, 1/4–3/8 in. (7–10 mm) long, with the lobes
spreading and the top about 3/8 in. (8–10 mm) wide, each lobe notched. This plant is a very
attractive part of the spring flora and worthy of cultivation.
Range and Habitat: Texas to Utah, California, and Mexico. Usually found on dry slopes or
in washes and riverbeds throughout most of New Mexico; 3,500–6,000 ft.
Key Characters: Southwestern vervain is characterized by the stems and leaves with long
hairs, the 3-lobed leaves, and the dense heads of conspicuous pinkish flowers.

272. **Redbush lippia**   *Lippia graveolens*   Vervain family

Aromatic shrub, the stems slender, to 12 ft. (4 m) tall, both stems and leaves hairy and
densely marked with resinous dots. *Leaves* opposite or whorled, oblong to elliptic, to about 3
in. (7 cm) long, with rounded marginal teeth. *Flowers* in dense spikes, the corolla tubular,
yellow or white with a yellow center, the tube 1/8–1/4 in. (3–6 mm) long, externally hairy.
This plant has potential medicinal use.
Range and Habitat: Texas and New Mexico to Central America. Associated with dry, rocky
hills, canyons, arroyos, and mesas of southern New Mexico; 3,000–5,500 ft.
Key Characters: Redbush lippia may be recognized by the hairy, resinous-dotted stems and
leaves and spikes of yellowish flowers.

Verbena bipinnatifida

Verbena bracteata

Verbena gooddingii

Lippia graveolens

273.   **Spotted horsemint**   *Monarda punctata*   Mint family

Square-stemmed annual or perennial herb, the stems to 16 in. (40 cm) tall, both stems and
leaves minutely hairy. *Leaves* opposite, lance-shaped, ³/₄–2 in. (20–50 mm) long, the margins
sometimes toothed. *Flowers* in clusters in the axils of the upper leaves, subtended by
conspicuous purplish or whitish floral bracts, the corolla mostly pale yellow with purple
spots, somewhat tubular, ³/₄–1 in. (20–25 mm) long, 2-lipped, the upper lip sickle-shaped.
Range and Habitat: Illinois to Kansas, southwestward to Mexico. Usually in dry, sandy
soils on plains and low hills throughout New Mexico; 5,000–7,000 ft.
Key Characters: Spotted horsemint is distinguished by the conspicuous purplish or whitish
floral bracts subtending the flower clusters and the purple-spotted flowers.

274.   **Drummond false pennyroyal**   *Hedeoma drummondii*   Mint family

Square-stemmed perennial herb, the stems with spreading branches, to 1¹/₄ in. (30 mm) tall,
covered with short, recurved hairs. *Leaves* opposite, narrowly linear to oblong or oval, ¹/₄–³/₄
in. (6–20 mm) long, ¹/₈ in. (1–4 mm) wide, the margins without teeth. *Flowers* in small,
axillary clusters, pink to purple, ¹/₄–¹/₂ in. (5–12 mm) long, somewhat tubular and 2-lipped,
the calyx teeth converging after flowers drop.
Range and Habitat: North Dakota and Montana to Mexico. Common on dry plains, slopes
and hills throughout New Mexico; 3,500–7,500 ft.
Key Characters: Drummond false pennyroyal can be identified by the narrow, untoothed
leaves, the recurved hairs of the stem, and the pink or purple 2-lipped flowers.
Related Species: The usually smaller *H. pulchella* of southern New Mexico differs in having
long, straight stem hairs and conspicuously toothed leaves.

275.   **Davidson sage**   *Salvia davidsonii*   Mint family

Square-stemmed perennial herb, the stems to 16 in. (40 cm) tall. *Leaves* opposite, pinnately
compound, to about 3 in. (7 cm) long, the 3 leaflets usually rounded or triangular and
coarsely toothed, the terminal leaflet larger than the others. *Flowers* conspicuous, somewhat
tubular, 1–1³/₈ in. (25–35 mm) long, red, 2-lipped, the upper lip arched.
Range and Habitat: New Mexico and Arizona. Associated with rocky slopes in extreme
southwestern New Mexico; 5,000–7,000 ft.
Key Characters: Davidson sage is characterized by the pinnately compound leaves with 3
coarsely toothed leaflets and the conspicuous, red, tubular, 2-lipped flowers.
Related Species: Another early blooming sage is *Salvia summa,* the spectacularly beautiful
but rare pink-flowered species found on limestone slopes in southeastern New Mexico.

276.   **Mealycup sage**   *Salvia farinacea*   Mint family

Square-stemmed perennial, the stems to 3 ft. (1 m) tall, covered with short hairs. *Leaves*
opposite, linear, 1¹/₈–3¹/₈ in. (30–80 mm) long, ¹/₁₆–³/₈ in. (2–10 mm) wide. *Flowers* in
dense, often woolly clusters at the upper nodes, bluish or purplish, somewhat tubular, ³/₄–1
in. (20–25 mm) long, 2-lipped, the calyx with whitish or bluish hairs, squared-off at the
top.
Range and Habitat: Western Texas and New Mexico. Usually found in limestone soils of
plains, slopes, and canyons of southern New Mexico; 3,500–6,000 ft.
Key Characters: Mealycup sage may be recognized by the long, narrow leaves, the dense
clusters of bluish or purplish flowers, and the calyx that is whitish or bluish and hairy.

Monarda punctata

Hedeoma drummondii

Salvia davidsonii

Salvia farinacea

277. **Cutleaf germander** *Teucrium laciniatum* Mint family

Perennial square-stemmed herb, the stems hairy, leafy, to 8 in. (20 cm) tall, branched at the base. *Leaves* opposite, pinnately divided to the middle into narrow lobes. *Flowers* scattered, somewhat funnel-shaped, bluish or purplish, $^1/_2$–$^3/_4$ in. (12–20 mm) long, 2-lipped, with the upper lip much shorter than the lower, the calyx with 10 ribs.

Range and Habitat: Oklahoma to Texas, westward to Colorado and New Mexico. Associated with open plains and meadows in all but western New Mexico; 4,000–7,500 ft.

Key Characters: Cutleaf germander is characterized by the leaves deeply divided into narrow lateral lobes and by the flowers with the upper lip much shorter than the lower one.

278. **Dead nettle** *Lamium amplexicaule* Mint family

Slender, square-stemmed annual, the stems, 4–20 in. (10–50 cm) tall. *Leaves* opposite, broadly oval to nearly round, often flattened to shallowly indented at the base, $^1/_4$–$^1/_2$ in. (7–16 mm) long, on petioles usually longer than the blades, the margins with rounded teeth or lobes. *Flowers* in the axils of the upper leaves, somewhat tubular, strongly 2-lipped, purple or red, about $^3/_8$–$^5/_8$ in. (10–15 mm) long, the lower lip spotted.

Range and Habitat: Introduced from the Old World and established throughout temperate North America. Typically found in waste ground throughout New Mexico: 4,500–6,500 ft.

Key Characters: Dead nettle is distinguished by the usually broad leaf blades with rounded teeth or lobes, the upper leaves sessile and clasping the stem, and the purplish red 2-lipped flowers.

279. **Drummond skullcap** *Scutellaria drummondii* Mint family

Slender, square-stemmed annual, the stems to about 11 in. (25 cm) tall, both stems and leaves densely covered with spreading hairs. *Leaves* opposite, oval or broader above the middle, $^5/_{16}$–$^3/_4$ in. (7–18 mm) long. *Flowers* solitary in the axils of upper leaves, 2-lipped, hairy externally, blue to violet, $^1/_4$–$^3/_8$ in. (6–10 mm) long.

Range and Habitat: Kansas to Texas and New Mexico. Usually found in canyons and on dry slopes in southern New Mexico; 4,000–6,000 ft.

Key Characters: Drummond skullcap is characterized by the hairy, square stems and the irregularly tubular, 2-lipped, bluish flowers.

280. **Desert tobacco** *Nicotiana trigonophylla* Nightshade family

Stout herb with few branches, to about 32 in. (80 cm) tall, sticky with gland-tipped hairs. *Leaves* scattered, the basal leaves petioled, the stem leaves sessile, clasping the stem by earlike lobes at the base, $^3/_4$–$2^3/_8$ in. (2–8 cm) long. *Flowers* in loose clusters, the corolla greenish white, tubular, about $^3/_4$ in. (20 mm) long, constricted at the base of the lobes, about $^3/_8$ in. (8–10 mm) wide at the top. *Fruit* a many-seeded capsule about $^3/_8$ in. (10 mm) long.

Range and Habitat: Western Texas to California and Mexico. Found mostly in canyons and gravelly washes, often in the shade, in southern New Mexico; 3,500–6,000 ft.

Key Characters: Desert tobacco may be recognized by the stems with sticky hairs, the upper leaves clasping the stem, and the greenish white tubular corolla.

Related Species: The uncommon tree tobacco, *N. glauca,* differs in having smooth stems, oval leaves, and a longer, yellowish corolla.

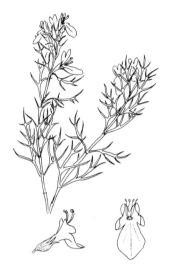

Teucrium laciniatum

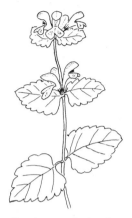

Lamium amplexicaule

Scutellaria drummondii

Nicotiana trigonophylla

281. **Pale wolfberry**   *Lycium pallidum*   Nightshade family

Upright-spreading, much-branched shrub, to about 6 ft. (2 m) tall, with slender, sharp spines to ³/₈ in. (10 mm) long. *Leaves* pale, usually in clusters (fascicles), mostly broadest above the middle and tapering to the base, smooth, ³/₈–1¹/₂ in. (10–40 mm) long and ¹/₈–¹/₂ in. (4–15 mm) wide. *Flowers* solitary or in pairs, the corolla greenish white or tinged with purple, narrowly funnel-shaped, ⁵/₈–³/₄ in. (15–20 mm) long, the lobes about ¹/₈ in. (3–4 mm) long, the stamens slightly longer than the corolla. *Fruit* a red berry about ³/₈ in. (8–10 mm) long.

Range and Habitat: Texas to Colorado, California, and Mexico. Scattered on dry plains or steep, rocky slopes throughout New Mexico; 4,500–7,000 ft.

Key Characters: Pale wolfberry is distinguished by the slender, sharp spines, pale leaves, and older bark that is dark reddish brown.

282. **Torrey wolfberry**   *Lycium torreyi*   Nightshade family

Shrub with spreading branches and usually stout spines, densely leafy. *Leaves* usually in clusters (fascicles), mostly broadest toward the tip and tapering to the base, ³/₈–2 in. (10–50 mm) long and ¹/₈–³/₈ in. (3–10 mm) wide. *Flowers* solitary or in small clusters, the corolla purplish, funnel-shaped, ³/₈–⁵/₈ in. (10–15 mm) long, the lobes woolly on the margins, ¹/₈ in. (3–4 mm) long, the stamens about as long as the corolla. *Fruit* a red berry ¹/₄–³/₈ in. (7–10 mm) long.

Range and Habitat: Western Texas to Nevada, Arizona, California, and Mexico. Usually found in relatively dry valleys and plains in central and southern New Mexico; 3,500–5,000 ft.

Key Characters: Torrey wolfberry is distinguished by stout spines, funnel-form purplish flowers not exceeding ⁵/₈ in. (15 mm) in length, and leaves often 1 in. (25 mm) or more in length.

283. **Anderson wolfberry**   *Lycium andersonii*   Nightshade family

Rounded, much-branched shrub, to about 6 ft. (2 m) tall, bearing slender spines. *Leaves* alternate, often in clusters (fascicles), narrowly linear or broadest toward the tip and tapering to the base, ¹/₈–⁵/₈ in. (3–15 mm) long and to ¹/₈ in. (1–3 mm) wide. *Flowers* solitary or in small axillary clusters, the corolla whitish, tinged with lavender, narrowly funnel-shaped, ¹/₂–³/₄ in. (12–18 mm) long, the lobes very short, the stamens longer than the corolla. *Fruit* a red berry about ¹/₄ in. (6–8 mm) long.

Range and Habitat: New Mexico to California and Mexico. Scattered on dry plains and hills in western New Mexico; 4,500–5,500 ft.

Key Characters: Anderson wolfberry is distinguished by the very slender spines and the narrowly funnel-shaped whitish flowers not exceeding ¹/₂ in. (14 mm) in length, and very narrow leaves.

Related Species: Berlandier wolfberry (*L. berlandieri*) differs in having much smaller flowers, only ¹/₈–⁵/₁₆ in. (4–7 mm) long and strongly constricted at the base.

Lycium pallidum

Lycium torreyi

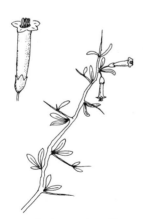

Lycium andersonii

284. **Virginia groundcherry**   *Physalis virginiana hispida*   Nightshade family

Perennial herb, the stems to about 16 in. (40 cm) tall, both stems and leaves bearing stiff, spreading hairs. *Leaves* scattered, lance-shaped, sometimes with a few teeth. *Flowers* solitary or in small clusters, yellow with dark spots at the base, about ⁵/₈–1 in. (15–25 mm) wide, the calyx becoming greatly inflated, papery, and strongly ribbed in fruit, the corolla somewhat bell-shaped, the border having 5 short, broad lobes, the anthers yellow. *Fruit* a globelike, pulpy berry. There are many varieties of this species, but they tend to be summer-blooming types. Groundcherries are usually regarded as edible at maturity. They are widely utilized by Indians in both raw and cooked form.

Range and Habitat: Oklahoma, Kansas, and Colorado to Texas and Arizona. Usually scattered in sandy, open, often disturbed ground throughout New Mexico; 4,500–5,500 ft.

Key Characters: Virginia groundcherry is distinguished by the lance-shaped leaves, the stiff, spreading hairs, the yellow flowers with dark spots, and the greatly inflated calyx.

285. **Horsenettle**   *Solanum elaeagnifolium*   Nightshade family

Perennial herb, the stems to nearly 3 ft. (1 m) tall, both stems and leaves covered with silvery, star-shaped hairs and often bearing slender, sharp spines. *Leaves* scattered, oblong to lance-shaped, 1¹/₂–4 in. (4–10 cm) long, the margins often wavy-toothed. *Flowers* in small clusters, usually purple, 5-lobed, about ³/₄–1¹/₄ in. (20–30 mm) wide, with 5 conspicuous anthers about ⁵/₁₆ in. (8 mm) long. *Fruit* a globelike berry about ⁵/₁₆–⁵/₈ in. (8–15 mm) in diameter. This is an attractive but very weedy plant.

Range and Habitat: Kansas to California, southward to tropical America. Typically associated with waste ground throughout New Mexico; 3,500–6,500 ft.

Key Characters: Horsenettle is easily distinguished by the silvery leaves and stems, usually with slender spines, and the purplish (rarely white) flowers with conspicuous yellow anthers.

286. **Prostrate groundcherry**   *Chamaesaracha conioides*   Nightshade family

Low perennial herb, the stems branching, to 8 in. (20 cm) long, both stems and leaves sticky and glandular. *Leaves* scattered, lance-shaped to rhombic, to 2 in. (50 mm) long and ³/₄ in. (20 mm) wide, usually with lobed or wavy margins. *Flowers* solitary or in small clusters, the corolla with 5 short, broad lobes, hairy inside, yellowish to purplish, about ⁵/₁₆–¹/₂ in. (8–12 mm) wide. *Fruit* a fleshy berry about ¹/₄–⁵/₁₆ in. (6–8 mm) in diameter.

Range and Habitat: Kansas and Colorado to Texas, Arizona, and Mexico. Scattered on dry plains and slopes throughout New Mexico; 3,500–6,000 ft.

Key Characters: Prostrate groundcherry is characterized by the low-growing habit, the somewhat sticky herbage, and the corolla with short, broad lobes.

287. **Blue toadflax**   *Linaria texana*   Figwort family

Annual or biennial herb, the stems erect, to about 32 in. (80 cm) tall, both stems and leaves smooth. *Leaves* opposite, or scattered, mostly linear or narrowly oblong, ³/₈–1¹/₄ in. (10–30 mm) long, the margins without teeth. *Flowers* scattered on short stalks along the upper stem, the corolla blue, irregularly funnel-shaped, strongly 2-lipped, ⁵/₁₆–¹/₂ in. (8–12 mm) long, the tube with a curved spur at the base, the throat with a pale raised pad within. *Fruit* a globe-shaped, many-seeded capsule.

Range and Habitat: Widespread in much of North America. Usually associated with sandy plains and slopes at scattered locations in New Mexico; 4,500–6,000 ft.

Key Characters: Blue toadflax is easily distinguished by the erect stems, the narrow leaves, and the blue snapdragonlike spurred flowers.

Related Species: The dalmatian toadflax (*L. dalmatica*) sometimes found along roadsides, differs in having much larger, yellow flowers, and usually lance-shaped leaves.

Physalis virginiana hispida

Solanum elaeagnifolium

Chamaesaracha conioides

Linaria texana

288. **False snapdragon**   *Maurandya antirrhiniflora*   Figwort family

Vining or prostrate perennial herb, the stems elongate. *Leaves* scattered, with petioles about as long as the triangular blades, the blades about ³/₈–1 in. (10–25 mm) long, the base broadly notched and spreading into a pair of pointed lobes. *Flowers* conspicuous, solitary, the corolla purple or pink, irregularly funnelform, 5-lobed, 1–1¹/₄ in. (25–30 mm) long, bearing within a yellowish, hairy projection which nearly closes the throat. *Fruit* a globe-shaped capsule about ⁵/₁₆ in. (7–8 mm) in diameter. This is an attractive adjunct to the flora of sandy slopes.
Range and Habitat: Texas to California and Mexico. Mostly associated with sandy slopes and rocky hills of central and southern New Mexico; 4,000–7,500 ft.
Key Characters: False snapdragon is easily recognized by the elongate vining stems, the triangular leaves, and the conspicuous snapdragonlike flower.
Related Species: The very similar *M. wislizenii* differs mainly in the lack of a hairy projection in the corolla throat.

289. **Perfoliate beardtongue**   *Penstemon pseudospectabilis*   Figwort family

Stout perennial herb, the stems clustered, to about 3 ft. (1 m) tall, both stems and leaves smooth. *Leaves* opposite, usually somewhat toothed on the margins, oval, the upper pairs of leaves fused at the base and completely surrounding the stem. *Flowers* in an elongate cluster often half as long as the stem, pink with darker pink lines in the throat, about ³/₄–1³/₈ in. (20–35 mm) long, the corolla funnel-shaped but only slightly 2-lipped, both inner and outer surfaces with gland-tipped hairs, and with 4 stamens plus an additional filament, this without an anther and smooth throughout. *Fruit* a short, many-seeded capsule.
Range and Habitat: New Mexico and Arizona. Usually found on dryish, rocky slopes and canyon walls in southwestern New Mexico; 6,000–7,000 ft.
Key Characters: Perfoliate beardtongue is easily distinguished by the upper pairs of leaves united at their bases around the stem and the pink funnel-shaped flowers.

290. **Eaton beardtongue**   *Penstemon eatonii*   Figwort family

Perennial herb, the stems to about 24 in. (60 cm) tall. *Leaves* opposite, lance-shaped or oval, often with the base clasping the stem. *Flowers* tubular, in a narrow, spikelike cluster with very small floral bracts, scarlet, mostly ³/₄–1¹/₄ in. (20–30 mm) long, with the corolla only slightly 2-lipped, the lobes erect or spreading, and with 4 stamens plus a fifth sterile filament, usually without hairs. *Fruit* a many-seeded capsule.
Range and Habitat: Colorado and Utah to New Mexico and Arizona. Usually found in canyons in northwestern New Mexico; 6,000–7,000 ft.
Key Characters: Eaton beardtongue is distinguished by the narrow, spikelike cluster of tubular scarlet flowers.

291. **Buckley beardtongue**   *Penstemon buckleyi*   Figwort family

Perennial herb, the stems to about 16 in. (40 cm) tall, both stems and leaves smooth and with a waxy bloom. *Leaves* opposite, the lower leaves usually broadest above the middle and tapering to a petiole, the upper leaves lance-shaped or oval. *Flowers* in a narrow, symmetrical, spikelike cluster, each flower in the axil of a conspicuous floral bract, with the corolla pale blue to lavender, with prominent lines in the throat, irregularly funnel-shaped, ⁵/₈–³/₄ in. (15–20 mm) long, 2-lipped, with both upper and lower lips spreading, and with 4 stamens plus an additional filament, this without an anther and bearded with yellowish hairs. *Fruit* a short, many-seeded capsule.
Range and Habitat: Kansas and Texas to New Mexico. Scattered on open plains, usually in sand dunes of central and southern New Mexico; 3,500–6,000 ft.
Key Characters: Buckley beardtongue is distinguished by the smooth stems and leaves with a waxy bloom, the bluish or lavender flowers, and the yellowish beard on the sterile filament.

Maurandya antirrhiniflora

Penstemon pseudospectabilis

Penstemon eatonii

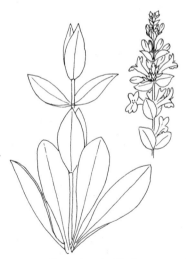

Penstemon buckleyi

292. **James beardtongue** *Penstemon jamesii* Figwort family

Perennial herb, the stems to about 20 in. (50 cm) tall. L̲ opp͞o͟s͟i͟c͟, narrow, the lower leaves petioled, linear to lance-shaped, or broadest towar ͟ ͟p, the upper ones narrower. *Flowers* in a narrow, one-sided, spikelike cluster, each flc ͟ ͟n the axil of a leaflike bract, the corolla blue to lavender, with conspicuous lines in the thɪuat, irregularly funnel-shaped, 1–1³/₈ in. (25–35 mm) long, 2-lipped, the upper lobes projecting forward, the lower lobes often recurved and bearing long whitish hairs, with 4 stamens plus an additional filament, this without an anther and bearing a cluster of yellowish hairs at the tip. *Fruit* a short, many-seeded capsule.
Range and Habitat: Colorado and Utah to Texas, New Mexico, and Arizona. Usually found on dry plains and hills throughout much of New Mexico; 5,000–7,000 ft.
Key Characters: James beardtongue is distinguished by the one-sided flower spike with large blue to lavender flowers having prominent lines in the throat and an extra filament bearing a tuft of yellowish hairs.

293. **American brooklime** *Veronica americana* Figwort family

Perennial herb, the stems often prostrate, to about 24 in. (60 cm) long, smooth. *Leaves* opposite, lance-shaped or oval, toothed, mostly ³/₈–3¹/₈ in. (1–8 cm) long. *Flowers* in the axils of bracts along the upper stems, violet to nearly white, about ¹/₄–³/₈ in. (7–10 mm) wide, with 4 sepals and petals. *Fruit* a swollen, rounded, notched capsule. This is probably the most attractive of our native speedwells.
Range and Habitat: Widespread in North America. Found mostly in shallow water of streams throughout New Mexico; 5,000–7,500 ft.
Key Characters: American brooklime may be identified by the prostrate purplish stems and the violet to pale blue flowers with whitish centers.

294. **Purslane speedwell** *Veronica peregrina xalapensis* Figwort family

Annual, the stems usually erect, bearing gland-tipped hairs. *Lower leaves* often opposite, oblong or broadest above the middle, ³/₈–³/₄ in. (10–20 mm) long, sometimes toothed, the *upper leaves* much smaller, scattered, linear or narrowly lance-shaped. *Flowers* solitary in the axils of the upper leaves, white, less than ¹/₈ in. (2–3 mm) wide, with 4 sepals and petals. *Fruit* a flattened, notched capsule bearing short, gland-tipped hairs.
Range and Habitat: Widespread in North America. Typically found in moist, often waste ground throughout New Mexico; 6,500–8,000 ft.
Key Characters: Purslane speedwell is distinguished by the erect stems, tiny white flowers, and glandular fruits.
Related Species: A similar species, corn speedwell (*V. arvensis*), an introduction from Europe, differs in having blue flowers and smooth fruits.

295. **Smooth monkeyflower** *Mimulus glabratus* Figwort family

Perennial herb, the stems creeping and rooting at the nodes, to about 16 in. (40 cm) long, smooth. *Leaves* opposite, oval to nearly round, irregularly toothed. *Flowers* yellow, often spotted within, about ⁵/₁₆–⁵/₈ in. (8–15 mm) long, irregularly funnel-shaped, 2-lipped, the lobes not toothed, the calyx asymmetrical, the teeth blunt and not converging. *Fruit* a many-seeded capsule. This is a beautiful little plant certainly worthy of cultivation. This description includes the var. *fremontii*.
Range and Habitat: Alaska southward to Texas, Arizona, and Mexico. Of aquatic or marshy habitats in or near streams, seeps, or springs throughout New Mexico; 4,000–7,500 ft.
Key Characters: Smooth monkeyflower is distinguished by the smooth, creeping stems, the often nearly round leaves, and the yellow flowers with red spots within and untoothed lobes.
Related Species: The rare crimson monkeyflower (*M. cardinalis*), which may bloom from spring to fall, differs in the scarlet flowers, often erect stems, and glandular leaves and stems.

Penstemon jamesii

Veronica americana

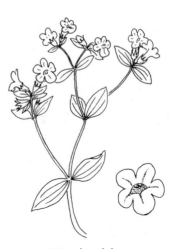

Veronica peregrina xalapensis

Mimulus glabratus

296. **Toothpetal monkeyflower**   *Mimulus dentilobus*   Figwort family

Perennial herb, the stems creeping and rooting at the nodes, to about 3 1/8 in. (8 cm) long. *Leaves* opposite, oval to nearly round, 3/16–3/8 in. (4–9 mm) long. *Flowers* bright yellow, about 3/8 in. (8–10 mm) long, the irregularly funnel-shaped, 2-lipped lobes irregularly toothed or sometimes deeply cut, with the calyx in fruit strongly asymmetrical, the teeth strongly converging, and with 4 stamens. *Fruit* a many-seeded capsule.
Range and Habitat: New Mexico and Arizona to Mexico. Occasionally found in wet ground in southwestern New Mexico; 4,000–5,500 ft.
Key Characters: This monkeyflower is distinguished by the slender, creeping stems and yellow flowers with irregularly toothed or deeply cut lobes.

297. **Wood betony**   *Pedicularis canadensis*   Figwort family

Perennial herb, the stems to 18 in. (45 cm) tall. *Leaves* scattered, 2–4 3/4 in. (5–12 cm) long, pinnately lobed, each lobe blunt at the tip and toothed or deeply cut. *Flowers* in spikelike clusters, the lower ones subtended by leaflike bracts, the calyx split on the lower side and toothed on the upper side, the corolla yellow to nearly white or reddish-tinged, 5/8–1 in. (15–25 mm) long, strongly 2-lipped, the upper lip arched and curved inward. *Fruit* a flattened capsule about 5/8 in. (15 mm) long.
Range and Habitat: Canada to Florida, New Mexico, and Mexico. Usually associated with damp woods, meadows, and prairies in the mountains of northern New Mexico; 7,000–10,000 ft.
Key Characters: Wood betony is distinguished by the fernlike leaves and the usually yellowish, irregular flowers with a strongly arched upper lip.
Related Species: Dwarf lousewort (*P. centranthera*) differs in that the stems usually are not more than 6 in. (15 cm) tall, the finely divided leaves are mostly crowded in a basal cluster, and the flowers are purplish.

298. **Plains paintbrush**   *Castilleja sessiliflora*   Figwort family

Perennial herb, the stems to about 16 in. (40 cm) tall, both stems and leaves densely hairy, often woolly. *Leaves* alternate, linear to narrowly lance-shaped, 3/4–2 in. (2–5 cm) long, the upper ones with a pair of lobes. *Flowers* in a densely hairy spike, inconspicuous but subtended by usually greenish, 3- to 5-lobed floral bracts marked with purplish veins and covered with gland-tipped hairs, the individual flowers yellowish or tinged with pink, irregularly tubular, 1 3/8–2 in. (40–50 mm) long.
Range and Habitat: Southern Canada to Illinois, Montana, Texas, and Arizona. Usually found on plains, prairies, or pinyon-juniper slopes, often in sandy areas, in all but western New Mexico; 4,500–7,000 ft.
Key Characters: Plains paintbrush is distinguished by the densely hairy stems and leaves, the upper leaves with a pair of lobes, and the greenish, lobed floral bracts marked with purplish veins.
Related Species: Laxleaf paintbrush (*C. laxa*), of southwestern New Mexico, differs in having somewhat drooping leaves and unlobed floral bracts.

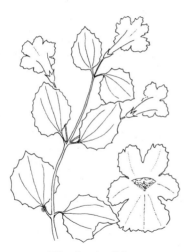

Mimulus dentilobus

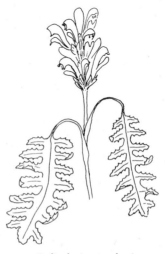

Pedicularis canadensis

Castilleja sessiliflora

299. Scarlettip paintbrush *Castilleja chromosa* Figwort family

Perennial herb, the stems mostly erect, to about 16 in. (40 cm) tall, both stems and leaves with straight hairs. *Leaves* alternate, linear or narrowly lance-shaped, 1 1/4–3 1/4 in. (3–7 cm) long, with short hairs, the upper ones usually with 1 or 2 pairs of spreading slender lobes. *Flowers* in a dense spike, inconspicuous but subtended by conspicuous, pinnately lobed, greenish but scarlet-tipped floral bracts, the individual flowers green with reddish margins, projecting beyond the bracts, irregularly tubular, 3/4–1 in. (20–25 mm) long.
Range and Habitat: Wyoming to New Mexico, westward to Utah and Arizona. Scattered in sandy areas, often among sagebrush, in northwestern New Mexico; 5,000–8,000 ft.
Key Characters: Scarlettip paintbrush is distinguished by the hairy stems and leaves, the upper leaves lobed, and the floral bracts lobed and scarlet-tipped.
Related Species: *Castilleja miniata,* from the mountains of New Mexico, differs in that the hairs of the stems usually point backward and the flower cluster is covered with glandular hairs.

300. Wholeleaf paintbrush *Castilleja integra* Figwort family

Perennial herb, the stems mostly erect, to 16 in. (40 cm) tall. *Leaves* alternate, narrow, to about 2 3/4 in. (7 cm) long, smooth above but hairy beneath, the margins without teeth. *Flowers* in a dense spike, inconspicuous but subtended by showy, red floral bracts, the individual flowers greenish, irregularly tubular, 1–1 3/8 in. (25–35 mm) long. These handsome plants provide splashes of scarlet on otherwise uninteresting dry slopes.
Range and Habitat: Texas to Colorado, New Mexico, Arizona, and Mexico. Usually scattered on dryish, often rocky slopes throughout New Mexico; 4,500–10,000 ft.
Key Characters: Wholeleaf paintbrush is distinguished by the thickish, narrow, untoothed leaves and the floral bracts which are scarlet or various shades of red and mostly without teeth or lobes.
Related Species: The closely related woolly paintbrush (*C. lanata*) from canyon areas of southern New Mexico differs in having densely woolly stems and leaves and in the usually lobed floral bracts.

301. Desert willow *Chilopsis linearis* Catalpa family

Large shrub or small tree to about 12 ft. (4 m) or more tall, the twigs slender and spreading or drooping. *Leaves* alternate, linear to narrowly lance-shaped, without teeth, about 4–6 in. (10–15 cm) long, narrowly tapering to a point. *Flowers* showy, in short terminal clusters, irregularly funnel-shaped, 1–1 3/8 in. (25–35 mm) long, variously lavender to whitish, often with purple markings, the lobes irregularly toothed or wavy. *Fruit* a slender pod to 12 in. (30 cm) long, with numerous fringe-margined seeds. The desert willow is often cultivated in the Southwest for the willowlike foliage and orchidlike flowers.
Range and Habitat: Western Texas to California, southward into Mexico. Scattered or common in gravelly soils along water courses in central and southern New Mexico; 4,000–5,500 ft.
Key Characters: Desert willow may be recognized by the narrow, willowlike leaves, the conspicuous, somewhat orchidlike flowers, and the elongate, slender, drooping pods.

Castilleja chromosa

Castilleja integra

Chilopsis linearis

302. **Yellow elder**   *Tecoma stans*   Catalpa family

Large shrub, to about 6 ft. (2 m) tall. *Leaves* opposite, pinnately compound, mostly 2¹/₈–4³/₄
in. (8–12 cm) long, the 5–13 leaflets mostly lance-shaped, toothed, and long-pointed. *Flowers*
in small clusters, bright yellow, 1¹/₄–2 in. (30–50 mm) long, irregularly funnel-shaped, with
rounded lobes. *Fruit* a slender pod 6–8 in. (15–20 cm) long, with winged seeds. This is a
most attractive shrub and is often cultivated in warm-temperate or subtropical areas.
Range and Habitat: Texas to New Mexico and Arizona to tropical America. Rocky slopes in
hills and mountains of southern New Mexico; 3,500–5,000 ft.
Key Characters: Yellow elder is characterized by the compound opposite leaves, large bright
yellow flowers, and the slender pods.

303. **Small-flowered unicorn-plant**   *Proboscidea parviflora*   Unicorn-plant family

Annual, the stems spreading, to about 32 in. (80 cm) long, densely covered with gland-
tipped hairs, as are the leaves and fruits. *Leaves* broadly triangular to somewhat rounded,
shallowly wavy on the margins, about 3¹/₈–6 in. (8–15 cm) wide. *Flowers* few, showy, to
about 1³/₈ in. (35 mm) long, and 1 in. (25 mm) wide at the top, irregularly funnel-shaped,
the 5 lobes flaring, reddish purple or sometimes whitish, often with streaks of yellow. *Fruit* a
capsule with an elongate curved beak which splits into two parts at maturity. This plant, in
flower, attracts attention. The young pods reputedly have been used as food by certain Indian
tribes.
Range and Habitat: Western Texas to California and Mexico. Usually found on dry slopes
and mesas in central and southern New Mexico; 4,000–5,500 ft.
Key Characters: This unicorn-plant is distinguished by the sticky, glandular stems and
leaves, the rounded-triangular leaves, and the showy, funnel-shaped flowers.

304. **Desert cancerroot**   *Orobanche multiflora*   Broomrape family

Parasitic perennial herb, the stems 4–12 in. (10–30 cm) long, with several scalelike bracts
and covered with sticky gland-tipped hairs. *Leaves* reduced to alternate, scalelike, nongreen
bracts. *Flowers* in dense spikes, brownish purple, the corolla about ⁵/₈–1³/₈ in. (15–35 mm)
long, curved and tubular, the lobes 2-lipped, rounded at the tip, the calyx about ³/₈–⁵/₈ in.
(10–15 mm) long, the lobes about equal in length. *Fruit* a one-celled capsule with numerous
seeds. There are several very similar varieties of this species in New Mexico. Members of this
genus have been used in the treatment of ulcers.
Range and Habitat: Texas and New Mexico, to Washington and California. Mostly found in
sandy soils on open plains throughout New Mexico; 3,500–7,000 ft.
Key Characters: Desert cancerroot is characterized by the sticky, scaly stems, and the dense
spikes of brownish purple curved tubular flowers.
Related Species: The superficially similar Mexican squawroot (*Conopholis mexicana*) differs in
having smooth, nonsticky hairs and the calyx split along the lower side.

305. **One-flowered cancerroot**   *Orobanche uniflora*   Broomrape family

Parasitic perennial herb, the stems scaly, mostly underground, sending up one or more naked
flower stalks, mostly 1–4³/₄ in. (2.5–12.0 cm) tall, each bearing a single flower. *Leaves*
reduced to scales. *Flowers* irregularly funnel-shaped, with 5 triangular lobes, usually dull
purplish or whitish, with a pair of yellowish ridges within, ⁵/₈–1 in. (15–25 mm) long, the
calyx hairy, dull yellow. *Fruit* an ovoid capsule with numerous seeds. This pretty but delicate
little plant is never common.
Range and Habitat: Widespread in North America. Occasionally found in wooded areas of
New Mexico; 5,000–6,000 ft.
Key Characters: One-flowered cancerroot is easily distinguished by the short, slender flower
stalks, the scaly underground stems, and the purplish or yellowish hairy flowers.

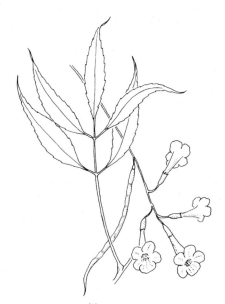

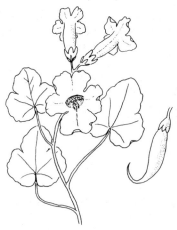

Tecoma stans

Proboscidea parviflora

Orobanche multiflora

Orobanche uniflora

306. Woolly stenandrium   *Stenandrium barbatum*   Acanthus family

Low perennial herb, with numerous shaggy white hairs, the stems to about 2³/₈ in. (6 cm) tall, with several branches from the base. *Leaves* opposite, narrow, the upper leaves lance-shaped, the lower ones broadest above the middle and tapering to the base. *Flowers* crowded among leaflike bracts at the summit of the stem, purplish, about ⁵/₈ in. (15 mm) long, with a slender tube and 5 abruptly spreading notched lobes. *Fruit* a 2-celled capsule with 2 seeds in each cell.

Range and Habitat: Texas and New Mexico. Usually found on dry, rocky slopes (usually limestone) in southern New Mexico; 3,500–4,500 ft.

Key Characters: Woolly stenandrium is distinguished by the multibranched base, the shaggy-hairy stems and leaves, and the purplish flowers.

307. Desert honeysuckle   *Anisacanthus thurberi*   Acanthus family

Stiff shrub, to about 3 ft. (1 m) tall, the bark whitish and scaling off. *Leaves* opposite, lance-shaped, about ³/₄–2 in. (20–50 mm) long, often narrowly tapering to a point at the tip. *Flowers* orange to purplish red, about 1¹/₄–2 in. (30–50 mm) long, with the corolla irregularly funnel-shaped and 2-lipped, the upper lip notched, the lower lip 3-lobed, and with 2 stamens. *Fruit* of flattened capsules about ³/₄ in. (20 mm) long. This is one of our most conspicuous shrubs but is often heavily browsed by livestock.

Range and Habitat: New Mexico and Arizona to Mexico. Usually found on dry, often gravelly or rocky slopes or mesas in southwestern New Mexico; 4,000–4,500 ft.

Key Characters: Desert honeysuckle may be identified by the shrubby condition, the whitish scaly bark, and the showy, honeysucklelike flowers.

308. Spreading dyschoriste   *Dyschoriste decumbens*   Acanthus family

Simple or branched perennial, the stems often spreading to prostrate, to about 12 in. (30 cm) long. *Leaves* opposite, oblong or broadest above the middle, blunt to pointed at the tip. *Flowers* irregularly funnel-shaped, purplish, about ³/₄ in. (20 mm) long and ⁵/₈–³/₄ in. (15–20 mm) wide at the top, the lobes flattened or notched at the tip, the calyx lobes slender. *Fruit* of narrowly oblong capsules with 2–4 seeds.

Range and Habitat: New Mexico and southern Arizona to Mexico. In open or brushy areas on plains and dry slopes in southern New Mexico; 4,500–5,000 ft.

Key Characters: Spreading dyschoriste is distinguished by the low-spreading growth pattern, the opposite, nearly sessile leaves, and the conspicuous purplish flowers.

Related Species: The closely related snakeherb (*D. linearis*) differs in having narrower leaves and corolla lobes rounded or notched at the tip.

309. Smooth bouvardia   *Bouvardia glaberrima*   Madder family

Perennial, the stems woody at the base, to about 3 ft. (1 m) tall. *Leaves* in whorls of 3 or 4 or sometimes opposite, 1–3¹/₄ in. (25–80 mm) long, the margins without teeth. *Flowers* red to pink or white, tubelike, ³/₄–1¹/₄ in. (20–30 mm) long, with 4 lobes ¹/₈ in. (2–3 mm) long at the top, the 4 sepals awl-shaped. *Fruit* of short 2-lobed capsules. This is a lovely little shrub, the flowers somewhat like those of the honeysuckle.

Range and Habitat: New Mexico to Arizona and Mexico. Usually found on dry, exposed slopes in southern New Mexico; 4,500–9,000 ft.

Key Characters: Smooth bouvardia is characterized by the somewhat shrubby nature, by the whorls of 3 or 4 leaves, and by the tubelike conspicuous flowers.

Related Species: The closely related scarlet bouvardia (*B. ternifolia*) differs in having the older bark that is grayish or whitish instead of brownish and leaves with short hairs on the upper surface.

Stenandrium barbatum

Anisacanthus thurberi

Dyschoriste decumbens

Bouvardia glaberrima

310. **Needleleaf bluets** *Hedyotis acerosa* Madder family

Perennial herb, the stems much-branched, somewhat woody at the base, to about 10 in. (25 cm) tall. *Leaves* whorled, with 3 or 4 leaves in each whorl, or sometimes opposite, needle-shaped, about ¼–⅜ in. (6–10 mm) long. *Flowers* white to pink or bluish, about ⅜ in. (10 mm) long, with a slender tube and 4 oval lobes projecting at right angles at the top, the flowers hairy within. *Fruit* of small capsules about ⅛ in. (3 mm) in diameter, the seeds shallowly cup-shaped.

Range and Habitat: Texas to New Mexico and Mexico. Usually found in sandy or rocky areas of central and southeastern New Mexico; 3,500–4,500 ft.

Key Characters: Needleleaf bluets is easily distinguished by the much-branched, clustered stems and stiff, needle-shaped leaves.

311. **Dwarf bluets** *Hedyotis humifusa* Madder family

Much-branched annual, the stems often spreading, to 4 in. (10 cm) long, with short, gland-tipped hairs. *Leaves* opposite, linear, sometimes broader toward the tip, to about ⅝ in. (15 mm) long and ⅛ in. (3 mm) wide, tipped with a rigid point. *Flowers* white to pink or purple, in the axils of leaves and branches, showy, funnel-shaped, ¼–⁵⁄₁₆ in. (6–8 mm) long, the sepals about half as long. *Fruit* of small capsules less than ⅛ in. (2–3 mm) in diameter, covered with small bumps.

Range and Habitat: Western Texas and eastern New Mexico. Typically found in sandy soils of plains, prairies, and dunes in eastern New Mexico; 3,500–4,000 ft.

Key Characters: Dwarf bluets can be recognized by the stems with short gland-tipped hairs, the funnel-shaped showy flowers, and the fruits covered with small bumps.

312. **Desert innocence** *Hedyotis rubra* Madder family

Perennial herb, stems clustered, to 4 in. (10 cm) tall. *Leaves* opposite or in basal clusters, stiff, linear to narrowly lance-shaped. *Flowers* deep rose pink or, rarely, white, with a slender tube ¾–1¼ in. (20–30 mm) long and 4 lobes projecting at right angles at the top, the flower about ⅜ in. (10 mm) wide, with 4 purplish stamens. *Fruit* of small 2-lobed capsules, usually nodding. This is a very pretty little desert plant, among the smallest members of the genus.

Range and Habitat: New Mexico and Arizona to Mexico. Found on dry, sandy plains and slopes throughout New Mexico; 4,000–6,500 ft.

Key Characters: Desert innocence is distinguished by the short, tufted stems with stiffish, erect leaves and conspicuous, long-tubed deep pink flowers.

313. **Blackbead elder** *Sambucus melanocarpa* Honeysuckle family

Shrub, the stems to about 10 ft. (3 m) tall, the young branches hairy. *Leaves* opposite, pinnately compound, the 5 or 7 leaflets lance-shaped to oval, about 2–6 in. (5–15 cm) long, hairy on the lower surface, long-pointed at the tip, the margins toothed. *Flowers* in dense, somewhat pyramid-shaped clusters, with 3–5 white petals, and with 5 stamens attached at the base of the petals. *Fruit* berrylike, black at maturity, about ¼ in. (5–6 mm) in diameter.

Range and Habitat: British Columbia to New Mexico and California. Found on moist slopes, often near streams in northern New Mexico; 7,500–10,000 ft.

Key Characters: Blackbead elder is distinguished by the pinnately compound leaves with leaflets hairy beneath, the large clusters of white flowers, and by the black berries.

Related Species: The Mexican elder (*S. mexicanus*) differs in having stems as tall as 33 ft. (10 m) and flowers in flat-topped clusters.

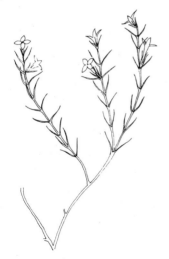

Hedyotis acerosa

Hedyotis humifusa

Hedyotis rubra

Sambucus melanocarpa

314. **Rocky Mountain red elder**   *Sambucus microbotrys*   Honeysuckle family

Shrub, the stems to about 6 ft. (2 m) tall. *Leaves* opposite, pinnately compound, the 5 or 7 leaflets broadly lance-shaped, mostly 2³/₈–4³/₄ in. (6–12 cm) long, without hairs, rounded at the base, pointed at the tip, the margins coarsely toothed. *Flowers* in dense, somewhat pyramid-shaped clusters, with 3–5 pale yellow petals, and with 5 stamens attached at the base of the petals. *Fruit* berrylike, bright red, about ⁵/₁₆ in. (5 mm) in diameter.

Range and Habitat: Wyoming to New Mexico, westward to California. Usually in scattered populations in moist woods in the mountains of northern, central, south-central, and western New Mexico; 8,000–12,000 ft.

Key Characters: Rocky Mountain red elder can be identified by the pinnately compound leaves with smooth, coarsely toothed leaflets, the large clusters of pale yellow flowers, and the bright red berries.

315. **Roundleaf snowberry**   *Symphoricarpos rotundifolius*   Honeysuckle family

Erect to spreading shrub, to about 3 ft. (1 m) or more tall, the young twigs densely hairy. *Leaves* opposite, oval or nearly round, mostly ³/₈–1¹/₄ in. (10–30 mm) long, bluntly pointed or rounded at the tip, short-petioled with short hairs on the upper surface and long, soft hairs beneath, the margins usually without teeth. *Flowers* in small axillary clusters, pink, narrowly funnel-shaped, about ³/₈ in. (10 mm) long, the lobes with a fringe of marginal hairs. *Fruit* berrylike, ovoid or ellipsoid, white, about ³/₈ in. (10 mm) long.

Range and Habitat: Colorado to New Mexico and Arizona. Usually associated with rocky slopes in the mountains throughout all except the eastern part of New Mexico; 7,000–10,000 ft.

Key Characters: Roundleaf snowberry is distinguished by the often nearly round leaves, the lobes of the corolla with a fringe of marginal hairs, and the densely hairy young twigs.

Related Species: The white snowberry (*S. albus*) differs in having the young twigs with short, curved hairs, the flowers bell-shaped and not more than ¹/₄ in. (6 mm) long, and the leaves often with wavy margins.

316. **Utah snowberry**   *Symphoricarpos utahensis*   Honeysuckle family

Much-branched shrub, to about 6 ft. (2 m) tall. *Leaves* opposite, oval, mostly ³/₄–1¹/₂ in. (2–4 cm) long, acutely or bluntly pointed at the tip, with very short hairs on both surfaces, short-petioled, the margins usually without teeth. *Flowers* in small axillary clusters, pinkish, narrowly funnel-shaped, about ³/₈–¹/₂ in. (8–12 mm) long, hairy within. *Fruit* berrylike, ellipsoid, white, about ³/₈ in. (8–10 mm) long. This plant is potentially a good ornamental shrub and the fruits are eaten by birds.

Range and Habitat: Wyoming to New Mexico, westward to Utah and Arizona. Usually found in canyons and on slopes in the mountains from north-central to south-central New Mexico; 7,000–9,000 ft.

Key Characters: Utah snowberry may be recognized by the much-branched shrubby habit, the oval leaves, and the pink funnel-shaped flowers.

Related Species: The closely related *S. palmeri* differs in having trailing rather than erect branches and lower leaf surfaces much paler than the upper surfaces.

Sambucus microbotrys

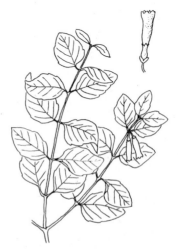

Symphoricarpos rotundifolius

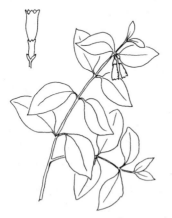

Symphoricarpos utahensis

317. **Western white-flowered honeysuckle** *Lonicera albiflora* Honeysuckle family

Woody vine or shrub with shreddy bark, the stems often 6–9 ft. (2–3 m) long. *Leaves* opposite, broadly oval to nearly round, without teeth or lobes, mostly ⁵/₈–1¹/₄ in. (15–30 mm) long, rounded or somewhat pointed at the tip, smooth or nearly so on both surfaces (a variety of this species, var. *dumosa,* has hairy leaves), sometimes the upper pair of leaves united at the base. *Flowers* in terminal clusters, whitish to yellowish, ³/₈–³/₄ in. (10–20 mm) long, funnel-shaped but strongly 2-lipped, the lower lip often somewhat recurved. *Fruit* berrylike, globe-shaped, hairy, usually ¹/₄–³/₈ in. (6–10 mm) long.
Range and Habitat: Oklahoma to Arizona, southward to northern Mexico. Usually found on rocky mountain slopes, in canyons, or near streams in southern New Mexico; 6,000–9,000 ft.
Key Characters: Western white-flowered honeysuckle is distinguished by the shreddy barked stems, the whitish or yellowish, strongly 2-lipped flowers, and the globelike, hairy fruit.

318. **Arizona honeysuckle** *Lonicera arizonica* Honeysuckle family

Woody vine, with shreddy bark. *Leaves* opposite, without teeth or lobes, oval to elliptic, mostly 2–2³/₈ in. (5–6 cm) long, pointed to rounded at the tip, the upper pairs of leaves sessile and united at the base, thus the stem appears to pass through the leaf. *Flowers* in small terminal clusters, the corolla narrowly funnel-shaped, reddish to orange, mostly ³/₄–1⁵/₈ in. (20–35 mm) long. *Fruit* berrylike, red, globose. This plant is one of our most spectacular shrubs in flower and is worthy of cultivation.
Range and Habitat: Western Texas to southern Utah and Arizona. Usually associated with open coniferous forests in the mountains of south-central and western New Mexico; 6,500–9,000 ft.
Key Characters: Arizona honeysuckle is distinguished by the upper pairs of leaves united at the base and the reddish to orange trumpetlike flowers in small clusters at the ends of the branches.

319. **Rocky Mountain valerian** *Valeriana capitata* Valerian family

Perennial herb, the stems erect, mostly 6–16 in. (15–40 cm) tall, usually smooth. *Leaves* opposite, or in basal clusters, the lower leaves broadest above the middle, long-petioled, usually without teeth, the upper leaves sessile, in 2–4 pairs, usually with 2–4 lobes on each side. *Flowers* in dense clusters at the top of the stem, white to pink, the corolla funnel-shaped, about ³/₁₆–¹/₄ in. (4–7 mm) long. *Fruit* achenelike, about ³/₁₆ in. (4 mm) long, crowned by a series of bristles. Although attractive in the field, these plants, when dried, exhibit a persistent unpleasant odor.
Range and Habitat: Wyoming to New Mexico and Arizona. Usually found in partial shade of damp woods in mountains from north-central to south-central and western New Mexico; 7,000–9,500 ft.
Key Characters: Rocky Mountain valerian may be identified by the erect, smooth stems with 2–4 pairs of lobed stem leaves and the dense clusters of small flowers at the summit of the stem.
Related Species: Close relatives include Texas valerian (*V. texana*), which differs in having yellowish flowers and stem leaves without lobes, and Arizona valerian (*V. arizonica*), which differs in having a much larger corolla and basal leaves that are mostly elliptic to nearly round.

Lonicera albiflora

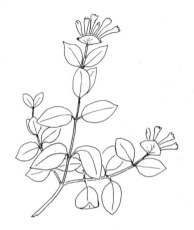

Lonicera arizonica

Valeriana capitata

320. **Buffalo gourd** *Cucurbita foetidissima* Melon family

Perennial herbaceous vine, the stems prostrate, harshly pubescent, with branched tendrils opposite the leaves. *Leaves* coarse, petioled, roughly triangular, with shallow angled lobes, flattened or notched at the base, 4–10 in. (10–25 cm) long, ill-smelling. *Flowers* unisexual, large, solitary, the staminate (male) flowers yellow, with 3 stamens, the pistillate (female) flowers yellow, ridged, harshly pubescent, the corolla mostly 3¹/₈–6 in. (8–15 cm) long. *Fruit* globe-shaped, about 2¹/₂–4 in. (5–10 cm) in diameter, smooth, striped or mottled in different shades of green. This plant is rapidly spreading in roadside areas throughout the Southwest.

Range and Habitat: Western Missouri to California, southward to Mexico. Usually found on open plains or in waste ground throughout New Mexico; 4,000–6,500 ft.

Key Characters: Buffalo gourd is distinguished by the harshly pubescent, ill-smelling stems and leaves, the large, coarse, roughly triangular leaves, and the conspicuous yellow flowers.

321. **Bigroot cucumber** *Marah gilensis* Melon family

Perennial herbaceous vine, the stems climbing, from large roots, with tendrils opposite the leaves. *Leaves* palmately divided into triangular lobes. *Flowers* unisexual, greenish white, 5- or 6-lobed, the staminate (male) flowers in clusters and with 2 or 3 stamens having filaments united and the anthers spreading horizontally, the pistillate (female) flowers usually solitary. *Fruit* berrylike, ³/₄–1¹/₄ in. (20–30 mm) in diameter at maturity, rounded, covered with soft spines.

Range and Habitat: New Mexico and Arizona. Usually associated with sandy soils near streams, often in shaded areas in southwestern New Mexico; 4,000–5,000 ft.

Key Characters: Bigroot cucumber is distinguished by the conspicuous leaves with usually 5 palmately arranged, triangular lobes, the greenish white flowers, and the spiny fruit.

322. **Cupleaf Venus's looking glass** *Triodanis perfoliata* Bluebell family

Slender annual, the stems mostly 6–32 in. (15–80 cm) tall, stiffly hairy. *Leaves* alternate, triangular to nearly round, about ³/₈–³/₄ in. (10–20 mm) wide, usually the leaf base clasping the stem, the margins stiffly hairy and with small teeth. *Flowers* in the axils of the upper leaflike bracts, those at the lower nodes often remaining closed and smaller than the expanded upper flowers, the sepals ¹/₄–⁵/₁₆ in. (5–8 mm) long, the corolla bluish, 5-lobed, ³/₈–¹/₂ in. (10–12 mm) wide. *Fruit* a capsule about ¹/₄–³/₈ in. (5–10 mm) long, with brownish, nearly smooth seeds.

Range and Habitat: Widespread in the Western Hemisphere. Usually found in disturbed areas but could be nearly anywhere in New Mexico; 5,000–7,500 ft.

Key Characters: Cupleaf Venus's looking glass is distinguished by the broadly triangular or nearly round, clasping leaves and the blue flowers in the axils of leaflike bracts.

323. **Roughstem Venus's looking glass** *Triodanis biflora* Bluebell family

Slender annual, the stems mostly 6–24 in. (15–60 cm) tall, with stiff, backward-pointing hairs. *Leaves* alternate, sessile, lance-shaped to ovate or oblong, to about 1¹/₄ in. (30 mm) long and ³/₈ in. (10 mm) wide, the margins hairy, sometimes with small teeth. *Flowers* 1 or 2 in the axils of several leaflike bracts, some of the flowers remaining closed and smaller than the expanded flowers, the calyx of open flowers with 4 or 5 narrowly lance-shaped lobes ¹/₁₆ in. (1–2 mm) long, the corolla blue, 5-lobed, about ⁵/₈ in. (15 mm) wide. *Fruit* a capsule, ¹/₄–³/₈ in. (6–10 mm) long, with smooth, shiny seeds.

Range and Habitat: Widespread in North America. Usually found in plains, prairies, or open fields in southern New Mexico; 4,000–5,000 ft.

Key Characters: This plant is characterized by the slender, rough, hairy stems, the hairy-margined leaves, the two kinds of flowers, and the smooth, shiny seeds.

Related Species: The similar *T. holzingeri* differs in that the leaves are broader above the middle, the calyx lobes are ¹/₈–¹/₄ in. (4–6 mm) long, and the seeds are not smooth.

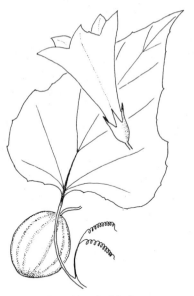

Cucurbita foetidissima

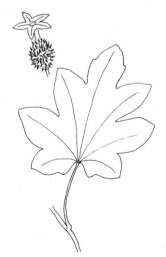

Marah gilensis

Triodanis perfoliata

Triodanis biflora

324. Small-flowered wire-lettuce   *Stephanomeria pauciflora*   Sunflower family

Perennial herb, the stems to 20 in. (50 cm) tall, stiffly branched. *Leaves* alternate, linear or narrowly lance-shaped, mostly smooth, the lower ones sharply pinnately lobed, the upper leaves becoming gradually smaller upward. *Flower heads* pinkish, the flowers all raylike, the flower head bracts in 2 series, with about 5 linear inner bracts, blunt at the tip and larger than the outer bracts. *Fruits* of slender achenes with 5 longitudinal ribs and a crown of brownish, feathery bristles.

Range and Habitat: Kansas and Texas to California. Mostly associated with dry, often sandy plains and slopes throughout New Mexico; 3,000–7,000 ft.

Key Characters: Small-flowered wire-lettuce is distinguished by the smooth stems and leaves, except for a tuft of hairs often at the base of the leaves, the margins of the lower leaves sharply pinnately lobed, and the pinkish flower heads.

Related Species: New Mexico wire-lettuce (*S. neomexicana*) differs in having unlobed leaves and fruits with a crown of white bristles.

325. Annual wire-lettuce   *Stephanomeria exigua*   Sunflower family

Branching annual, the stems to 20 in. (50 cm) tall. *Leaves* alternate, narrowly oblong in outline, coarsely toothed to lobed, to about 2 in. (5 cm) long, the upper ones gradually reduced in size upward. *Flower heads* with 5–8 flowers, scattered, pinkish, the subtending bracts of 2 lengths, the 4–6 inner ones much longer than the outer. *Fruits* of slender, 5-angled achenes crowned by feathery whitish or brownish bristles.

Range and Habitat: Wyoming to New Mexico, westward to California. Usually found on dry plains and slopes throughout New Mexico; 3,000–8,000 ft.

Key Characters: Annual wire-lettuce is distinguished by the coarsely toothed or lobed leaves, the pinkish flower heads with flowers all alike, and the fruits 5-angled and crowned with feathery bristles.

Related Species: Thurber wire-lettuce (*S. thurberi*) differs in being a perennial and having larger flower heads with 10–20 flowers.

326. Desert chicory   *Rafinesquia neomexicana*   Sunflower family

Branching annual, the stems to about 20 in. (50 cm) tall. *Leaves* alternate, pinnately sharply lobed or sometimes toothed, to about 3 in. (8 cm) long. *Flower heads* (including rays) 1½–2 in. (40–50 mm) wide, mostly whitish, dandelionlike, all flowers raylike, the subtending bracts in 2 series, the inner ones much longer than the outer, somewhat recurved, bracts, the rays white with purplish veins. *Fruits* of slender achenes, ½–⅝ in. (12–15 mm) long, tapering to a slender beak at the top and crowned by conspicuous, feathery bristles.

Range and Habitat: Western Texas to Utah and California. Usually scattered on dry mesas and slopes in north-central to southern New Mexico; 3,500–5,000 ft.

Key Characters: Desert chicory is distinguished by the dandelionlike leaves and flower heads, the white rays with purple veins, and the feathery bristles crowning the fruits.

Stephanomeria pauciflora

Stephanomeria exigua

Rafinesquia neomexicana

327. Wright desert dandelion   *Calycoseris wrightii*   Sunflower family

Slender, branching annual, the stems smooth except for conspicuous knobby glands on the upper part, to about 12 in. (30 cm) tall. *Leaves* alternate, to about 4 in. (10 cm) long, with several narrow lobes on each side. *Flower heads* (including rays) about 1⅝–2 in. (40–50 mm) wide, whitish or tinged with pink, dandelionlike, the subtending bracts linear, gradually tapering to a point at the tip, in 2 series, the inner bracts with whitish margins and much longer than the outer, often recurved bracts, the rays ⅝–¾ in. (15–20 mm) long, white with purplish pink markings beneath. *Fruits* of dark brown achenes with 5 or 6 roughened longitudinal ribs and crowned with numerous white, slender bristles.

Range and Habitat: Western Texas to California. Usually found on rocky slopes, plains, and mesas of southern New Mexico; 3,500–4,500 ft.

Key Characters: Wright desert dandelion can be identified by the smooth stems with conspicuous knobby glands on the upper part, the whitish rays with purplish pink markings, and the fruits with 5 or 6 roughened ribs.

328. Dandelion   *Taraxacum officinale*   Sunflower family

Perennial herb, without true stems but with slender, naked flower head stalks (scapes) to about 12 in. (30 cm) tall. *Leaves* basal, broader toward the tip, to about 12 in. (30 cm) long, with somewhat triangular lobes, the lobes often toothed. *Flower heads* (including rays) about ¾–2 in. (20–50 mm) wide, yellow, many-flowered, all raylike, the subtending bracts narrowly lance-shaped, usually reflexed (recurved). *Fruits* of slender, grayish or greenish achenes with roughened surfaces near the tips and tapering to slender beaks at the top and crowned with numerous soft, slender bristles.

Range and Habitat: Cosmopolitan. Mostly found in open fields, lawns, and waste ground throughout New Mexico; 3,000–10,000 ft.

Key Characters: Common dandelion is distinguished by the leaves with somewhat triangular lobes and the conspicuous yellow flower heads on naked flowering stalks.

Related Species: All species of *Taraxacum* are rather closely related, differing primarily in such characters as the presence of wings on the margins of the petioles, arrangement of the subtending bracts of the flower heads, and fruit color.

329. Smooth mountain dandelion   *Agoseris glauca*   Sunflower family

Smooth perennial herb, without true stems but with naked flower head stalks mostly 4–20 in. (10–50 cm) tall. *Leaves* narrow and linear, or broadest above the middle and tapering to the base, to about 10 in. (25 cm) long and 1¼ in. (30 mm) wide, without teeth or sometimes shallowly lobed on the margins, bluntish at the tip. *Flower heads* yellow, dandelionlike, the bracts about ¾ in. (20 mm) long, lance-shaped, sometimes purplish. *Fruits* of longitudinally ribbed achenes, narrowed into a beak at the top and crowned by numerous white, slender bristles.

Range and Habitat: Montana to California, southward to New Mexico and Nevada. Mostly found in mountain meadows in northern, central, and south-central New Mexico; 7,000–10,000 ft.

Key Characters: Smooth mountain dandelion may be recognized by the smooth stems and leaves, the lower leaves bluntish at the tip, the yellow dandelionlike flower heads, and the fruits tapering at the top to form a beaklike structure.

Related Species: The closely related *A. arizonica* differs in having the beak of the fruit at least as long as the body of the fruit and *A. heterophylla* differs in its annual habit and in the usually gland-tipped hairs on the subtending bracts of the flower heads.

Calycoseris wrightii

Taraxacum officinale

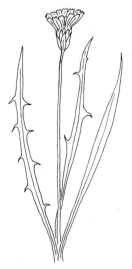

Agoseris glauca

330. **Fendler hawkweed**   *Hieracium fendleri*   Sunflower family

Perennial herb, the stems hairy, to 12 in. (30 cm) tall. *Basal leaves* broadest above the middle
and tapering to the base, to about 3¼ in. (80 mm) long and ¾ in. (18 mm) wide, the
margins with minute teeth or none, the *upper leaves* ranging from lance-shaped to very small
and linear. *Flower heads* (including rays) yellow, dandelionlike, in loose clusters, the
subtending bracts in 2 series, the inner bracts narrow and about ½–⅝ in. (12–14 mm) long.
Fruits of reddish or blackish achenes with 10 or more longitudinal ridges and a crown of
slender whitish or brownish bristles.
Range and Habitat: South Dakota to Mexico. Mostly associated with open or wooded slopes
in the mountains of New Mexico; 6,000–10,000 ft.
Key Characters: Fendler hawkweed is identified by the hairy stems, the lower leaves
unlobed and tapering to the base, the yellowish dandelionlike flower heads, and the reddish
fruits, especially when young.
Related Species: A variety of this species from the Mogollon Mountains differs in having the
inner flower head bracts only 10 mm long.

331. **Annual skeleton plant**   *Lygodesmia exigua*   Sunflower family

Smooth annual, the stems branching, to about 12 in. (30 cm) tall. *Leaves* mostly at the base
of the stem, usually broadest toward the tip, often lobed but sometimes with neither lobes
nor teeth, to about 1⅝ in. (40 mm) long, the upper leaves few, gradually reduced to bracts
toward the summit. *Flower heads* at the tips of short branches, the 4–6 flowers all raylike,
pinkish, the 4–6 inner subtending bracts narrowly linear or lance-shaped, the outer ones very
small. *Fruits* of slender, smooth achenes about 3 mm long, crowned with bright white slender
bristles.
Range and Habitat: Texas to Colorado, New Mexico, and California. Usually found in dry
ground in southern and western New Mexico; 4,000–6,000 ft.
Key Characters: Annual skeleton plant may be recognized by the basal leaves broadest
toward the tip and often lobed, and the upper leaves reduced to small bracts, the small pink
flower heads, and the bright white bristles crowning the fruits.

332. **Big-flowered skeleton plant**   *Lygodesmia grandiflora*   Sunflower family

Perennial herb, the stems to about 12 in. (30 cm) tall, marked with longitudinal lines. *Leaves*
narrow and grasslike, without teeth or lobes, to about 4 in. (10 cm) long, the upper ones
sometimes very small. *Flower heads* solitary on the flowering stalks, the inner series of
subtending bracts linear, about ¾ in. (20 mm) long, much larger than the outer ones, with
5–10 flowers, all raylike, the rays pinkish, very showy, about ¾ in. (20 mm) long. *Fruits* of
slender cylindrical achenes about ⅜ in. (10 mm) long, crowned with numerous brownish-
tinged, slender bristles.
Range and Habitat: Idaho to New Mexico and Arizona. Scattered on open, usually gravelly
plains and slopes in northwestern New Mexico; 5,000–6,500 ft.
Key Characters: Big-flowered skeleton plant may be identified by the narrow, often
grasslike basal leaves and the large, showy, pinkish flower heads with the outer subtending
bracts much shorter than the inner series.

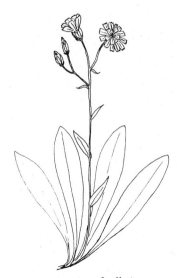

Hieracium fendleri

Lygodesmia exigua

Lygodesmia grandiflora

333. **Narrow-leaf microseris**   *Microseris linearifolia*   Sunflower family

Annuals without true stems, but with slender, naked flower head stalks to 24 in. (60 cm) tall. *Leaves* clustered at the base, elongate, narrow, without teeth or lobes or with a few narrow, spreading lobes on each side. *Flower heads* dandelionlike, the bracts in 2 or 3 series, 3/8–3/4 in. (1–2 cm) long, yellow but often purplish when dry. *Fruits* of cylindrical, slender achenes with about 10 longitudinal nerves, blunt at the top and crowned with 5 narrowly lance-shaped scales divided into 2 lobes and with a slender, bristlelike awn projecting between them.

Range and Habitat: Idaho and Washington to New Mexico, California, and Baja California. Usually found on dry, open plains and slopes, often in sandy soils, in western and southern New Mexico; 3,500–5,000 ft.

Key Characters: Narrow-leaf microseris is distinguished by the basal cluster of narrow leaves, unlobed or with a few narrow spreading lobes, the yellow flower heads on slender, naked stalks, and the fruits crowned with 5 narrowly lance-shaped scales.

334. **Lance-leaf microseris**   *Microseris cuspidata*   Sunflower family

Perennial herb, without true stems but with slender, naked stalks (scapes) 4–14 in. (10–35 cm) tall, bearing the flower heads. *Leaves* clustered at ground level, narrowly lance-shaped, mostly 4–7 1/2 in. (10–18 cm) long, with whitish hairs. *Flower heads* with the subtending bracts about 3/4 in. (20 mm) long, with pale margins, the tips narrowly tapering to a point, all flowers raylike, the rays yellow and with 5 teeth at the tip. *Fruits* of cylindrical achenes with 10 longitudinal ridges and crowned with numerous soft, white, slender bristles, each bristle flattened at the base.

Range and Habitat: Wisconsin to Montana, southward to Texas and New Mexico. Found mostly on open plains and slopes in sandy soils in northeastern New Mexico; 4,000–6,000 ft.

Key Characters: Lance-leaf microseris may be identified by the slender, elongate, unlobed leaves in a basal cluster, the yellowish dandelionlike flower heads on slender, naked stalks, and the fruits crowned with soft bristles which are flattened at the base.

335. **Fendler desert dandelion**   *Malacothrix fendleri*   Sunflower family

Annual, the stems smooth, somewhat branched, to about 12 in. (30 cm) tall. *Leaves* mostly glabrous, with coarse, wavy teeth or lobes, roughly oblong in outline, the basal leaves to 3 1/8 in. (8 cm) long, often with woolly hairs at the base, the upper leaves smaller than the basal ones, sometimes without teeth or lobes. *Flower heads* (including rays) 3/4–1 1/8 in. (2–3 cm) wide, all flowers raylike as in dandelions, the rays yellow but tinged with purple beneath, 1/4–3/8 in. (7–10 mm) long, the subtending bracts with an outer series much shorter than the thinner, membranelike, purplish-tipped inner series. *Fruits* of cylindrical achenes with 15 prominent longitudinal ribs and crowned with soft, slender bristles.

Range and Habitat: Western Texas to southern Arizona and northern Mexico. Occurring on sandy or rocky slopes, flats, or plains; 4,000–6,000 ft.

Key Characters: Fendler desert dandelion is characterized by the basal cluster of usually wavy-toothed or lobed leaves and reduced upper leaves, the dandelionlike yellow flower heads, and the 15-ribbed fruits.

Related Species: The closely related *M. sonchoides* differs mostly in having longer rays, 3/5–1/2 in. (10–12 mm) long and fruits with only 5 prominent longitudinal ribs.

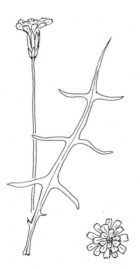

Microseris linearifolia

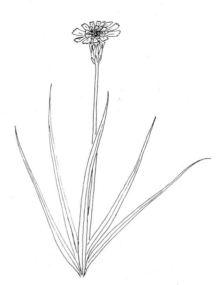

Microseris cuspidata

Malacothrix fendleri

336. **Dwarf dandelion**   *Krigia biflora*   Sunflower family

Perennial herb, the stems forked above, smooth, to about 24 in. (60 cm) tall. *Leaves* mostly basal, broadest above the middle and tapering to winged petioles, the few upper leaves much smaller than the basal ones, clasping the stem. *Flower heads* (including rays) 1/2–5/8 in. (12–15 mm) wide, on long stalks, all flowers raylike as in dandelions, yellow to orange, the subtending bracts often reflexed in age. *Fruits* of short, slender achenes with numerous longitudinal ribs and crowned with 10–15 narrow, blunt scales and numerous slender bristles.
Range and Habitat: Widespread in North America except southeastern, south-central, and extreme western areas. Occasionally found in meadows, prairies, and open woods in New Mexico; 7,000–8,000 ft.
Key Characters: Dwarf dandelion is distinguished by the dandelionlike yellow or orange heads and the clasping stem leaves.

337. **Dwarf desert-holly**   *Perezia nana*   Sunflower family

Perennial herb, the stems sometimes branched, to about 8 in. (20 cm) tall. *Leaves* often nearly round, leathery, to about 2 in. (5 cm) long, conspicuously veined, coarsely spiny-toothed and hollylike. *Flower heads* solitary on stems and branches, about 5/8 in. (15 mm) wide, the flowers all with 2-lipped purplish corollas, the subtending bracts woolly on the margins at the base. *Fruits* of slender achenes crowned with numerous slender bristles. The common name describes this plant perfectly.
Range and Habitat: Western Texas to Arizona and northern Mexico. Usually found on dry plains, flats, or slopes throughout all but northern New Mexico; 3,000–6,000 ft.
Key Characters: Dwarf desert-holly may be recognized by the leathery, hollylike leaves with a conspicuous network of veins.

338. **Dwarf pussytoes**   *Antennaria rosulata*   Sunflower family

Matted perennial herb, the stems very short, to 3/8 in. (1 cm) tall, mostly shorter than the basal cluster of leaves. *Leaves* broadest above the middle and tapering to the base, blunt or pointed at the tip, 1/4–3/8 in. (6–10 mm) long, silvery hairs on both surfaces. *Flower heads* without rays, projecting only slightly above the leaves, sometimes 2 or 3 in a cluster, about 1/4 in. (6–7 mm) wide, the subtending bracts rounded or pointed at the tip, the inner ones whitish at the tip. *Fruits* of smooth, slender achenes, crowned with a ring of slender bristles.
Range and Habitat: Colorado and Utah to New Mexico and Arizona. Found in open meadows and slopes in the mountains from north-central to south-central New Mexico; 6,000–9,000 ft.
Key Characters: Dwarf pussytoes is distinguished by the matlike cluster of silvery-haired leaves surrounding small, rounded flower heads with papery bracts.
Related Species: The closely related *A. rosea* may also have a matted growth form but the stems project conspicuously above the basal leaf cluster.

339. **Cottony everlasting**   *Gnaphalium chilense*   Sunflower family

Annual or biennial, usually aromatic herb, the stems erect, loosely woolly, to 24 in. (60 cm) tall. *Leaves* usually broadest above the middle and tapering to the somewhat clasping base, woolly, to about 2 in. (50 mm) long and 3/8 in. (10 mm) wide. *Flower heads* in compact clusters, the subtending bracts papery and whitish to yellowish, the rays absent. These plants are more pleasing in appearance from a distance than at close range.
Range and Habitat: Montana, Idaho, and Washington to Texas, Arizona, and California. Scattered in damp ground throughout New Mexico; 4,000–7,000 ft.
Key Characters: Cottony everlasting is distinguished by the loosely woolly stems and leaves, the dense clusters of small, rayless flower heads, and the conspicuous papery flower head bracts.
Related Species: The closest relatives of this species include *G. macounii* and *G. pringlei,* with greenish, nonwoolly leaves, and *G. wrightii,* with leaf bases never clasping the stem.

Krigia biflora

Perezia nana

Antennaria rosulata

Gnaphalium chilense

340. Snakeweed   *Gutierrezia sarothrae*   Sunflower family

Perennial herb, sometimes woody at the base, the stems mostly erect, to about 24 in. (60 cm) tall, with resinous dots on the surface. *Leaves* alternate, often with clusters of smaller leaves in the leaf axils, linear, gland-dotted, to about 2³/₄ in. (7 cm) long and ¹/₈ in. (1–3 mm) wide, the margins not toothed. *Flower heads* (including rays) ¹/₄–¹/₂ in. (6–12 mm) wide, numerous, the subtending bracts yellowish with greenish tips, with 4–6 yellow rays ¹/₈–³/₁₆ in. (2–5 mm) long, and with 4 or 5 disk flowers. *Fruits* of hairy achenes crowned with several scales. This plant is a common invader after habitats have been disturbed, as in overgrazing, and often occurs in dense populations.

Range and Habitat: Manitoba and Minnesota to California, southward to Mexico. Common on dry plains and slopes in heavier soils throughout New Mexico; 3,000–8,000 ft.

Key Characters: Snakeweed is distinguished by the slender, gland-dotted leaves, the clusters of axillary leaves, and the numerous small yellow flower heads with only 4–6 rays.

Related Species: The closest relative of this species is the small-headed snakeweed (*G. microcephala*), which differs in having smaller flower heads, 1 or 2 rays, and 1–3 disk flowers.

341. Golden aster   *Chrysopsis villosa*   Sunflower family

Perennial herb, the stems leafy, mostly 4–24 in. (10–60 cm) tall, densely hairy. *Leaves* narrow and linear or broadest above the middle and tapering to the base, densely hairy, to 2³/₈ in. (60 mm) long, the lower ones petioled, the margins without teeth or lobes. *Flower heads* (including rays) ³/₄–1³/₈ in. (20–35 mm) wide, in loose or dense clusters, the subtending bracts linear or awl-shaped, with stiff hairs, the rays yellow, ⁵/₁₆–¹/₂ in. (7–12 mm) long. *Fruits* of hairy achenes crowned with brownish bristles.

Range and Habitat: Minnesota to Washington, southward to Texas and Arizona. Usually found on dry, rocky, or sandy slopes throughout New Mexico; 5,000–8,000 ft.

Key Characters: Golden aster is distinguished by the densely hairy stems and leaves and the clusters of yellow flower heads.

Related Species: Several similar but difficult-to-separate species occur in New Mexico; these tend to bloom later in the growing season. The closest relative is the sticky golden aster (*C. viscida*), which has numerous viscid, glandular hairs.

342. Spinyleaf goldenweed   *Haplopappus spinulosus*   Sunflower family

Perennial herb, the stems leafy, branching, 8–24 in. (20–60 cm) tall. *Leaves* alternate, sometimes woolly, narrow, broadest above the middle and tapering to the base, to about 2³/₈ in. (6 cm) long and ³/₈ in. (10 mm) wide, with bristle-tipped teeth or lobes. *Flower heads* (including rays) 1–1¹/₄ in. (25–30 mm) wide, borne at the tips of the branches, the subtending bracts in several series, linear, usually bristle-tipped, greenish in the center, the rays yellow, ⁵/₁₆–³/₈ in. (8–10 mm) long. *Fruits* of hairy achenes crowned with numerous slender, brownish bristles.

Range and Habitat: Southern Canada to Texas, New Mexico, Arizona, and Mexico. Usually found on dry plains, prairies, and open slopes throughout New Mexico; 3,500–6,500 ft.

Key Characters: Spinyleaf goldenweed is distinguished by the leaves with spiny-tipped teeth or lobes, the usually many yellow-rayed flower heads, and the green-centered flower head bracts.

Related Species: Several varieties of this species occur in New Mexico, differing from the typical form in one or more relatively small features. A close relative, *H. gracilis*, differs in being annual or biennial and in having a conspicuous green spot at the tip of the subtending bracts.

Gutierrezia sarothrae

Chrysopsis villosa

Haplopappus spinulosus

343. **Naked-headed spreading fleabane**   *Erigeron nudiflorus*   Sunflower family

Biennial herb, the stems to 20 in. (50 cm) tall, leafy, terminating in a naked flower head stalk at the summit, the base forming elongate, leafy creeping laterals (stolons) late in the growing season. *Leaves* narrow, tapering to the base from near the tip, densely hairy, ³/₈–³/₄ in. (10–20 mm) long, the margins with or without teeth. *Flower heads* (including rays) ¹/₂–1 in. (12–25 mm) wide, with usually 75–100 white or pinkish rays about ³/₁₆–³/₈ in. (5–10 mm) long. *Fruits* of sparsely hairy achenes crowned with an outer series of scales and an inner series of slender bristles. This plant often forms large populations but individually is not among the most conspicuous of our spring wildflowers.

Range and Habitat: Kansas to Nevada, southward to Texas and Arizona. Most common on dry slopes, often in sandy soils, from north-central and northwestern to south-central and southwestern New Mexico; 5,500–8,000 ft.

Key Characters: Naked-headed spreading fleabane is distinguished by the stout, naked flower head stalks, the whitish or pinkish rays, and the leafy, creeping lateral branches produced after midseason.

Related Species: The closely related spreading fleabane (*E. divergens*) differs in lacking the late-season lateral creeping branches.

344. **Bigelow fleabane**   *Erigeron bigelovii*   Sunflower family

Perennial herb, the stems erect, leafy, 4–8 in. (10–20 cm) tall, with numerous branches from the base. *Leaves* alternate, narrow, broadest toward the tip or the upper ones sometimes linear, to about 1 in. (25 mm) long, usually petioled. *Flower heads* (including rays) ⁵/₈–³/₄ in. (15–20 mm) wide, scattered on the branches, the subtending bracts stiffly lance-shaped and tapering to a point, the usually 40–50 purplish rays about ¹/₄ in. (6 mm) long. *Fruits* of achenes crowned by an outer series of narrowly lance-shaped scales and an inner series of threadlike bristles. This is one of the earliest-blooming members of the sunflower family in our area.

Range and Habitat: Texas and New Mexico to Mexico. Locally abundant in valleys and along streams, often in silty soils, in southeastern New Mexico; 3,000–4,000 ft.

Key Characters: Bigelow fleabane is distinguished by the 40–50 very narrow purplish rays, the branches from the base of the plant, and the narrow petioled leaves, often broadest toward the tip.

345. **Pretty fleabane**   *Erigeron pulcherrimus*   Sunflower family

Perennial herb, the stems erect, mostly 2–14 in. (5–35 cm) tall. *Leaves* alternate, the basal ones in tufts, narrowly linear or broadest toward the tip and tapering to the base, to about 2³/₄ in. (7 cm) long and less than ¹/₈ in. (1–2 mm) wide, the upper leaves much shorter than the basal ones. *Flower heads* (including rays) 1–2 in. (25–50 mm) wide, solitary on the stems, the subtending bracts in 3 or 4 series, long-pointed, with numerous segmented hairs, the 25–60 pink, white, or bluish rays about ³/₈–⁵/₈ in. (8–15 mm) long and ¹/₈ in. (2–4 mm) wide. *Fruits* of densely hairy achenes, with 2–5 longitudinal ridges and crowned with many slender bristles. This is our loveliest daisy fleabane, worthy of cultivation.

Range and Habitat: Wyoming to Colorado, Utah, and New Mexico. This plant is found on dry slopes in the foothills of northern New Mexico; 5,500–6,500 ft.

Key Characters: Pretty fleabane is distinguished by the short stems, the very slender leaves, and the large, very conspicuous flower heads, these often fully 2 in. (50 mm) wide.

Erigeron nudiflorus

Erigeron bigelovii

Erigeron pulcherrimus

346. **Common fleabane**   *Erigeron philadelphicus*   Sunflower family

Biennial herb, the stems to 39 in. (1 m) tall, with short offsets at the base. *Leaves* alternate, the basal ones broadest above the middle and tapering to the base, to 5⅞ in. (15 cm) long and 1¼ in. (30 mm) wide, the margins usually toothed, the upper leaves usually oblong, their bases rounded and often clasping the stem. *Flower heads* (including rays) ⅝–1⅜ in. (15–35 mm) wide, usually numerous, nodding before opening fully, the subtending bracts linear and often purplish, the rays very slender, 150–200 or more, white to pinkish or purplish, ¼–⅜ in. (5–10 mm) long. *Fruits* of sparsely hairy achenes with a pair of longitudinal ridges and crowned with a single series of threadlike bristles. This plant is one of the most noticeable of our spring flowers.
Range and Habitat: Much of North America except Mexico. Usually found in open fields and open areas in woods in all except eastern New Mexico; 6,000–8,500 ft.
Key Characters: Common fleabane is distinguished by the tall, robust stems with short offset branches at the base, the large basal leaves tapering to the base, and the conspicuous flower heads, often with 200 or more white to purplish rays and yellow centers.

347. **Bushy fleabane**   *Erigeron bellidiastrum*   Sunflower family

Annual or biennial herb, the stems usually much-branched, to about 20 in. (50 cm) tall, mostly with incurved hairs. *Leaves* narrow, linear or broadest toward the tip, rarely toothed. *Flower heads* (including rays) ½–¾ in. (12–18 mm) wide, numerous, the subtending bracts similar in length, with numerous glandular dots and small incurved hairs, the 30–70 very narrow, white to pinkish rays about ⅕–¼ in. (4–6 mm) long. *Fruits* of hairy achenes, with 2 longitudinal ridges and crowned with a single series of threadlike bristles. This little fleabane is locally abundant and relatively conspicuous when in large populations.
Range and Habitat: South Dakota to Oklahoma, Wyoming, Colorado, Utah, Nevada, and New Mexico. Usually found in sandy soils on open plains or hills throughout New Mexico; 5,000–8,000 ft.
Key Characters: Bushy fleabane is distinguished by the relatively short, much-branched stems, the short, incurved hairs on all parts, and the small flower heads with whitish or pinkish rays and yellowish centers.

348. **Small-flowered mountain aster**   *Machaeranthera parviflora*   Sunflower family

Annual, the stems erect, branching, mostly 8–20 in. (20–50 cm) tall. *Leaves* alternate, mostly ¼–⅝ in. (7–15 mm) long and less than ⅛ in. (1.0–2.5 mm) wide, pinnately divided into minute linear segments. *Flower heads* (including rays) about ½–⅝ in. (12–15 mm) wide, the subtending bracts green at the tip and whitish at the base, not reflexed, the rays purplish, about 3/16 in. (5 mm) long. *Fruits* of short, hairy achenes crowned with numerous threadlike bristles. This species is one of the few early-flowering asters in our area but continues to bloom until autumn.
Range and Habitat: Colorado and Utah to New Mexico and Arizona. Found usually in sandy soils on open plains, slopes, and mesas throughout New Mexico; 4,000–7,500 ft.
Key Characters: This aster is distinguished by the annual habit, the small, narrow leaves with tiny lobes, and the small, purple-rayed flower heads.

Erigeron philadelphicus

Erigeron bellidiastrum

Machaeranthera parviflora

349. **Bigelow aster**   *Machaeranthera bigelovii*   Sunflower family

Annual or biennial herb, the stems branching, to 39 in. (1 m) tall, with gland-tipped hairs in the upper part. *Leaves* mostly oblong or lance-shaped but sometimes with the broadest dimension above the middle and tapering to the base, about 2–4 in. (5–10 cm) long, the margins with a few teeth. *Flower heads* (including rays) 1–1½ in. (25–40 mm) wide, the subtending bracts slender, in several series, conspicuously green-tipped, mostly reflexed, the rays purplish, ⅓–⅗ in. (8–15 mm) long. *Fruits* of smooth or sparsely hairy achenes, crowned with numerous threadlike bristles at the top. This is our most conspicuous spring-blooming aster.

Range and Habitat: Colorado to New Mexico and Arizona. Found mostly in mountain meadows throughout New Mexico; 7,000–9,000 ft.

Key Characters: Bigelow aster is distinguished by the tall stems, the large leaves with few teeth, and the conspicuous flower heads with purplish rays and yellowish centers.

350. **Heartleaf arnica**   *Arnica cordifolia*   Sunflower family

Perennial herb, the stems erect, 8–16 in. (20–40 cm) tall. *Leaves* mostly opposite, the lower ones with blades to about 4 in. (10 cm) long and sometimes almost as wide, acutely pointed or blunt at the tip, notched or flattened at the base, the margins smooth or coarsely toothed, on petioles about as long as or longer than the blades, the upper leaves often sessile and lance- or egg-shaped and usually in not more than 3 pairs. *Flower heads* (including rays) 2–2½ in. (50–65 mm) wide, the subtending bracts with soft, spreading hairs, the rays yellow, ¾–1⅛ in. (20–30 mm) long, toothed at the tip. *Fruits* of hairy achenes about ¼ in. (7 mm) long, crowned with numerous feathery bristles.

Range and Habitat: Alaska to New Mexico and California. Scattered on protected or exposed, usually moist slopes in northern New Mexico; 8,000–10,000 ft.

Key Characters: Heartleaf arnica is distinguished by the opposite leaf arrangement, the lower leaves notched or flattened at the base and often coarsely toothed, and the large yellow flower heads.

351. **Bigtooth butterweed**   *Senecio eurypterus*   Sunflower family

Perennial herb, the stems mostly 6–16 in. (15–40 cm) tall. *Leaves* alternate, often woolly, broadest above the middle and tapering to a petioled base, to about 5½ in. (14 cm) long and 1 in. (25 mm) wide, the margins sharply toothed, the bases of the upper leaves somewhat clasping the stem. *Flower heads* (including rays) about 1¼–1⅜ in. (30–35 mm) wide, erect, several in a cluster at the summit of the stem, with about 13 subtending bracts and usually 13 yellow rays. *Fruits* of smooth achenes crowned with numerous very slender bristles.

Range and Habitat: Restricted to the mountains of central, western, and southern New Mexico; 7,000–9,000 ft.

Key Characters: Bigtooth butterweed is distinguished by the sharply toothed leaves which are broadest above the middle and tapering to the base and usually by the 13 yellow ray flowers.

Machaeranthera bigelovii

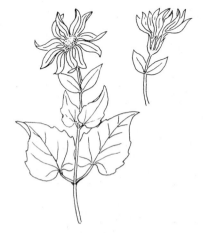

Arnica cordifolia

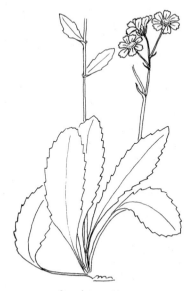

Senecio eurypterus

352. Wooton butterweed *Senecio wootonii* Sunflower family

Perennial herb, the stems erect, smooth, 8–20 in. (20–50 cm) tall. *Leaves* alternate, the basal leaves broadest above the middle and tapering to a slightly winged petiole, to 10 in. (25 cm) long, sometimes toothed, rounded at the tip, the stem leaves sessile and without teeth. *Flower heads* (including rays) about ³/₄–1 in. (20–25 mm) wide, erect, with about 13 subtending bracts, and 6–10 yellow rays about ¹/₄ in. (7 mm) long. *Fruits* of smooth achenes crowned with numerous very slender bristles. This plant flowers all summer.
Range and Habitat: Colorado to northern New Mexico. Usually found in open areas in dry or moist soils in the mountains throughout New Mexico; 6,000–9,000 ft.
Key Characters: Wooton butterweed is distinguished by the hairless stems and leaves, the basal leaves broadest above the middle, and the flower heads with 6–10 yellow rays and about 13 subtending bracts.

353. Cress-leaved butterweed *Senecio cardamine* Sunflower family

Perennial herb, the stems smooth, 4–14 in. (10–35 cm) tall. *Leaves* mostly at the base of the stem and often lying on the ground, slender-petioled, heart-shaped, notched at the base and pointed or rounded at the tip, to about 4 in. (10 cm) long, purplish on the lower surface, the upper leaves much reduced in size, their bases clasping the stem. *Flower heads* (including rays) ³/₄–1 in. (20–25 mm) wide, erect, in small clusters or solitary, the rays yellow, ¹/₄–⁵/₁₆ in. (6–8 mm) long. *Fruits* of smooth achenes crowned with numerous soft, slender bristles.
Range and Habitat: Open slopes in the Mogollon Mountains of southwestern New Mexico; 8,000–10,000 ft.
Key Characters: Cress-leaved butterweed is distinguished by the heart-shaped, wavy-toothed basal leaves having purplish pigment on the underside.

354. Western yarrow *Achillea lanulosa* Sunflower family

Perennial herb, the stems mostly 10–26 in. (25–65 cm) tall. *Leaves* alternate, mostly 2–4 in. (5–10 cm) long, finely divided into very slender spine-tipped segments, strongly aromatic. *Flower heads* (including rays) small, ⁵/₁₆–³/₈ in. (8–10 mm) wide, the subtending bracts blunt at the tip, yellowish brown on the margins, the 2–6 rays somewhat rounded, about ¹/₈ in. (3–4 mm) long, white or pinkish-tinged. *Fruits* of flattened, smooth achenes with thickish margins. This plant is valued for its reputed healing properties and has been used by certain Indian tribes in ceremonial functions.
Range and Habitat: Western Canada to New Mexico, California, and Mexico. Scattered or abundant in meadows or in wet ground in the mountains throughout most of New Mexico; 6,000–10,500 ft.
Key Characters: Western yarrow is distinguished by the numerous flower heads arranged in flattish clusters, small whitish or pinkish rays, and the pleasantly aromatic, finely divided leaves. (This plant is sometimes confused with Queen Anne's lace in the carrot family.)

Senecio wootonii

Senecio cardamine

Achillea lanulosa

355. **Woolly paperflower**   *Psilostrophe tagetina*   Sunflower family

Perennial herb, the stems hairy, to 20 in. (50 cm) tall. *Leaves* alternate, petioled, with long hairs, mostly broader above the middle and tapering to the base, or the upper ones sometimes linear, to about 4 in. (10 cm) long, the margins without teeth or sometimes pinnately lobed. *Flower heads* (including rays) 5/8–1 in. (15–25 mm) wide, the subtending bracts densely woolly, the 3–5 yellow rays about 3/16–3/8 in. (5–9 mm) long, shallowly lobed at the tip. *Fruits* of slender, nearly smooth achenes, crowned with several lance-shaped scales. The massed flower clusters make this plant a conspicuous element of both spring and summer flora. It is reputedly poisonous to sheep.

Range and Habitat: Western Texas to Utah, southward to northern Mexico. Found in several habitats on open plains, mesas, and slopes throughout New Mexico; 4,000–7,000 ft.

Key Characters: Woolly paperflower is distinguished by the compact, diffusely branched habit, the profusion of yellow flower heads with broad, shallowly lobed rays, which become persistent and papery in texture, and the usually woolly leaves and stems.

Related Species: The closely related *P. villosa* differs in having rays 1/8–3/16 in. (3–5 mm) long and deeply lobed at the tip, for about half the length of the rays.

356. **Barestem rubberweed**   *Hymenoxys acaulis*   Sunflower family

Perennial herb without true stems but with hairy flower head stalks to 8 in. (20 cm) tall. *Leaves* clustered at the base of the plant, usually moderately or densely hairy, narrow and linear or broadened toward the tip, to about 2 3/8 in. (60 mm) long and 1/8–3/16 in. (3–6 mm) wide, the margins without teeth. *Flower heads* (including rays) 3/4–1 5/8 in. (20–40 mm) wide, the subtending bracts hairy, nearly equal in length, the rays yellow, 1/4–5/8 in. (6–15 mm) long, toothed at the tip. *Fruits* of 5-angled, hairy achenes, crowned with 5–7 scales. This is a very handsome little plant.

Range and Habitat: Southern Canada to Texas and New Mexico. Usually in scattered clumps on rocky slopes and plains throughout New Mexico; 4,500–7,000 ft.

Key Characters: Barestem rubberweed is easily recognized by the conspicuous yellow-rayed flower heads in solitary arrangement at the top of each stalk and the leaves in dense clusters at the base.

Related Species: The very similar *H. scaposa* has leaves that are attached to an unbranched base, while the leaves of *H. acaulis* are attached to several short, spreading branches at ground level.

357. **Bitterweed**   *Hymenoxys odorata*   Sunflower family

Annual, the stems erect, much-branched, hairy, to about 20 in. (50 cm) tall. *Leaves* alternate, glandular-dotted, mostly 3/4–2 in. (20–50 mm) long, deeply divided into 3–5 narrow lobes. *Flower heads* (including rays) 5/8–1 in. (15–25 mm) wide, at the ends of the branches, the subtending bracts in 2 series, lance-shaped, united below the middle, glandular-dotted, the rays yellow, 3/16–3/8 in. (5–10 mm) long, toothed at the tip. *Fruits* of 5-angled, hairy achenes, crowned with 5–10 lance-shaped, slender-pointed scales. This plant is one of the earliest-blooming members of the sunflower family, tinting the slopes with splashes of yellow.

Range and Habitat: Kansas and Texas to California and Mexico. Often abundant on dry plains, hills, or valleys in New Mexico except in the extreme northern and northwestern areas; 3,500–6,000 ft.

Key Characters: Bitterweed is distinguished by the narrowly lobed, glandular-dotted leaves and usually by several to many rounded yellowish flower heads.

Related Species: This plant most closely resembles Richardson bitterweed (*H. richardsonii*), which differs in being perennial and having copious tufts of woolly hairs in the axils of the basal leaves.

Psilostrophe tagetina

Hymenoxys acaulis

Hymenoxys odorata

358. Rosy palafoxia   *Palafoxia rosea*   Sunflower family

Annual, the stems branched, to 24 in. (60 cm) tall. *Leaves* alternate, lance-shaped or oblong, finely hairy, with 3 main veins extending upward from the base, petioled, to about 3 1/8 in. (8 cm) long and 1 in. (25 mm) wide, the margins smooth or wavy. *Flower heads* 1/4–3/8 in. (7–10 mm) wide, without rays, solitary at the ends of glandular branches, with 8–12 subtending bracts broadest toward the tip, rose-colored, the corolla lobes of the disk flowers 1/8–3/16 in. (4–5 mm) long. *Fruits* of linear, tapering achenes crowned with several papery scales.

Range and Habitat: Wyoming to Texas and New Mexico. Usually found in sandy soils on the plains of eastern New Mexico; 4,000–5,000 ft.

Key Characters: Rosy palafoxia is distinguished by the flower heads without rays, the rose-colored subtending bracts, and sticky, glandular flowering branches.

359. **Small-headed sneezeweed**   *Helenium microcephalum*   Sunflower family

Annual or biennial herb, the stems erect, branched, mostly 20–32 in. (50–80 cm) tall. *Leaves* alternate, lance-shaped to elliptic, sessile, with the base extending a distance along the stem, 1 1/4–2 3/8 in. (30–60 mm) long, the margins with or without teeth. *Flower heads* (including rays) 5/16–3/8 in. (8–10 mm) wide, the subtending bracts slender, recurved, the rays yellow, inconspicuous, 1/8–1/4 in. (3–5 mm) long. *Fruits* of 4- or 5-angled achenes crowned with several oval scales.

Range and Habitat: Texas and New Mexico to Mexico. Found occasionally in moist soils in southeastern New Mexico; 3,000–4,000 ft.

Key Characters: Small-headed sneezeweed is distinguished by the relatively small flower heads with short rays, domed center, and recurved subtending bracts.

360. **Goldfields**   *Baeria chrysostoma*   Sunflower family

Low annual, the stems 4–10 in. (10–25 cm) tall, hairy, often branched. *Leaves* opposite, sessile, narrowly linear, pointed at the tip, somewhat clasping the stem at the base, 3/8–3/4 in. (10–20 mm) long. *Flower heads* (including rays) about 3/8–5/8 in. (9–15 mm) wide, the subtending bracts lance-shaped, pointed at the tip, the rays yellow, mostly 1/8–3/8 in. (4–10 mm) long. *Fruits* of slender, usually 4-angled achenes. Because of the small stems and flower heads, these plants are easily overlooked individually but are frequently so numerous as to form a spectacular golden yellow carpet over large areas of desert.

Range and Habitat: Nevada, New Mexico, and Arizona to Oregon, California, and Baja California. Scattered or abundant in dry, open plains and mesas of southwestern New Mexico; 4,000–5,000 ft.

Key Characters: Goldfields is distinguished by the low habit of growth, the slender leaves less than 1/8 in. (2 mm) wide, and the usually small flower heads.

361. **Plains bahia**   *Bahia oblongifolia*   Sunflower family

Perennial herb, the stems to about 8 in. (20 cm) tall. *Leaves* alternate, oblong to elliptic or often broadest above the middle and tapering to the base, sparsely hairy, 3/4–2 in. (20–50 mm) long and to 5/8 in. (15 mm) wide, the margins without teeth. *Flower heads* (including rays) 1–1 3/8 in. (25–35 mm) wide, on long stalks, the subtending bracts broadest toward the tip, the rays conspicuous, yellow, 5/16–1/2 in. (8–12 mm) long. *Fruits* of slender, tapering, 4-angled achenes crowned with 8–10 narrow scales.

Range and Habitat: Colorado and Utah to New Mexico and Arizona. Scattered locally on dry slopes and plains in northwestern New Mexico; 5,000–6,500 ft.

Key Characters: Plains bahia is distinguished by the low growth habit, the flowering head bracts broader above the middle, and the fruits 4-angled and crowned with a cluster of narrow scales.

Related Species: Similar species differ in the leaves either opposite or variously lobed or dissected.

Palafoxia rosea

Helenium microcephalum

Baeria chrysostoma

Bahia oblongifolia

362. **Rocky Mountain zinnia**   *Zinnia grandiflora*   Sunflower family

Perennial herb, the stems branching, to about 8 in. (20 cm) tall. *Leaves* opposite, sessile, linear to narrowly lance-shaped or awllike, to 1 in. (25 mm) long and $^1/_8$ in. (3 mm) wide, the margins without teeth. *Flower heads* (including rays) 1–2 in. (25–55 mm) wide, the subtending bracts rounded at the tip, the rays bright yellow, $^3/_8$–$^3/_4$ in. (10–20 mm) long and $^3/_8$–$^5/_8$ in. (10–15 mm) wide, becoming papery and remaining attached for several months. *Fruits* compressed and angled. This plant is potentially useful as a desert landscape item.

Range and Habitat: Texas to Colorado, New Mexico, and Arizona. Locally abundant on dry slopes and plains throughout New Mexico; 3,000–6,500 ft.

Key Characters: Rocky Mountain zinnia is distinguished by its low bushy shape, the bright yellow rays which become papery and persistent, and the dark yellow or orange flower head centers.

363. **Hopi tea**   *Thelesperma megapotamicum*   Sunflower family

Erect perennial herb, the stems branching, smooth, mostly 12–28 in. (30–70 cm) tall. *Leaves* opposite, $1^1/_2$–$3^1/_2$ in. (40–90 mm) long, divided into 3 or more slender, untoothed segments or sometimes unlobed and linear. *Flower heads* about $^1/_3$–$^5/_8$ in. (8–15 mm) wide, the outer subtending bracts blunt and white-margined, the inner ones reddish-brown or blackish, united for about half their length or more, the rays none or rarely present. *Fruits* of slender blackish or brownish achenes crowned with a pair of triangular bristles. Used by many people for making tea.

Range and Habitat: Nebraska to Utah, southward to Mexico and South America. Usually found on open plains, mesas, and slopes throughout New Mexico; 4,000–7,000 ft.

Key Characters: Hopi tea is distinguished by the leaves usually divided into slender segments and by the flower heads without rays and with subtending bracts united.

Related Species: Other species of this genus have either conspicuous flower head rays or broader leaf lobes.

364. **Dwarf crownbeard**   *Verbesina nana*   Sunflower family

Perennial herb, the stems mostly 6–10 in. (15–25 cm) tall. *Leaves* mostly opposite, oval, blunt at the tip, narrowed at the base, usually $1^1/_2$–$2^3/_8$ in. (35–60 mm) long, the margins irregularly toothed. *Flower heads* (including rays) about $^3/_4$ in. (20 mm) wide, solitary at the ends of the branches, the subtending bracts slightly unequal in length, the rays orange yellow, about $^1/_3$ in. (8 mm) long, 3-toothed at the tip. *Fruits* of nearly round, flattish, broadly winged, hairy achenes.

Range and Habitat: Western Texas to New Mexico and Mexico. Occasionally found on dry, open plains in southeastern New Mexico; 3,000–4,000 ft.

Key Characters: Dwarf crownbeard is characterized by the oval leaves with irregular teeth, the orange yellow rays, and the broadly winged fruits.

Related Species: Other species of crownbeard are typically much larger and usually bloom much later in the season.

Zinnia grandiflora

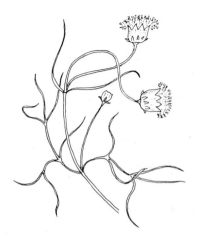

Thelesperma megapotamicum

Verbesina nana

365. **Mexican sunflower**   *Zexmenia brevifolia*   Sunflower family

Small, rounded shrub, to 39 in. (1 m) tall. *Leaves* usually opposite, ovate, 3/4–1 1/4 in. (20–30 mm) long, blunt at the tip, the margins not toothed. *Flower heads* (including rays) about 1 1/4 in. (30 mm) wide, solitary on long stalks, with the subtending bracts ovate and often recurved and with 5–8 yellow or orange rays about 3/8 in. (10 mm) long. *Fruits* of achenes with winged margins, often necklike at the top and crowned with 2 or 3 stiff bristles.
Range and Habitat: Texas and New Mexico to Mexico. Usually found on rocky, often brushy slopes in southern New Mexico; 4,500–8,000 ft.
Key Characters: Mexican sunflower is distinguished by its shrubby nature, the yellow or orange rays, the recurved flower head bracts, and the winged fruits.

366. **Blackfoot**   *Melampodium leucanthum*   Sunflower family

Perennial herb, the stems much-branched, to 16 in. (40 cm) tall. *Leaves* opposite, sessile, linear to oblong, 3/4–2 in. (20–50 mm) long, the margins without teeth or sometimes pinnately lobed. *Flower heads* (including rays) 3/4–1 3/8 in. (20–35 mm) wide, the subtending bracts united for at least half their length, with 8–10 whitish rays 5/16–1/2 in. (8–12 mm) long. *Fruits* of curved achenes, the outermost ones surrounded by a hoodlike covering.
Range and Habitat: Oklahoma and Colorado to Mexico. Usually found on open, dryish slopes, mostly in limestone soils, throughout New Mexico; 3,500–6,500 ft.
Key Characters: Blackfoot is distinguished by the habit of growth, the white rays with usually purple veins beneath, and the united bracts beneath the flower heads.

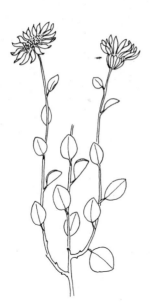

Zexmenia brevifolia *Melampodium leucanthum*

Index

*refers to wildflowers illustrated in color